THE LIBRARY OF TRADITIONAL WISDOM

The Library of Traditional Wisdom has as its aim to present a series
of works founded on Tradition, this term being defined as the trans-
mission, over time, of permanent and universal truths, whose written
sources are the revealed Scriptures as well as the writings of great
spiritual masters.

This series is thus dedicated to the *Sophia Perennis* or *Religio Perennis*
which is the timeless metaphysical truth underlying the diverse religions, together with its essential methodological consequences.

It is in the light of the *Sophia Perennis*, which views every religion
"from within," that may be found the keys for an adequate understanding which, joined to the sense of the sacred, alone can safeguard
the irreplaceable values and genuine spiritual possibilities of the great
religions.

D1157897

IN THE FACE
OF THE ABSOLUTE

FRITHJOF SCHUON

WORLD WISDOM BOOKS

Certain chapters of this book
were first published in:
Approches du Phénomène Religieux
© Le Courrier du Livre, Paris, 1984

In the Face of the Absolute
Translated from the French
Copyright © 1989 by Frithjof Schuon

Library of Congress Cataloging-in-Publication Data

Schuon, Frithjof, 1907-
    [Approches du phénomène religieux. English]
    In the face of the absolute / Frithjof Schuon

    249 p. -- (The Library of traditional wisdom)
    Translation of: *Approches du Phénomène Religieux*.
    ISBN 0-941532-07-0: $12.00
    1. Religion. 2. Spirituality I. Title. II. Series.
BL48.S37813 1989   89-5422

Printed in the United States of America
For information address World Wisdom Books
P.O. Box 2682, Bloomington, Indiana 47402-2682

Table of Contents

Preface

Assuredly there are no such things as "problems of our time" in the philosophers' sense of the expression; that is to say, there is no thought that one could describe as "new" in its very foundations; there are however some questions that arose when "science" and "faith" began to part company, and which "belong to our time" because they have never ceased to engage people's attention.

Faith is the acceptance of that which we do not see, or rather, of that which transcends the experience of the average man; science is the experience of that which we do see, or at least of that whereof we can have an empirical knowledge. Traditional faith has been shaken or lost for reasons both subjective and objective; the "intellectual worldliness" inaugurated during the Renaissance and voiced by Descartes brought as its consequence a general diminishing of contemplative intelligence and of the religious instinct, while new facts, all manner of discoveries and inventions, took advantage of this weakening and seemed to inflict a more or less flagrant contradiction upon the propositions of faith. In other words, modern man was not — and is not — "intelligent" enough to offer intellectual resistance to such specious suggestions as are liable to follow from contact with facts which, though natural, normally lie beyond the range of common experience; in order to combine, in one and the same consciousness, both the religious symbolism of the sky and the astronomical fact of

1

the Milky Way, a more than just rational intelligence is required, and this brings us back to the crucial matter of intellection and, as a further consequence, to the topics of gnosis and esoterism.

However, modern scepticism, in order to take root, does not always require the prior misdeeds of Cartesianism; every sort of "worldliness," when aided by circumstances, is an opening for the spirit of doubt and the denial of the supernatural. Experience goes to prove that no people, however contemplative, is able in the long run to withstand the psychological effects of the modern discoveries, a fact that clearly demonstrates their "abnormality" in relation to human nature generally; in Europe, the hostility of the medieval Church towards the new astronomical theses does not appear, in the light of subsequent events, to have been altogether unreasonable, to say the least. It is evident that no kind of knowledge is bad in principle or in itself; but many forms of knowledge can be harmful in practice as soon as they cease to correspond to the hereditary experience of man and are imposed on him without his being spiritually prepared to receive them; the human soul finds difficulty in coping with facts that are not offered to its experience in the ordinary course of nature. The same holds true of art: it has need of limits imposed by nature, at least insofar as it is the prerogative of a collectivity, which by definition is "passive" and "unconscious"; one has but to put at the disposition of a people or a caste the resources of machinery and the chemical industry, and their art, regarded in the broadest sense, will be corrupted, not in its every manifestation of course, but insofar as it belongs to all. This does not mean to say that the majority of an artistic people are totally lacking in discernment, but rather that the seductive attraction of novel possibilities proves in the long run more powerful than hereditary taste; fineness of soul yields to the clamor of what is easy and offered in quantity, just as happens on the intellectual plane and other planes besides. Human nature is weak and prone to corruption; it is not possible for a whole people to be holy or even simply clear-sighted.

Howbeit, the tragic dilemma of the modern mind results from the fact that the majority of men are not capable of grasping a priori the compatibility of the symbolic expressions of tradition with the material observations of science; these observations incite modern man to want to understand the "why and wherefore" of all things, but he wishes this "wherefore" to remain as external and easy as scientific phenomena themselves, or in other words, he wants all the answers to be on the level of his own experiences; and as these are purely material, his consciousness closes itself in advance against all that might transcend them.

One of the great errors of our time is to speak of the "failure" of religion or the religions; this amounts to imputing to the truth our own refusal to accept it and at the same time to denying man both his liberty and his intelligence. The latter depends, in large measure, on his will, therefore on free will, in the sense that the will can contribute towards rendering intelligence effective or else towards paralyzing it; it is therefore not without good reason that medieval theologians situated heresy in the will. Intelligence can in fact slip into error, but its own nature does not allow it to resist truth indefinitely; for this to happen the intervention of a volitional factor is required or, to be more precise, of a passional factor, namely prejudice, a sentimental interest, individualism under its many forms. Every error contains an element of irrational "mysticism," a tendency that has nothing to do with concepts but which uses concepts or invents them. Behind every philosophical opinion is to be found some particular "savor" or "color"; errors are born of psychic "hardenings," "dissipations," "explosions" or "heavinesses" and these are, each in its own way, obstacles to the shining forth of the Intellect and to the vision of the "Eye of the Heart."

The darkening of our world — whether of the West properly speaking or of its extensions into the East or elsewhere — is apparent also in the fact that mental nimble-ness for the most part goes hand in hand with intellectual shallowness: people are in the habit of treating concepts like mental playthings that commit one to nothing; ideas no longer "bite" into the intelligence and the latter glides over concepts without giving itself time to grasp them. The modern spirit proceeds "along the surface," hence a continual toying with mental images without awareness of the part these really play; the traditional spirit, on the other hand, proceeds in depth, whence arise doctrines that may be apparently "dogmatic" but which nonetheless remain fully satisfying and effective.

*

* *

In reading the essays contained in this collection, it will be noted that we have in view, not traditional information pure and simple so much as intrinsic doctrinal explana-tions; that is to say, the expression of truths of which the traditional dialectics are the vestitures; hence it is not as a historian of ideas, but as a spokesman of the *philosophia perennis* that we expound diverse formulations of the truth that is everywhere and always the same.

One point that always seems to escape philosophical ra-tionalists, is that there is of necessity a gap between the ex-pression and the thing expressed, hence between doctrine and reality. It is always possible to reproach a sufficient doctrine for being insufficient, since no doctrine can be identical to what it intends to express; no formulation can altogether take into account all that could be demanded, rightly or wrongly, by innumerable different needs for causal explanations. If an expression could be absolutely or in every respect adequate and exhaustive — as critical philosophy would have it — there no longer would be any difference between an image and its prototype and there no longer would be any point in speaking, or in thinking or even simply in language. In reality, doctrinal thought

4

exists in order to furnish a coherent scheme of points of reference more or less elliptical by definition but in any case sufficient to lead mental perception towards given aspects of the real. This is all that one has the right to demand of a doctrine; the rest is a matter of intellectual capacity, good will and grace.

Everything has already been said, and even well said; but it is always necessary to recall it anew, and in so doing, do what has always been done: to actualize in thought the certitudes contained, not in the thinking ego, but in the transpersonal substance of the human intelligence. Inasmuch as it is human, intelligence is total, hence essentially capable of the sense of the Absolute and, correspondingly, of the sense of the relative; to conceive the Absolute is also to conceive the relative as such, and consequently to perceive in the Absolute the roots of the relative and, within the relative, the reflections of the Absolute. Every metaphysic and every cosmology transcribes, in the final analysis, this play of complementarity pertaining to the universal *Māyā*, and thus inherent in the very substance of the intelligence.

To return to our book, we would say that its dialectic is necessarily bound up with its message; it could not take into account the exorbitant pretensions of a certain psychology — let alone a biology — which tends to substitute itself absurdly for philosophy and for thought itself. We cannot in good logic be reproached for using a naive and obsolete language, since our dialectic is essentially justified by its content, which pertains to the Immutable.

There is no spiritual extraterritoriality; since man exists, he is linked to all that implies Existence; since we know, we are called upon to know all that is intelligible; intelligible not in accordance with our comfort but in accordance with human capacity and with the nature of things.

Part One

General Doctrine

The Decisive Intuition

The content of religions and their reason for being is the relationship between God and man; between necessary Being and contingent existence. Now the Infinitude of Necessary Being, which is All-Possibility, implies an in principle limitless diversity of modes of this relationship; for to say Possibility as such, is to say diverse, and therefore multiple, possibilities. Consequently, the diversity of religions results from the diversity of the possibilities comprised in the relationship between God and man; and this relationship is both unique and innumerable.

It is this relationship which gives religions all their power and all their legitimacy; and, on the contrary, it is their confessional claim to absoluteness which constitutes their relativity; if they have something absolute, which is indisputable, it is by their principle, but not by their particular mode, nor *a fortiori* by their exclusivism and their formalism. For example, what gives Christianity all its force is the principial possibility upon which it is founded, namely that the relationship between God and man can take on a sacrificial, redemptive and sacramental form; in turn, what constitutes the limitation, and in a certain sense the fragility, of this religion, is that this form presents itself as the only one possible, whereas the relationship between God and man can, and consequently must, take on other forms, which it does much more often than not, given that the sacrificial and penitential possibility is more

9

particular than the legalistic and obediential possibility, although the one necessarily participates in the other. In other words: religion imposes itself with the force of absoluteness because it is a possibility — hence also a necessity — of the relationship Heaven-Earth, but it is limited and relative because it is, not the very possibility of this relationship, but one mode among others of this possibility, and because this mode must nonetheless present itself as the religious possibility as such, on pain of not being able to manifest effectively its reason for being. This paradox entails an exclusivism plainly contrary to total Truth, which alone is capable of satisfying all legitimate needs for causal explanations, and therein lies all the ambiguity of the exoterisms, with their disproportions and their divergences.

The *Religio* — the "link" that is both natural and supernatural — may, therefore, manifest more or less directly the very essence of the relationship Heaven-Earth, just as it may manifest it more or less indirectly and in an underlying manner by accentuating a particular mode of this relationship; this is what Christianity and Buddhism do, in presenting themselves as spiritual "innovations," whereas Islam, on the contrary, intends to be primordial and normative, universal and not original; it could also be said that the great argument of Christianity as well as of Buddhism is of the phenomenal order, whereas that of Islam is of the doctrinal order, if one may emphasize distinctive features at the risk of seeming to schematize things. Hinduism for its part tends to realize in its midst all the religious modes possible, whence its richness both dazzling and baffling; and the same holds true, in principle, for the other mythological traditions, those anchored in the night of time.

*

* *

In the rationalist critique of dogmatisms, not everything is to be rejected out of hand, for the inconsistencies —

even though extrinsic — that are encountered in religious imageries necessarily provoke doubts and protestations, in the absence of a sapiential esoterism which could bridge the gaps and bring the accidental dissonances back to the harmony of the substance. Moreover, not unrelated to the fatal limitation of dogmatisms is their disdain of intelligence — which they affect to reduce to "reason" — owing to their appeal to belief alone; this being the case, it goes without saying that one cannot blame those who cannot help noticing the misdeeds of pious unintelligence, of which the fideist camp offers only too many examples; that some draw from these observations the falsest conclusions and delight in the most abusive generalizations, is another question altogether. Be that as it may, the fact that the reactions of the unbeliever and the esoterist can coincide, does not excuse the errors of unbelief, any more than it invalidates the theses of the metaphysician.

The man who rejects religion because, if taken literally, it sometimes seems absurd — since truths have to be dosed out bit by bit and in time, given the demands of formal crystallization and of adaptation to an intellectually minimal collective mentality — such a man does not know one essential thing, despite the logic of his reaction: namely, that the imagery, contradictory though it may be at first sight, nonetheless conveys data that in the final analysis are coherent and even dazzlingly evident for those who are capable of having a presentiment of them or of grasping them. It is true that there is, a priori, a contradiction between an omniscient, omnipotent and infinitely good God Who created man without foreseeing the fall; Who grants him too great a freedom in proportion to his intelligence, or too small an intelligence in proportion to his freedom; Who finds no other means of saving man than to sacrifice His own Son, and without the immense majority of men being informed of this — or being able to be informed of it in time — whereas this information is the *conditio sine qua non* of salvation; Who after having

11

powerfully revealed that He is One, waits for centuries to reveal that He is Three; Who condemns man to an eternal hell for temporal faults; a God Who on the one hand "wants" man not to sin, and on the other "wills" that a particular sin be done,[1] or Who on the one hand predestines man to a particular sin and on the other punishes him for having committed it; or again, a God Who gives us intelligence and then forbids us to use it, as practically every fideism would have it, and so forth. But whatever may be the contradiction between an omniscient and omnipotent God and the actions attributed to Him by scriptural symbolism and anthropomorphist, voluntaristic and sentimental theology, there is, beyond all this imagery — whose contradictions are perfectly resolvable in metaphysics[2] — an Intelligence, or a Power, fundamentally good which — with or without predestination — is disposed to saving us from a *de facto* distress, on the sole condition that we resign ourselves to following its call; and this reality is a "categorical imperative" which is so to speak in the air that we breathe and which is independent of all requirements of logic and all need for coherence.[3] No doubt this assertion of ours comprises no rational proof, but it nonetheless has the meaning and the value of a concrete vision, as we shall make clearer in what follows.

*

* *

1. This is the Asharite thesis, determined by the obsession to safeguard the oneness of God at all costs, as if this oneness had need of a zeal that goes beyond all limits. More prudently, the Christians — who do not have this preoccupation — consider that God "permits" sin.

2. By the doctrine *Ātmā-Māyā*, making explicit All-Possibility, and therefore the hypostatic complexity of the Principle; all this we have treated with sufficient amplitude, it seems to us, in our books.

3. It is upon this imperative datum — "logical" or not — that Pascal's wager is based, reinforcing the universal and immemorial experience of men.

To be able to reply to the difficulties we have enumerated, one has first to understand the principal notions; to begin with, what must be understood by the term *"God"*? From the strictly human point of view, which alone is what religions as such have in view, "God" could not be the Absolute as such, for the Absolute has no interlocutor; we may, however, say that God is the hypostatic Face turned towards the human world, or towards a particular human world; in other words, God is Divinity which personalizes itself in view of man and insofar as it more or less takes on the countenance of a particular humanity. Another question: what does this personalized Divinity, this God become partner or interlocutor, or this Divine Face turned towards man "want" or "desire"? The most concise answer seems to us to be the following: if the Divine Essence, being infinite, tends to manifest itself by projecting its innumerable potentialities into the finite, the Divine Face, for its part, operates this projection and then — at a more relative level — projects within this first projection a principle of coordination, among other things a Law intended to regulate the human world and above all to regulate this miniature world that is the individual. This Face is thus like a sheaf of rays with diverse functions; a Face which, although it issues from the same Divine Order, does not amount to a single subjectivity with a moral intention; thus it is vain to seek behind the infinitely diverse combinations of the veil of *Māyā* an anthropomorphic and humanly graspable personality.[4]

Religious formulations limit themselves to enunciating points of reference without being too concerned with outward coherence, although from another point of view, the mythic and symbolical image always evokes a profound and lived reality: the history of Adam and Eve may clash with a certain need for logic, but we bear it deeply within ourselves, and it is this inherence of the sacred image

4. This is what the various "polytheisms" and, no less so, Mazdean dualism, are fundamentally aware of.

13

which on the one hand justifies it and on the other explains a relatively easy adherence to it. Aside from this, it is precisely the surface contradictions, the fissures so to speak which, by a crowning paradox, offer the decisive points of reference for the discovery of the metaphysical homogeneity of doctrines or symbols that are at first sight disparate.

*

* *

A few lines above we expressed a crucial truth which answers the following question: why is it that the Revelations, by accepting the inconvenience of certain contradictions in their postulates and symbols, and thereby the risk of scandal, yet have not deemed it necessary to forestall the danger of unbelief? There are two reasons for this: firstly — and this is the main reason — the sacred truth is part of our soul; the archetypal symbol is to be found in the deepest layer of our consciousness or being; secondly, in disdaining a certain logical plausibility, Revelation subjects us to a quasi-initiatory trial, which shows that faith coincides in the final analysis with virtue; not with a superficial moral quality, but with the virtue of our substance;[5] and this second reason is obviously linked to the first. Man realizes or actualizes his substantial virtue by practicing the virtues that are accessible to his immediate will, and he does so in and by faith, precisely; and it is this underlying virtue, joined to immanent and archetypal truth, that produces in the consciousness what we may term the "decisive intuition"; thus our mental and volitive comportment actualizes the values of our substance, just as these values determine our

5. Before the fall man identified with this substance, but has been separated from it ever since, which requires a methodic effort of realization; all of which is at the antipodes of Rousseau's simplifications. It is this initial separation that the anthropological pessimism of St. Augustine wishes to take account of.

comportment. Of course, the object of the decisive intuition is not the extrinsic limitations of the religions — the over-accentuations, narrownesses and ostracisms — but their intrinsic and therefore universal truths, for an error could not be an archetype, nor could it stem from a virtue; nevertheless, the exoterist acceptance of these "providential errors" could hinder neither the intuition in question, nor, obviously, virtue, otherwise exoterism would not exist.

The inherence of Truth in our spirit is, in principle, of a nature capable of conferring direct and plenary certitude, without an element of "meritorious obscurity"; if a priori it offers only a sufficient minimal intuition — decisive in any case — it is because in fallen, hence exteriorized, man there is a veil separating him from the inner light, while allowing a glimmer to filter through; unless the veil — or series of veils — is torn and gives rise to the Platonic anamnesis, which the religions situate in the beyond — it is then the "beatific vision" — but which plenary esoterism aims at rendering possible in this very life, if only to a degree which, if it is not unitive, at least already pertains to supernatural participation.[6]

An important factor resulting from our previous considerations, is that the absence of religious intuition is all too often, and even necessarily, the result of a fault of character, of pride above all; and it is known that pride puts up with all the virtues provided it can poison them and thus empty them of their substance. In the midst of a traditional society the pressure of the surroundings excludes unbelief, or almost so; whereas in a world where this pressure scarcely exists or even no longer exists at all, moral defects act much more easily upon thought, to the point of influencing it in a decisive manner. Under normal psychological and social conditions, to have virtue is

6. As Virgil said: "Happy is he who has been able to know the profound reasons of things." This association between happiness and knowledge is far from being fortuitous, on the contrary it indicates the profound — and moreover evident — identity between wisdom and beatitude. *Sat, Chit, Ānanda.*

practically speaking to have faith; not necessarily a particular faith, but certainly faith as such. It is true that in surroundings of unbelief one often, or almost always, affects certain moral qualities, but at bottom it is to prove to oneself that one has no need of religion and that man is good by nature.

*

* *

The virtues that on the one hand ennoble the individual and on the other render collective life possible, result fundamentally, whether one is conscious of it or not, from the convictions of a transcendent Absolute and of the immortality of the soul;[7] these two convictions, to the degree they are sincere and concrete, necessarily produce the essential moral qualities in man, and if these convictions come to be lacking, the qualities disappear *ipso facto,* slowly perhaps, but inexorably. Doubtless, a virtue unattached to any doctrinal root is conceivable, but even in this case it is, by its very nature, predisposed to the two convictions in question, which is to say that virtue pertains to man in the same way as does religion. Consequently, their disassociation can be only artificial and accidental. In this sense virtue is a proof of God, as is intelligence: virtue which permits man to surpass himself, and intelligence which is capable of conceiving the Absolute. And in effect, it is moral liberty and intellectual objectivity which constitute a priori man's deiformity.

Another point that we wish to raise is the following: two unimpeachable proofs in favor of religion and conse-

---

7. We say "transcendent Absolute" and not "God" in order to forestall the objection that the Buddhists are "atheists," which is the case neither from the point of view of metaphysical reality nor from that of the human attitude, whether mystical or simply moral. The same remark holds true, *mutatis mutandis,* for the immortality of the soul, the reality of which is not negated by the insistence upon our relativity.

quently of that decisive intuition that is faith — unimpeachable for one who has grasped the language of phenomena and who for that reason possesses both the sense of the sacred and the sense of proportions — these two proofs are the phenomena of sanctity and of art; for the saints and sacred art are theophanies before being human glories; these two phenomena greatly, and in a certain sense even infinitely, surpass the capacity of the ordinary man, which obviously is not the case for natural virtues nor for specifically profane works.[8] Sanctity is diverse as art is diverse, but both attest to one and the same spiritual reality; it is thus that the Divine Face turned towards man makes itself diverse, because God is infinite, and that it fundamentally remains one, because He is absolute.

If sanctity and sacred art did not prove anything as regards religion, hence as regards the immortal soul and the metaphysical capacities of man, sanctity and sacred art would be nothing, and man himself would be nothing. For it is in man's theomorphic nature, as man as such and in God's creative intention, that he cannot be something fragmentary or incomplete — which cuts short the absurdities of transformist evolution[9] — but that on the contrary he must be something that is all, and which would be nothing if it were not all; and it is in this sense that it can be said that man's fundamental vocation is to "become what he is."

8. As regards art, the comparison between the styles before and after the Renaissance is particularly eloquent in relation to the point being made here. It should not be overlooked that traditional artisanship always keeps a certain contact with the sacred and the spiritual.

9. Which basically asserts that the center of a circumference is as relative as any other point on the surface.

The Ambiguity of Exoterism

Cathedrals often, and perhaps even always, comprise intentional irregularities signifying that God alone is perfect and capable of perfection; that human works, like man himself, are necessarily imperfect. And this applies to the entire universe, hence to all that is not God; "Why callest thou me good?" said Christ. It is not surprising, therefore, that this principle also includes the domain of the sacred — we have just mentioned cathedrals — and above all religions themselves; thus humility as well as the sense of reality demand that we not be scandalized disproportionately by the dissonances we may encounter in celestial ambiences on earth; that we not be shocked, for example, by particular "providential excesses." The natural shadows, in a particular earthly beauty, do not prevent us from seeing that beauty; to see it with gratitude and to sense that the earthly reflection transmits a flawless archetype. Since he who judges is himself not exempt from imperfection and must be aware of it, by what right and with what logic would he require that other cosmic phenomena be exempt from it? "God alone is good."

*

* *

The term "exoterism" designates three different orders: firstly, a system of symbols and means; secondly, a way; and thirdly, a mentality. The first category embraces

19

dogmas and rites, then legal, moral and other prescriptions, and liturgy in the widest sense; the second embraces the general religious practices, those which are incumbent upon all; and the third category comprises the psychism corresponding to a particular religious climate, thus all the manifestations of sentimentality and imagination determined by a particular religion, a particular piety and particular social conventions.

In other words, it is important to distinguish the following aspects in exoterism: the formal system, which offers symbols and means; the exoteric way, which is based exclusively upon this system; the exoteric mentality, which is formalistic, voluntaristic and individualistic, and which adds all kinds of restrictive sentimentalities to the simple forms. These are three altogether different meanings of the term "exoterism": according to the first, the religious Law is necessary and venerable, and it becomes a constitutive element of esoterism; according to the second meaning, the Law is different from esoterism without necessarily excluding certain elements of the latter; according to the third meaning, there is an antinomy between the "outward" and the "inward," or between the "letter" and the "spirit."

It is of the highest importance not to confuse these three levels; in particular, not to lose sight of the fact that the first — Dogma and Law — is available to esoterism as regards both interpretation and practice. In order to determine whether a spiritual support is exoteric or esoteric, we need to ask not only what doctrinal and legal forms are involved, but also "who" accepts and practices them, and thus "how" they are accepted and practiced. In Dogma and Law, only those aspects are exoteric that are restrictive if taken literally, but not the aspects of pure symbolism and thus of universality.

When, on the contrary, there is an exclusively literal interpretation of the ideas and symbols on the one hand, and a voluntaristic and sentimental practice of the rites and prescriptions on the other — and this individualism corresponds to an anthropomorphic conception of the Divinity — then the way itself pertains to exoterism; the believer accomplishes what the Divine Person has ordained, and abstains from what He has forbidden, in view of salvation and without necessarily concerning himself directly with the nature of things as regards human attitudes and divine intentions.

What we have just said shows that the exoteric way cannot be entirely disassociated from the exoterist mentality; nevertheless, extremes — notably pedantry and fanaticism — are independent of religious practice as such; religious practice can inspire human temperaments and comportments, but quite obviously, it is not inseparably linked to them by definition. Dogmatic and legal exoterism is of divine institution; the exoterist mentality has a right to exist so long as piety wards off abuses, but it has nothing supernatural about it; its rights coincide more or less with those of human nature.

Dogmatic exoterism, as we have mentioned more than once, exhibits providential limitations determined by its mission and thus by its reason for being. To begin with, it excludes the idea of universal relativity — of *Māyā* — and therefore is unaware of the diverse and at times antinomic aspects of things, as well as of the points of view which take them into account; this amounts to saying that it identifies itself with a particular point of view determined by a particular aspect. By excluding the notion of *Māyā,* exoterism situates itself entirely within *Māyā,* the summit of which is the personal God who creates and legislates; *Paramātmā,* the supreme Self — Boehme's *Ungrund* — could not produce a world or found a religion. But religion could not be closed to the total truth, for God is one, and where the Divine Person is, there also is the Divine Essence;[1] the latter is accessible through esoterism, precisely,

1. When it is said that the personal God is situated in *Māyā,* which runs the risk of sounding offensive, one must be careful to make it

21

by full right and despite a certain inevitable opposition on
the part of the exoteric framework.

One has to realize that outward religion is not disinterested; it wants to save souls, no more no less, and at the
cost of the truths that do not serve its holy strategy.
Sapience, by contrast, wants only the truth, and the truth
necessarily coincides with our final interests because it coincides with the Sovereign Good.

*

* *

In Hinduism, as in other archaic traditions — to the extent that they have kept a sufficient vitality — the relationship between exoterism and esoterism presents itself in
another way than the Semitic religions: what is merely of
social relevance, or what is taken literally, is exoteric;
whereas the esoteric is not what of itself pertains to pure
metaphysics — *Advaita Vedānta* is not technically an "esoterism" — but what for some reason or other — social reasons above all — must be kept secret.

Hinduism — like the religions of ancient Europe — is
not exclusively interested in the salvation of souls; it is
true that it tries to prevent men from falling into hell, but
it abandons them to transmigration, which in monotheistic language amounts to the same thing. Among the ancient Europeans — Greeks, Romans, Celts, Germans —
only the initiates go to Paradise, and possibly also the he-
roes, who then are assimilated to the initiates; the others
remain in the darkness, in some underworld Hades,
which in practice combines the state of the perishable psychic elements with the great unknown that is transmigration through non-human and extraterrestrial states. Thus

clear that this God is the Supreme Principle "entering" into universal
Relativity, hence still "Supreme" despite the "entering," which enables
one to affirm that God the Creator and Legislator is at one and the
same time *Ātmā* and *Māyā*, or *Ātmā* in *Māyā*, but never simply *Māyā*.

the reproach of "paganism" on the part of the Semitic religions is not altogether unjustified, except of course as regards initiates, Platonists and Vedantists.

But it is not enough to acknowledge the difference — or even the divergences — between religious perspectives and their exoteric-esoteric structures; we need essentially to know their causes, which a priori result from the refraction of the Divine Light in the cosmic darkness. The "descent" *(tanzīl)* of the Koran signifies that the ordaining Will of the Personal God — the Principle which, upon contact with *Māyā*, becomes personalized, and thus limits itself by virtue of the universal radiation required by the very nature of the Sovereign Good — enters into a collective soul determined by particular racial and ethnic factors; it enters therein with "temporal" as well as "spatial" purposes, that is to say that it has in view eschatological destinies as well as immediate social situations; succession and the afterlife as well as simultaneity and the earthly city. In descending into a collective soul, the Divine Word becomes refracted into the possibilities of this soul: it becomes Judaized, Arabized, Hinduized or Mongolized, according to case; and in making itself human it cannot maintain, in every respect or modality, its original majesty and beauty; the human requires the little and the ambiguous and cannot live without it; but greatness, transcendence and harmony without admixture subsist always in the supernatural substance of the revealed Word. Christ is "true man and true God"; the same is true for every Revelation; it is this that must never be forgotten when one encounters elements that at first sight seem too human — to the point of seeming unlikely — in the variform stream of the divine Messages.

To understand, at least morally, certain apparent contradictions in the Scriptures, the following principial situation must be borne in mind: Divine All-Possibility, ontologically "prior" to the Divine Personification, pours into creation what is ontologically possible; it is a manifestation of Infinitude, and necessarily involves contrasting and amoral aspects because in a certain manner it includes the impossible, owing to the limitlessness of Possibility itself; whereas the Divine Personification, which hypostatically reflects the essential Goodness of the Essence, coordinates the chaos of possibilities and "desires" the good, whence precisely the half-divine, half-human phenomenon that is Revelation.[2]

The ambiguity of exoterism is largely a consequence of the complexity of the Divine Order; we say "Divine Order" to indicate that we have in mind here not the Principle in itself, but in respect to its "extension" within universal Relativity. Now exoterism, which must restrict itself to being a minimal doctrine, so to speak — whatever the mode of its emphasis — could not render an account of this Divine Order, both transcendent and relative,[3] without allowing enigmas and pitfalls to remain, or rather, without creating them.

*

* *

A typical feature of the monotheistic exoterisms is their dogmatization of theological speculations; it is the fixed

2. This precisely is the Moslem point of distinction between the ontological "Will" of God and His moral "Desire"; the weak point in the theory is that it attributes two hypostatic degrees to one and the same anthropomorphic subjectivity, as we have noted more than once. According to Ibn 'Arabi, God confines Himself to "bringing into existence" that which "wants to exist"; He is not "personally" responsible for the possibilities as such.

3. Purely transcendent at its summit, relative in its reverberation in accordance with *Māyā* and yet transcendent in this aspect as well, at least in relation to the world. The mystery of mysteries — pointed out in the West by Eckhart — is that there is in our Intellect a "divine point" which is linked to pure Transcendence, of which otherwise we would have no notion; and moreover it is this point which explains the possibility of the "central" phenomenon that is man.

prejudice that not only wishes to "dot all the i's," but to do so at the level of "faith," and hence of dogmatic constraint — this being the role of the councils and of promulgations *ex cathedra* — whereas it would suffice in many a case to let the scriptural enunciations stand as they are, in a holy indetermination that excludes no aspect of truth and does not crystallize one aspect to the detriment of the others. In fact, the evil lies less in the existence of speculations and precisions — for man cannot be prevented from thinking — than in their dogmatic fixation; one threatens with hell not only those who doubt God and immortality, but also those who dare doubt some exorbitant theological conclusion; and this threat is all the less plausible in that one postulates the incomprehensibility of God and always holds in reserve this substitute for a reply that is "mystery." The more one adds precisions *ex cathedra*, the more one increases the chances of scission and the risks of persecution, which would not be the case if one remained content with a level of "admissible" or "probable opinions" in varying degrees.[4] There is no point in objecting that pure metaphysicians do as much, for it is not the action of explaining or specifying which is at issue here, but the formalistic and therefore restrictive character of the specification, and above all the constraining dogmatization that is added to it, and that in no way forms part of the intentions and functions of pure and disinterested knowledge.[5]

4. One example of ostracism by exoterists is the case of the Pope Honorius I, accused of "heresy" in a disproportionate manner, to say the least; for the idea that Christ has only one will, the Divine — this is the Monothelite thesis — takes nothing away from the glory of Christ, quite the contrary, since it is based upon the axiom that there is nothing in the nature of Christ that could be opposed to the Divine Will. All in all, it is a simplistic and "implausible" theological opinion — since the human will certainly exists in the soul of Jesus — but the opinion is not subversive for all that; it is an ellipsis, and it suffices to take note of the intention, or to put it in parentheses.

5. Those American Indians who retain a traditional outlook point out, against disputatious confessionalism, that one can always argue

Given its mission, exoterism has to take into account the weaknesses of men, and thus also, be it said without euphemism, their stupidity; like it or not, it must itself take on something of these shortcomings, or at least it must allow them some room, on pain of not being able to survive in human surroundings. Thus one must not be too surprised, nor above all scandalized, at the paradoxical phenomenon of pious stupidity; to be sure, this phenomenon is far from being harmless, for it sometimes affects the canonical domain, but it cannot but exist since religion addresses itself to everyone and everyone must be able to recognize himself in it, if one may so express matters. A climate of religious belief appeals to emotivity, and emotivity is obviously opposed to perfect objectivity, at least when it goes beyond its rightful limits; when it does so, excessive emotivity damages the power of reflection or even — with all due reservations — intelligence itself, while plainly favoring a fundamental sentimentalism, extending from an initial biased attitude to harmless prejudices.[6] However: re-

about concepts, but not about the immutable symbols of virgin nature; and that books are perishable, whereas the symbols of the Great Spirit abide; what matters is to understand them. When one goes to the root of things, one sees that the argument is far from simplistic, and it even coincides with the Koranic doctrine of the divine "signs" *(ayāt)* in the world.

6. Very typical of the sentimental, and paradoxically individualistic humilitarianism, is this Hesychast's opinion: to remember God constantly is not a great thing; on the contrary, what is great, is to believe oneself lower than all other creatures. A surprising ignorance of the sacramental quality of the Name of God is here combined with a strange misappreciation of the qualities and merits of holy perseverance, and with a no less strange abdication of intelligence in the name of virtue. "He that raiseth up himself shall be brought low": which could not mean that humility is incompatible with that prerogative of man which is discernment, hence objectivity; besides, one may well wonder whether "to make oneself low in order to be raised up" is really humility. Such inconsequences, it is true, are not the prerogative of any religion.

move emotivity from religion and you kill it; moreover, a stream has need of banks in order to flow, and thus it is that exoterism, or the religious form, has need of limitations in order to be a living influence; "grasp all, lose all," as a proverb has it.

The exoterist mentality is largely the result of associations of ideas inspired by religious imagery: for example, in Islam, the sun does not enjoy an unmixed prestige, because of the danger of becoming a rival with God and because of the sun-worship which existed in the Near East, and this is attested to by certain symbols very unflattering to the sun. Aside from this imagery, and prior to it, the Koran speaks of the sun, moon and stars as slaves upon whom God has imposed forced labor *(sakhara)* in the service of men, and it moreover enjoins men not to bow down to the heavenly bodies; thus it is considered advisable, whenever one looks upon the sun or the moon, to say that "God is greater" *(Allāhu albar)*. Analogous remarks apply to fire: whereas for the Indo-Iranian, or simply Aryan traditions, fire is sacred like the sun — *Agni* and *Surya* being theophanies — in the monotheism of the Semites it takes on a baleful coloration because of its association with hell.[7] Christianity, which is not based upon jealous zeal for Unity, does not have such worries in relation to the sun, as is proved by the "Canticle to the Sun" of St. Francis of Assisi; for the Christian, it is all too evident that the sun is not God or that it is not Christ; thus he can love the sun in all innocence and without the least complex of guilt. A question that arises here incidentally is the following: would a Westerner who has serious motives for following the Sufic path be obliged to adopt the Moslem attitude towards the royal orb? — we chose this example among others — that is, should he feel obliged to experience an imaginative and sentimental reaction that he does not

---

7. This is far from Heraclitus, for whom fire — or rather its divine prototype — is at the origin of everything.

have and cannot have? Clearly not, and all the more so since essential Sufism would not require it; for the confessional mentality is one thing, and spiritual realization, another.

But let us return to the Arabs: by a curious derogation from the sensibility we have described above, the expressions "Sun of Princes" *(Shams al-Umarā'),* "Sun of the Learned" *(Shams al-'Ulamā'),* "Sun of (spiritual) Guidance" *(Shams al-Hudā),* are honorific titles; "Sun of Religion" *(Shams ad-Dīn)* is a man's name, and "Like unto the Sun" *(Shamsī or Shamsiyyah)* and "Sun of Daytime" *(Shams an-Nahār)* are women's names — all of which express the unanimous sentiment of primordial man, or of man as such, and thus of esoterism. Moreover, when the Koran declares that "God is the Light of the heavens and the earth" (Sura "Light"), it is impossible, by the very nature of things, for the sun to be excluded from this hierarchy, even though no Moslem could acknowledge this, except perhaps in esoteric surroundings. Besides, all these considerations on the solar orb also apply, to one degree or other and in an appropriate manner, to the moon and even to the stars: "Full Moon of the Religion" *(Badr ad-Dīn)* and "Star of the Religion" *(Najm ad-Dīn)* are masculine names; "Like the Full Moon" *(Badrī or Badriyyah),* "Star" *(Najmah)* and other images of the kind are feminine names.

In the Koran, the sun is described three times as a "lamp" *(sirāj),* and this word is also applied to the Prophet, whence his name *Sirāj,)* which — we have been told — establishes a scriptural and liturgical connection between Muhammad and the sun.[8] This "rehabilitation" of the

---

8. It should be noted, however, that the image of the lamp is less offensive to Moslem sentiment than that of the sun, for no one is tempted to worship a handmade object, even if it is a symbol of light. When praying in a mosque, the believer necessarily bows down in the direction of the lamp in the *miḥrāb;* he would not do so in the direction of the sun.

sun, and above all its indirect glorification by proper names and other metaphors, seems to indicate that the sensibility of Moslems is not greatly affected by the pejorative symbolism in question nor by the sacred ostracism of the theologians;[9] all of which has to be granted with some reservations, for the "evidence," namely certain classical formulations, cannot be brushed aside entirely. A further remark while we are on the subject: in Moslem imagery, rain is the most favored, as can be easily understood in a desert country; the Koran misses no opportunity to mention it with praise, and the Prophet loved to bare his head in the rain because of the blessing it brings.

In passing, and before going further, we would like to say a few words concerning the integration of a foreign element into a particular traditional formalism; this problem places us between syncretism, which is intrinsically heterodox, and esoterism, which in certain cases can admit such coincidences. This is because, in principle, esoterism is "open to all forms," as Ibn 'Arabi expressed himself in speaking of his heart; but in fact, such exceptions depend upon certain subjective as well as objective conditions; therefore we must ask, not only what has been done, but also by whom and for what reason.

In esoterism there are two principles which may be actualized sporadically and at different levels, but always in a partial and contained manner: the first is that fundamentally, there is only one religion with various forms, for humanity is one and the spirit is one; the second principle is that man bears everything within himself, potentially at least, by reason of the immanence of the one Truth.

*

* *

9. The same is true for the question of secondary causes: the average Moslem does not doubt that fire has the attribute of burning, despite Hanbalite or Asharite hairsplitting.

The only plausible explanation for the theological excesses of an 'Ashari — aside from religious zeal — is the principle of "functional" truth — not "informative" truth — of which we have spoken above; what is "true" is not necessarily what gives an adequate account of a reality, but what serves a particular psychological purpose in view of salvation and in relation to a particular mentality. From this standpoint, heresy is not objective error, it is subjective inopportuneness: it is better to reach Paradise with a limb missing than to be thrown into hell with all of one's limbs; this principle, purely moral and mystical in the intention of Christ, becomes intellectual or doctrinal in the domain of certain theological speculations. If 'Ashari maintains that fire does not burn by its own nature, that it burns only because God decides to bring about the burning, this is because the faithful have to be convinced that "God is without associate," despite the evidence that He surrounds Himself with Angels and Prophets;[10] and if this same doctrine goes so far as to affirm that evil comes from God and could not occur otherwise, or that God can impose obligations that man is incapable of accomplishing, or that God can make a creature suffer — or even punish it — for no reason and without compensation, or that, being free from all obligation, He can do "what He wills" with man, and that consequently it would not be unjust for Him to send the good to hell and the bad to Paradise[11] — if the Asharite doctrine upholds such enormities, this is, at bottom, in order to wage preventive warfare against certain vicious predispositions of man, rightly or wrongly, and in

10. Despite the idea that every single drop of rain is sent down by an angel, and other inconsequentialities of the kind.

11. Quite as absurd is Asharite atomism, which stems from a defective conception of causality: from the inability to see — or refusal to understand — that far from being excluded by metaphysical causes, physical causes on the contrary manifest or reflect them and are relatively real precisely by virtue of the absolute reality of their prototypes *in divinis*.

the context of a particular mentality — doubtless heroic, but prone to heedlessness and insubordination.[12]

Different opinions may be held as to the legitimacy or efficacy of such stratagems, but what matters here is not their quality, but their purpose, thus the principle of "functional truth," which is indirect and conditional and not direct, informative and categorical.[13] The non-interference of the Holy Spirit in theological matters — if one may so express it — can be explained, in short, by the necessity of having to accommodate the limited capacities of the majority and consequently of having to renounce the intellectual element to a greater or lesser extent, and to emphasize all the more the moral and emotional element as well as eschatological interests. Muhammad knew what he was saying when he asserted that "disagreements *(ikhtilāf)* between the doctors of the Law are a Mercy": differences of opinion are all the more useful in that it is impossible to satisfy the needs of a collectivity of believers by presenting a homogeneous metaphysical doctrine; something more is needed, even in religion, for "it takes all kinds to make a world."

12. All these excesses are contradicted by the Hanafite theologian Maturidi, who considers that man's freedom is relatively real and not imaginary, and that God "desires" *(riḍā,* "being pleased") only good actions; that when He demands something of the creature, God confers upon it *ipso facto* the capacity to do it; that injustice is incompatible with the Divine Nature, and not that injustice is justice when the doer is God. Let us add that prior to Maturidi, the Mutazilites had the merit of teaching unambiguously that God is obliged to be just to men; an obligation freely assumed and resulting on the one hand from the Divine Perfection itself, and on the other from the intelligent and responsible nature bestowed by God upon the human creature. It could be said, paradoxically: if the Divine Nature allows God to claim all rights in all circumstances, He would not have created man; a formulation worthy of Zeno of Elea, yet nevertheless without being devoid of meaning.

13. Despite the warrant given by Ghazali to the extreme opinions we have quoted above, Sunnite theology has hardly retained them; the great majority of Sunnites, despite being Asharites, side in practice with the ideas of Maturidi which can be described as "reasonable."

There is no room for polytheism or idolatry in Islam; and yet they are to be found in it, insofar as they have a positive and thus legitimate meaning: "Moslem polytheism" is represented by the ninety-nine Names of God, and "Moslem idolatry," by the Kaaba and the Black Stone, the Kaaba being prolonged by the prayer niche in mosques. One could object that these are not images; no doubt, but nonetheless they are material objects, situated in space; a tree is not an image either, and yet if one were to pray towards a particular tree intentionally, while disregarding the canonical direction — the *qiblah* — Islam would term it an idol. Logically, and strictly speaking, Moslems ought to pray with their eyes closed — which they do not — and without regard to a ritual direction; abstraction would then be complete; but in fact, they pray before one visible thing — the *miḥrāb* — and in the direction of another thing — the Kaaba. Thus it can be seen that the purism of a religion is necessarily relative when it is a question of things that are justified in themselves and, moreover, opportune.

Iranian and Indian Moslems,[14] and even certain Arabs, are not afraid to practice painting, whereas the Sunna forbids it; it is true that there are differences of opinion as to whether the indictment of images refers simply to statues, which "cast a shadow"; but the predominant attitude of the ulamas is plainly hostile towards figurative art, and admits no exceptions. Here again, one has to take into consideration the motive of the Law, namely the tendency of the Semites towards idolatry; the Aryans do not have this tendency, which means that they are not idolaters when they worship images; the Hindus — apart from cases of popular deviation — are at bottom no more idolaters than the Christians, who certainly are not. Logically, Christians should be as iconoclastic as Jews since they base them-

---

14. We mean the Iranians in the proper sense of the term, and not the Persians alone.

selves on the Bible, but in this case as in others, it is the instinct for the "nature of things" which has prevailed and which has even given rise to certain modes of spirituality; the sacramental icon conveys graces and works miracles.

Let us add that music and above all dancing fall into the same category of traditional ambiguities; disapproved in Islam, they are nonetheless practiced in Sufism, always by reason of the profound justification conferred upon them by that universal criterion which is the nature of things. Inopportuneness is neither error nor wickedness, and there can always be cases wherein opportuneness changes sides, not only because men differ, but also — and above all — because man is one.

An example of excessive formalism — and of a conventionalism which is definitely superstitious — is provided by certain garments of Moslem women: in Islamic India there are certain ways of veiling women that have something truly sinister about them — they are like walking prisons or phantoms — which to say the least is contrary to nature, and which demonstrates to what extent the exoteric spirit can be pedantic, blind and desiccated; by contrast, the veil of Moroccan women is morally and aesthetically acceptable, being so to speak "one point of view among others." In the Maghrib, Berber women go unveiled — this should be recalled here — and the same is true for many Moslems of the black and yellow races, not to mention other examples difficult to categorize; which shows that this convention of dress is in no way essential from the point of view of the Law.[15]

In all climates of formalistic super-saturation, the instinct for the "nature of things" or for the archetypal and primordial norm sporadically regains the upper hand; while this is not technically an expression of esoterism, it is

15. The prescription to "veil one's charms" allows of various interpretations, including the most paradoxical, since modesty is sometimes concentrated on the face alone.

nonetheless linked with its spirit, with the distinterested and universal vision of good and evil, useful and useless, beautiful and ugly, and also, it must be said, serious and ridiculous, or human and monstrous, as the case may be.[16] And it is normally one of the functions of esoterism, not to play the *mufti* or the *pandit,* but as far as possible to bring visible forms as well as moral comportments back to the serenity of a Paradise lost, but still accessible in the depth of our hearts.

*

* *

From the standpoint of pure or total truth, the unavoidable drawback of the Semitic or monotheistic religions is that they reduce man to a privative or negative aspect of the average man, to a "minimal aspect," so to speak: Christianity defines man as a "sinner" who must do penance, whereas Islam defines him as a "slave" who must simply obey and whose intelligence exists merely to register orders; it is true that this is not all of the religion, and also that it is not unjustified at a certain level or given a certain end in view, but in any case, this reduction suffices to create misunderstandings and uneasiness on a higher level, and above all, to open the door to the abuses of sentimentalism. Moreover, if it lies within human possibility to present the most stupid ideas in the most intelligent manner — which is the case of modern philosophers — the converse must be possible too, namely that the most intelligent ideas be presented in the most stupid manner, as happens precisely in religions.

---

16. As for the gratuitous hyperbolism of certain kinds of religious language, it is important not to confuse it with symbolism in the proper sense of the term, which in any case is not a matter of style. Let us note in this connection that for the Westerner it is difficult to conceive that exaggeration pure and simple can form part of eloquence; and yet, it suffices to think of it; it is as with Columbus' egg.

As for the general question of the balance between faith and intellection, or between their respective rights, it cannot be solved juridically, for it depends upon personal imponderables; the imbalance between the two points of view or domains is consequently a kind of natural calamity, but man is what he is.

And yet, it is in the nature of things that there be means of regulating this balance, by taking into account the factors of harmony in the world and in our spirit. We have in mind here the complementarity between the sense of the true and the sense of the beautiful; the sense of the evident and the sense of the sacred; now the second intuitive capacity contributes towards regulating the demands of the first. The wise man sometimes abstains from asking questions, not because he despairs of his intelligence, but because his sense of beauty imposes upon him a limit — not of darkness, but of light; moreover, there is no sacred science without some modes of holy ignorance. Otherwise, the Absolute would enter just as it is into the relative, and the Infinite into the finite; Necessary Being would cause contingency to burst and there no longer would be either relativity or, consequently, existence and existing wisdom.[17] To say manifestation is to say limitation.

*

* *

When two religions have to exist side by side, as in India, or in Palestine at the time of the Crusades, two things happen: on the one hand a stiffening on the part of the

17. The Koran expresses this as follows: "(O man), follow not that whereof thou hast no knowledge. Lo! the hearing and the sight and the heart — of each of these reckoning will be asked. . . . They will ask thee concerning the Spirit [the universal Spirit, *Rūḥ*]. Say: The Spirit is by command of my Lord [by radiation or hypostatic prolongation], and of knowledge [of divine mysteries] ye have been vouchsafed but little. And if We [God] willed We could withdraw that which We Have revealed unto thee. . . ."(Sura "The Children of Israel," 36, 85 and 86)

formal religion, and on the other a greater flexibility and a certain interpenetration in the domain of spirituality; it is true that religions exist side by side everywhere, but what we have in mind here are those cases where there is virulent antagonism, unmitigated by habit and indifference. A crucial truth emerges from such confrontations and reciprocities: when a man has grasped the validity of a religion other than his own — which comprehension results from concrete experience as much as from intellectual intuition — God cannot but take into account the widening of this man's spiritual perspective and the awareness he will have of the relativity of forms as such; God, therefore, will absolutely not demand of him what he asks of believers who are totally enclosed in the formal system of their religion, yet at the same time He will make new demands. Knowledge is not a gift that entails no obligations, for all knowledge has its price; the "minus" on the side of formal religion will have to be compensated by a "plus" on the side of non-formal religion, which coincides with the *sophia perennis*.

Esoterism, with its three dimensions of metaphysical discernment, mystical concentration and moral conformity, contains in the final analysis the only things that Heaven demands in an absolute fashion, all other demands being relative and therefore more or less conditional. The proof of this is that a man who would have no more than a few moments left to live could do nothing more than: firstly, look towards God with his intelligence; secondly, call upon God with his will; thirdly, love God with all his soul, and in loving Him realize every possible virtue. One may be surprised at this coincidence between what is most elementarily human and what pertains quintessentially to the highest wisdom, but what is most simple retraces precisely what is highest; *extremitates aequalitates*, "extremes meet."

The Problems of
Evil and Predestination

From the standpoint of a piety nourished by anthropomorphism, the question of predestination and the question of evil are the two great problems. But from the
standpoint of metaphysical knowledge, the only problem
is that of expression through language; the difficulty
therefore lies in the fact that the heaviness of language requires almost endless prolixities.[1] Be that as it may: on the
principial plane, there are no unsolvable questions, for all
that "is" can in principle be known, the human spirit being
total — not partial as is animal intelligence. The real and
the knowable coincide, not for the rational faculty to be
sure, but for the Intellect, whose presence — actual or
purely potential — constitutes the reason for being of the
human condition.

If the questions of evil and predestination appear as unsolvable problems to the average believer, it is because theology, owing to its anthropomorphism, halts midway; it
improperly personalizes the supreme Principle, and this
shows that it has an insufficient idea of what we term the
"Divine Order." Doubtless there is no impenetrable parti-

---

1. The extreme opposite of the inevitable complication of abstract
dialectics is visual symbolism, or simply symbolism, which exhibits all
the aspects of a problem at once, but without thereby furnishing the
keys allowing everything to be deciphered.

tion between reason and intelligence, but the latter cannot enter fully and decisively into a thinking that identifies with dogmatic crystallizations and their corresponding sentimentalities.

*
* *

The Absolute by definition includes the Infinite — their common content being Perfection or the Good — and the Infinite in its turn gives rise, at the degree of that "lesser Absolute" that is Being, to ontological All-Possibility. Being cannot not include efficient Possibility, because it cannot prevent the Absolute from including the Infinite.

Possibility has so to speak two dimensions, one "horizontal" and one "descending," or one "qualitative" and one "quantitative," analogically or metaphorically speaking. The first contains the indefinitely diverse qualities and archetypes, whereas the second projects them in the direction of "nothingness" or impossibility. In drawing away from its source — namely pure Being — the second dimension on the one hand coagulates the qualities and archetypes, and on the other manifests their contraries; whence ultimately the phenomenon of contrastive manifestation, and consequently of evil. Being, which coincides with the personal God, cannot prevent evil because, as we have said, It cannot abolish, and could not wish to abolish, the Infinitude of the pure Absolute.

And this resolves the following difficulty: if God is both good and omnipotent, why does He not abolish evil? Does He not wish to, or can He not do so? For the reasons we have just indicated, He cannot abolish evil as such — and He does not wish to abolish it because He knows its metaphysical necessity — but He is able and wishes to abolish particular evils, and in fact, all particular evils are transient;[2] the cosmogonic unfolding itself is transient since

2. Even hell: which theology, for reasons of moral opportuneness — and in this respect rightly so — could not acknowledge explicitly. We shall return to this topic further on.

universal Manifestation is subject to phases and becomes reabsorbed "periodically" into the Apocatastasis or the "Night of Brahman."

In one sense, the Absolute is beyond good and evil, but in another sense It is the very essence of goodness, which is to say that It is the Good as such. It is neither good nor evil insofar as It conditions, by the radiation of Its Infinitude, the genesis of what we term evil, but It is good in the sense that every conceivable good testifies to Its essential nature; evil as such could not have its root in the pure Absolute, nor in that "lesser Absolute" that is Being, the personal God. Moreover, evil ceases to be evil when it is seen as a metaphysical necessity contributing to that "greater good" which is, on the one hand, the contrastive manifestation of the good, and on the other the reabsorption that transforms every evil into the Good which is both origin and end; *ad majorem Dei gloriam*. As regards the root of the problem, we could also express ourselves as follows: the absolute Good has no opposite; a good that has an opposite is not the absolute good; "God alone is good."

If one were to say that supraontological Infinitude, or ontological Possibility which projects It, is "good" in the contrastive sense normally meant by this word, then the objection that evil does exist could be raised; but precisely, in relation to this indirect causation of evil — whether of privation or excess — one has to say that Possibility is beyond that opposition; it is "amoral," so to speak. In another respect however, as regards the intrinsic and positive nature of the supreme Principle, it has to be recognized that efficient Possibility or the personal God, as well as *a fortiori* the Infinitude of the impersonal or suprapersonal Divinity, must be defined as the "Sovereign Good."

Parallel to the problem of evil — which calls into question both the Omnipotence and the Goodness of God, and which exists only in virtue of the anthropomorphist confusion between the impersonal Divinity and the personal God — there is the problem of predestination, which calls

39

into question, on the one hand man's freedom and therefore his responsibility, and on the other hand both the Goodness and Justice of God. Here too, the solution of the difficulty lies in the distinction between Being and Beyond-Being, or between the "lesser Absolute" and the "pure Absolute": predestination could not stem from a "will" — which in that case would necessarily be arbitrary — of the personal God; it stems from pure Possibility, whose source, as we have said, lies in the Infinitude of the Absolute. From this standpoint we would say that a creature is a possibility, and a possibility is what it is; therefore, in a sense it is what it "wants to be"; destiny is one of its aspects among others. The individual "wants" to be what he "is," and it could even be said, more profoundly, that he "is" what he "wants": what his possibility, the very one he manifests, wants — or wanted initially.

Everybody agrees that man is distinguished from animals by free will; but also, no one can deny that compared to a bird in a cage, a bird who escapes is free; the relative character of this freedom takes nothing away from the reality it represents and possesses. Therefore, freedom unquestionably exists, even in the case of an animal, but it goes without saying that the existence of a thing does not mean that it is absolute; and to deny absoluteness does not amount to denying existence, as is only too obvious.

In addressing Himself to the individual and to the collectivity — which by definition is made up of individuals — the personal God makes Himself an individual: that is to say, He creates a religion which is necessarily particular and formalistic and which for that reason could not be universal as regards its form, any more than an individual as such can represent or realize universality. By contrast, the impersonal Divinity does not create religions: the Divine Self confers universal truth and the corresponding sanctity from within, by illuminating the Intellect and by penetrating into the Heart; this presupposes that the Heart be without blemish, without passions and

40

errors, and thus that it have reintegrated primordial purity.

But God is one, and there is no question of acceding to immanence while going counter to transcendence, or of approaching the impersonal Divinity against the will or requirements of the personal God; particularly outside a religious framework.

*

* *

Assuredly, theologies have the right to use simplifying and moralizing stratagems demanded by their sphere of action, but human intelligence — to the extent that it is capable of rejoining its own substance — has nonetheless the right to know, beyond moral and other interests, the simple nature of things, even within the Divine Order. The theological point of view cannot refrain, in practice, from attributing to the personal God — Who is within the domain of *Māyā* — the features of the impersonal Divinity, which alone is beyond *Māyā* or Relativity; but the pure Intellect — hence in principle, man — can go beyond *Māyā* since it is essentially capable of conceiving the pure Absolute, which is beyond *Māyā*, Relativity, Being. Therefore, man is not absolutely subject to God the Person, or to God-*Māyā;* he is subject insofar as he is an individual, but not in every other respect, and that is why the *pneumatikos* is "a Law unto himself," which evokes the whole question of the principial immanence of the Truth and the Way; we say "principial," thereby insisting strongly upon this reservation, for not every man is a *jīvan-mukta.*

Plainly, we are here at the limits of the expressible, where there is only one choice: either to take upon oneself the task of furnishing points of reference that cannot avoid paradox, complication, ellipsis and other drawbacks of thought or language, or else abstain from satisfying certain imperious needs for causal explanations, and confine oneself to asserting that "God does what He wills," and that the "potter" need not render account to the "pots" he has fashioned in accordance with his good pleasure. However, by refusing to take into account the needs for causal explanations to which man has a right in principle — since these needs stem from the total intelligence which characterizes the human species — one opens the door to luciferian usurpations and thereby to the most pernicious errors and denials — those which affect all that constitutes man's reason for being.

Therefore, man essentially has the right to ask certain questions: "in principle," as we have said, for in fact there is the original fall, which obliges religions — and thus theologies — to treat man like a child or like an invalid; yet fallen man is not all of man, and as a result there are problems — or rights and duties — against which it would be vain to legislate according to the "letter" of the Law.

In short, metaphysical explanations have two functions, one *de jure* and the other *de facto:* to furnish information — and thereby keys — to those who are qualified to receive it, and to free from errors those who have contracted them through contact with false ideologies; in the latter case, the function of wisdom will be a priori to allow those who have lost their faith to recover the capacity to believe in God, and all the graces that result from it.

Concerning the Notion of Eternity

If one conceives of Eternity according to the proper sense of the word, as being what is beyond duration and therefore having neither beginning nor end, one then understands that this quality could not be attributed to created things. Yet this is what the eschatological dogmas of monotheism do, or appear to do, when they teach us on the one hand that hell exists and, on the other, that it is eternal; we choose this example at the outset because it is, in practical terms, by far the most paradoxical and the most problematical. In other words, if religion sets out to inform, it also yields to a concern for moral efficacy, to the detriment of the metaphysical exactness of the message; which latter is not, in any case, a matter of urgency from the standpoint of exoterism. We readily agree that the notion of a hell situated in time, and therefore transitory, would lose its constraining power over many men, at least in a certain ethnic sector; but to attribute eternity to the infernal fire is nonetheless a two-edged sword in the long run, as the history of free thinking proves.

It is true that in Islam the notion of a hell that is all but absolute is mitigated, or even transcended, by reservations that are decisive in themselves but that are not necessarily given priority: thus the Koran calls hell "perpetual" *(khālid)*, but adds "unless God should will otherwise"; the Prophet even declares explicitly that hell will have an end.[1] 'Ashari bases this same idea on the essential Mercy *(Rahmah)* of God which, according to the Koran, "reacheth unto all things,"[2] and he had the merit of disseminating this thesis among most Sunni Moslems; according to other information though, the theologians do not agree on this point, despite the *hadīth* just quoted.[3]

Certain followers of the Asharite idea maintain that, while neither the Koran nor the Sunna provides any proof of the cessation of chastisement, neither do Divine Revelation and prophetic inspiration provide any proof to the contrary — the Koran would affirm only the perpetuity of hell and not of its torments — and they conclude from this that the question is better not debated in public. However, apart from the fact that their opinion appears hardly tenable to us, it must be realized that the contrast between the rigor of the Koran and the mildness of the Prophet — if one can so put it — is a dialectical antinomy and not an inconsistency: each of the traditional sources enunciates an aspect of the Real in an almost absolute fashion, as if it were a closed system, in order to forestall either facile solutions or positions of despair.[4] Ibn 'Arabi's conclusion is, in substance, that it is for the sages to break through this barrier of formal and providential incoherences.

In Christianity the preponderant and all but dogmatic view is in favor of eternal hell; sin, it is argued, has something infinite about it by reason of the infinite dignity of God which it offends, and consequently chastisement too

1. The same declaration is made by most doctors of the Torah, whose authority has carried weight in Jewish tradition since antiquity.

2. Or "encompasseth" *(wasi'at)* every thing (Sura "The Heights," 156). According to this principle of Mercy, the Dhyani-Bodhisattva Jizo *(Kshitigarbha)* makes his beneficent appearance even in the hells.

3. As regards the Koranic reservation, certain persons have interpreted it as meaning simply that God is all-powerful and "doeth what He will."

4. A classic example of this type of antinomy is the complementarity — a priori unresolved — between predestination and free will.

has to have something infinite about it. They forget that the sinner for his part has nothing infinite about him and is therefore not even capable of offending God infinitely; they forget above all — and this is the classic objection — that a thing which has a beginning must also have an end, or that a thing created cannot possibly have an attribute of the Increate. We could also say that man does not in fact measure up to the divine gift of freedom since he is capable of so misusing it as to damn himself, which proves that he cannot deserve a chastisement that is symmetrical with the dignity of God. Man is not unlimited; to man's limit corresponds the limit of chastisement; hell's limit is man's.

It seems inconceivable that no reservations should have been formulated in the Christian world regarding the "eternity" of the pains of hell, and in fact we recollect having read something of the sort in Saint Thomas Aquinas; however, supposing that no Christian authority has deemed it useful or possible to lay down such reservations, this does not mean that the motive was only moral opportunism or pure and simple ignorance; for the "eternity" of hell, or "damnation," does not only mean an endless punishment, it also, and even a priori, signifies final exclusion from the human state, this being what Brahmanists and Buddhists understand by "transmigration"; and this is not definitively infernal, but definitively non-human — in worlds other than our own — which in the monotheistic perspective amounts to the same thing; he who in the final count loses the human condition is "damned." Here, therefore, the word "eternal" is synonymous with the word "definitive," not as regards suffering but as regards exclusion from the human Paradise. This interpretation underlies, in principle and as an esoteric possibility, each of the monotheistic eschatologies.[5]

5. If, in the canonical prayer of Islam — the *Fātiḥah* — "those upon whom is Thy Grace" *(an'amta 'alayhim)* are saved, and "those upon whom is Thine Anger" *(maghḍūbi 'alayhim)* are the damned, "those that

But let us to return to the ordinary notion of an endless chastisement: this notion — which aside from its symbolism is specifically exoteric — is not unconnected with the temptation of atheism, and we have already alluded to this. In fact the argument concerning the infinite dignity of God which would, if offended against, demand a sanction proportionate to it — and therefore also infinite in a certain fashion — can only reinforce the position of the atheist who will then contend that a God who is perfect and thus essentially good could not avenge Himself infinitely and needlessly on a creature whose sin consisted only in forgetting God or in yielding to a passion. Our reply will be that the dogmatic image of a God who judges man "from without" is insufficient; in reality this image results from the fact that the sinner judges himself "from within," that is to say, from his own substance and by virtue of the relationship between cause and effect. On the one hand, man does what he is, and on the other, a particular fault has a psychological consequence entailing particular cosmic consequences, which religious anthropomorphism likens to a "judgement," and rightly so, since the universal Norm judges phenomena; yet "it is not God that wrongeth them, but they wrong themselves," the Koran says.

When Saint Thomas says that the chosen do not pity the damned, his intention is to stress the identity, in the damned, between the subjectivity and the perversion,[6]

go astray" *(aḍ-ḍallūn)* could well be they who are cast forth into the endless round of transmigration; that is, according to the inherent meaning and not to a traditional interpretation, which would be unthinkable in a monotheist milieu.

6. His purpose is likewise to suggest that nothing can diminish the beatitude of the chosen, which is nourished on the Divine Reality; for in that Reality there can be nothing privative, pure Being coinciding with Plenitude. This, at least, is the essential dimension of Beatitude; in fact, it does not preclude another dimension, turned towards even extra-paradisiacal contingencies, but not moving out of the climate of the "beatific vision."

whereas Buddhist compassion is based, on the contrary, on the phenomenon of suffering alone; both positions are justified from the standpoints that they respectively emphasize; what counts is to know how to put each thing in its place, that is, to conceive of the concrete modalities that these standpoints imply. Let us add that sceptics who deny afterlife, because they believe neither in a virtue that could deserve Paradise nor in a vice that could deserve hell, are fundamentally ignorant of human nature, its substance and its possibilities; it is the postulate of a leveling humanitarianism in whose name the highest human values are denied — those which constitute man's reason for being — in order to be able to declare the bad man good; from there on, to claim that he alone is good or "sincere" is but a single step.

From the viewpoint of Islam, a man is damned because he does not believe that God is One; one may well wonder what interest God has in our believing that He is One rather than manifold. In fact He has no such interest, but the idea of Unity determines and introduces a saving attitude of coherence and interiorization which detaches man from the hypnosis, both dispersive and compressive, of the outward and manifold world; without this unifying attitude man becomes inordinately outward and thereby dissipated, hardened and lost; it is man, and not God, who has an interest in believing that God is One. Inwardness, which cannot be imposed at the outset on every man, is foreshadowed in a framework of Law which makes human life coherent in relation to the Universal Norm and in view of the Sovereign Good; every religion takes the measures that are indispensable, but each with different points of emphasis, for the governing idea is not necessarily that of ontological unity as presented by Islam. Clearly it is not the diversity of points of emphasis that needs to be highlighted here, it is solely the fact that after the fall — however one may picture this — man is given over to the exteriorizing and imprisoning powers of the lower *māyā*, so that the only means of saving him is a priori a Key-Idea which opposes this *māyā* and which determines and introduces corrective and saving measures. Man damns himself not solely by reason of having sinned mortally, but because he remains in the initial state of sin — the state that is precisely the nature of fallen man and from which religion alone can deliver him. Man is not damned for not believing that God is One, or that Christ saves or that the world is illusory; he becomes lost because, not believing it, he remains at the mercy of the dehumanizing powers of centrifugal *māyā* which appear to be envious of the unique chance that is offered by the human state. When it is said that it "offends God" not to believe in this or that, this means basically that man courts perdition unless he grasps a particular "lifeline," as a verse of the Koran says.

"Unless God should will otherwise": this basic reservation in the Koran concerns not only the perpetuity of hell, but also that of Paradise which will be transcended — or "absorbed" — in the end by the mystery of *Riḍwān*, the "Divine Acceptance," and this leads us back to the eschatological cosmology of Origen. In this terminal dimension which in reality is "without beginning and without end," there can be no diminishment — quite the contrary: beings are reintegrated into their timeless and uncreated essences, into what they have never ceased to be in their quintessential reality. It follows from this that it is far less incorrect to speak of the eternity of Paradise than of the eternity of hell, and this asymmetry is indeed so obvious — when one takes into account the nature of the Sovereign Good — that we see no point in insisting on it with endless arguments of an apologetic trend. It is consequently the eternity of hell that constitutes a great religious problem; not that of Paradise, which opens out onto pure Being, onto That which is.

*

* *

Scriptural anthropomorphism does not disturb those who, while not necessarily being metaphysicians, have sufficient perspicacity to grasp intuitively its plausible intentions; but it does disturb those "strong minds" who apply a purely mechanical and therefore even ill-willed logic to the literal meaning of the symbolisms; this has nothing to do with the legitimate critical mind — that is, with the awareness we may have of the imperfection of a particular dogmatic or theological manner of speaking — for this awareness comes not from our ignorance but, on the contrary, from our knowledge of what these expressions imply.[7] Whatever the case, it is important not to confuse dogmatic expressions with theological explanations; we may accept the apparent contradiction of the former thanks to our intuition, but we are not bound to accept likewise every piece of theological reasoning — such as that of the consequences of the infinite dignity of God — and it is not even possible to do so when the opinion contains a flagrant absurdity, even if imperceptible to the simple believer. It is true that lame arguments are eroded by time, on the one hand because even the fideist is a thinking being, and on the other, because doubt increases with the decline of faith and so of intuition; what is left is mere rationality with no spiritual background and which is unjustified, evidently not because of its logic as such, but because of its superficial and fragmentary nature. It is then that pure metaphysics or gnosis if one will — so long vilified by the spokesmen of fideism — should intervene, for it alone offers the data needed in order to be able to combine the rights of intelligence with those of human weakness.

7. A marginal note: the images and accounts of the Sacred Scriptures, quite apart from their literal meaning and various symbolical significations of a principial nature, apply equally to an endless series of outward and inward situations; that is to say, they are like archetypes of everything that has a moral or spiritual meaning. Every type of holiness in particular and every saintly destiny is foreshadowed in that iconostasis which is Scripture.

We should like to insist once more upon the following point, at the risk of repeating ourselves: if ancient or medieval man — these epithets being approximate — found it easy to accept arguments that were naive and on the whole provisional, this was not only because he accepted in advance the dogmas that these arguments set out to illustrate, but also because these arguments themselves had the power to release in him intuitions of truth. But worldliness and material progress ended in weakening piety and therewith faith, hence also intuition.

On the one hand there is the man who is philosophically naive but intuitive as regards the supernatural;[8] on the other there is the man gifted with critical sense but insensitive to that which transcends him; the ideal, quite clearly, is a discernment that does not result from the merely outward rationality of the logician and empiricist, but from an intellection which, by its very supernaturalness, also coincides, in its dynamic dimension, with the "Faith that can remove mountains." It follows from all that we have said above that what is needed is a sense of causality that is realistic, intuitive, sober and thereby legitimate, as opposed to one that is arbitrary, aggressive, sceptical and thus illegitimate; and it goes without saying that the arguments of metaphysics have to satisfy only the former. When Saint Paul says that the pots must not argue with the potter, his intention is to close the door not so much to sapience as to a curiosity that is insatiable a priori; an attitude of principle which doubtless goes too far — the line of demarcation being nonetheless variable — but which has the advantage of putting a firm stop to a thinking that has lost the sense of the sacred and, for that very reason, the sense of proportions.

8. The sense of the supernatural and the sacred was not lacking in the pagan Semites, for they had an irresistible need to worship something, be it the golden calf or the idols of Mecca; the analogy between the pagans of antiquity and modern disbelievers is therefore only partial.

*

* *

The temptation to make Eternity a cosmic attribute would not occur if, through human preoccupations, one did not lose sight of the fact that Eternity is what we could call — for want of a better term — a "dimension of the Infinite." Eternity or Immutability, like Omnipresence or Immeasurability — God as "Time" or as "Space" — result in fact from Infinitude; Eternity relating rather to Transcendence and to Rigor, and Omnipresence, to Immanence and to Gentleness; relationships which call to mind the complementarity of *Shiva* and *Vishnu*.[9] Infinitude itself is, so to speak, substantially connected with the Absolute which radiates precisely through its dimension of Infinitude and by virtue of its nature as the Sovereign Good, therefore as a result of its essential tendency to communicate itself.

The Divine Omnipresence, while constituting a threat to the proud and the evil-doers — and there is no "mortal sin" without pride — has on the contrary something reassuring and consoling for the good, who in any case represent the norm; the Omnipresent is the refuge that is everywhere accessible; those who love God are nowhere separated from Him. In its turn, however, the Divine Eternity, while nourishing the hope of the man who knows he is in exile here below and who aspires to the heavenly homeland, has about it something cold and terrifying from the point of view of earthly dreams; for the Eternal is He who is enthroned immutably above the evanescent things of this world below; He seems to look upon them with the implacability

9. Too often has it been maintained that space and time are categories exclusively pertaining to the physical universe and that beyond these "limiting conditions" there is nothing of the kind; this is to forget, in the name of transcendence, the relationship of immanence, for which physical — or psychosomatic — categories are no more than a translation of heavenly and divine categories into perceptible terms.

of the stars. Moreover the name "Eternal" is synonymous with Majesty; whereas the Omnipresent is near, the Eternal is remote. The two aspects meet and merge in their common Infinitude, thus in Divinity as such.

When the Bible recounts that the "Eternal" speaks and acts, one might object that there is something contradictory in this, for that which has the quality of Eternity can no more enter into time than the Absolute can enter into contingency. Now this apparent contradiction is in fact the key to ontology: it signifies that, without the Eternal, temporal things would not exist; without the Absolute, there would be no contingent order; this is tantamount to saying that the Divine must always be able to make itself perceptible to men, either indirectly in its existential traces or directly through its theophanies. "Water takes on the color of its container," a Sufi said, and it is thus that Divine Reality, transcendent in itself, enters into the temporal order without leaving its Immutability. "True man and true God": here is the entire mystery of the "manifestation of the Void" *(Shunyāmūrti);* the sun is unaffected by what it shines upon. The phenomenon of the miracle is ontologically indispensable because the meeting between the Eternal and the temporal is possible and necessary; the archetype of the miracle is the irruption of the Absolute into contingency. And this irruption would not be conceivable if contingency were not, precisely, "something of the Absolute."

Ātmā-Māyā

The substance of knowledge is Knowledge of the Substance; that is, the substance of human intelligence, in its deepest and most real function, is the perception of the Divine Substance. The fundamental nature of our intelligence is quite evidently discernment between the substantial and the accidental, not the perception of the accidental exclusively; when the intelligence perceives the accident, it sees it as it were in relation to its corresponding substance — he who sees the raindrop also sees water — and ought to perceive it all the more so in relation to the Substance as such.[1]

To speak of the Divine Substance is necessarily to speak of its ontological prolongation since we who speak owe our very being to this prolongation, which is Existence, manifested Relativity, Cosmic *Māyā*. Absolute Substance prolongs itself by relativization, under the aspects of Radiation and Reverberation; that is to say, the Substance is accompa-

---

1. The terms substance and essence which — rightly or wrongly — are almost synonymous in practice, differ in that substance refers to the underlying, immanent, permanent and autonomous nature of a basic reality, whereas essence refers to the reality as such, that is, as "being," and secondarily as the absolutely fundamental nature of a thing. The notion of essence denotes an excellence which is as it were discontinuous in relation to accidents, whereas the notion of substance implies on the contrary a sort of continuity, and this is why it is used here in speaking of *Ātmā* in connection with *Māyā*.

nied — at a lesser degree of reality — by two emanations, one of which is dynamic, continuous and radiating, and the other static, discontinuous and formative. If, in addition to the Substance, there were no Radiation and Reverberation to prolong It by relativizing It, the world would not be.

But this projection of God — if one may put it thus — demands one element to make it possible, an element that explains why the Substance does not remain simply "a hidden treasure." This diversifying, exteriorizing or relativizing element is none other than *Māyā;* we could define its nature by a multitude of different terms such as Relativity, Contingency, Separativity, Objectification, Distinctification, Exteriorization, and more; even the term "Revelation" could apply here in an altogether fundamental and general sense.

In every existing thing there is the Substance, without which that thing would be a pure nonentity; now the fact that things do "exist" means that they are actualized by virtue of "Existence" in the highest sense this term is capable of;[2] and this "Existence" or this Relativity is brought about by the Substance in virtue of its Infinitude, which amounts to saying that Divine Reality would not be what it is unless it included the paradoxical dimension of a kind of tendency towards a nothingness which obviously is never attained; for this nothingness has no other reality than the quite indirect one of a point of reference, in itself ungraspable and unrealizable.

There is a first duality: the Substance and — principially within the Substance but in fact falling short of its

2. It is in this sense that we speak of the "existence of God." In this question of terminology, it is important to know in which connection a reality "exists." If it is in relation to the "Absolute," then this reality is relative; if it is in relation to nothingness, it is simply real, and can be principial as well as manifested. In the subconsciousness of current language, "existence" stands out with more immediacy from the negative and abstract void, which is non-existence, than from the concrete or positive Void, which is God.

Ātmā-Māyā

absolute Reality — Relativity, or *Māyā;* now *Māyā* comprises the two aspects previously mentioned: Radiation and Reverberation; it is in and through *Māyā* that both the "Holy Spirit" and the "Son"[3] are actualized; expressed in geometric terms, the Substance is the center, Radiation is the cluster of radii, and Reverberation, or the Image, is the circle; Existence or the "Virgin," is the surface which allows this unfolding to take place.

*

* *

Divine *Māyā,* which is both metacosmic and cosmic, comprises essentially the following powers or functions: firstly the function of separation or duplication — starting with the scission into subject and object — the aim of which is to bring about a plane for the manifestation of the two consecutive functions of Radiation and Reverberation, to which correspond movement and form. Just as in God — although outside the Absolute Substance — Relativity constitutes a plane for the actualization of Radiation and Reverberation as principles, so also in projecting itself outside this Divine Order it projects a further, eminently more relative plane, namely the entire Cosmos. Within the Cosmos, it repeats this same process of segmentation

---

3. The opinion that the trinitarian relationships — or the three hypostatic Persons — "constitute" the Absolute is not inherent in Christianity; it has come down to us from an Orthodox source, not a Catholic one; but it has possibly rather more the meaning of a "sublimation" than a strict definition. According to the Scholastics, Divine Reality is neither purely absolute nor purely relative, but contains *formaliter eminenter* both absoluteness and relativity; this has not prevented the theologians from being apparently disinclined to grasp the implication of these two terms, since they do not draw the obvious conclusions from them. We shall take this opportunity to make the following observation: that the hypostases should have a Personal character — or should be "Persons" — because the Substance imparts its own Personality to them, does not in any way prevent them from being in another respect, or from another point of view, Modes of the One Substance, as Sabellius maintained.

down to that end point which marks the material world; and on each of the planes projected in its descent — angelic world, animic world, material world — it manifests an appropriate mode of Radiation and Reverberation; there is no order of Relativity that does not comprise these two functions or dimensions. The element "Substance" is represented at each ontological or cosmic level in appropriate mode; and *a fortiori,* pure Substance or Substance as such underlies each of its secondary manifestations.

In the material world, *Māyā* will be the plane of space-time; the Substance will be ether; Reverberation, or Image, will be matter; and Radiation, energy. But there are, needless to say, much more restricted applications of this same symbolism; it could not be otherwise inasmuch as all matter, all form and all movement or change are to be ascribed respectively to the three principles in question. The complementary relationship "space-time" — which concretely speaking is "extension" and "duration" — shows moreover that in Relativity, or in Ex-sistence[4] as such there are two dimensions, the one expansive and conserving and the other transforming and destructive; hence the complementary relationship between worlds and cycles at all levels of the Universe. In God himself, the element "Space" is *Māyā* as container or conserver of possibilities, and the element "Time" is *Māyā* inasmuch as it transmits them to the world; the first face of *Māyā* is intrinsic and contemplative, and the second extrinsic and creative, or, in other words: the first face contemplates the undifferentiated foundation of possibilities in the Substance, whereas the second realizes these possibilities in view of their cosmic manifestation.

*

* *

4. We take the liberty of this graphic neologism in order to show that what is meant is not existence in the current sense of the term, which refers to cosmic manifestation.

Ātmā-Māyā

Relativity essentially brings into being a succession of planes, whence the hierarchy of universal orders; now it is important to understand that the nearer these planes or degrees are to the Substance, the more incommensurable they are. There is no common measure, or almost none, between the material world and the animic world which envelopes and, as it were, penetrates it and whose possibilities are vastly greater than those of space or matter; and the disproportion becomes almost absolute when we compare creation and Creator — "almost" because, speaking metaphysically but not theologically, these two planes are related in respect to their Relativity, that is in respect to their being determined by *Māyā*. *Māyā* in its turn is annihilated in relation to the Absolute Substance, that is, the Absolute as such; but this way of looking at things necessarily falls outside the perspective of theology[5] which, by definition, must consider the Divine Principle only in relation to the world and, more specifically, to man. It is the theological perspective, and the reality to which it refers, that has led us to have recourse more than once to the paradoxical notion of a "relative Absolute" — an unavoidably ill-sounding expression, but one that is metaphysically useful.

The error — born in the climate of monotheism — of a Divine Freedom able, thanks to its absoluteness, to not create the world or to create it without any inner necessity, this error is repeated — on a smaller scale and in grosser fashion — in the Asharite error of a Divine Power able — again thanks to its character of absoluteness — to punish the just and reward evildoers "if God so willed." In the first case it is forgotten that Necessity — not constraint — is a complementary quality of Freedom;[6] in the second, it is forgotten that Goodness and therefore also Justice — not impotence or subordination — is a complementary

---

5. However, a Meister Eckhart is perfectly aware of this mystery, and is doubtless not alone in this in scholastic and mystical circles.

6. Liberty is related to the Infinite, and Necessity to the Absolute.

quality of Omnipotence.[7] For the virtuous man, the need to practice the virtues is no constraint; all the more so, if God "must" do what His Perfection demands and "cannot" do what is contrary to it — namely to withhold creation or to punish the innocent — this is neither for lack of freedom nor for lack of power. God's Goodness implies that He may be above His Justice, but not below it; His Freedom implies that He can create everything, but not that He could not create at all. His transcendence in relation to creation resides in His undifferentiated Substance, in respect to which there is neither creation nor any attributes concerning it.

*

* *

In the celestial world, there is no place for those privative manifestations — or "existentiations of nothingness" — which we have the right to call "evil." Evil as such starts only with the animic world and extends to the world of matter;[8] it therefore pertains to the domain of form and change. Evil, as we have said more than once, arises from the distance separating the world of form from the supraformal Principle; this is to say that by its very nature form involves the danger of separation from, and opposition to, the Principle or the Substance; when this danger becomes actual — and it is prefigured in the separation and opposition implied by existence — the element Radiation, taking on an illusory autonomy, brings about remoteness from God, and the element Image, deifying itself, becomes idol. Form is nothing else than individuation; now the individual tends to seek his end in himself, in his accidentality and not in his principle, not in his Self.[9] The retribution for this is

---

7. God is just not because He owes account to man a priori, but because, being good, he is incapable of being unjust.

8. According to the Koran, Satan is a *jinn*, not an angel; he is made of "fire," not of "light."

9. The devil was the first being to say "I," according to some Sufis.

the presence, along with normal or perfect forms — of forms having some claim to being termed good — of privative or false and therefore ugly or vicious forms, on the psychic as well as on the physical level; ugliness is the price paid for ontological revolt, so to speak. The tendency towards evil is Radiation that has deviated or become inverted; the form of evil is Image falsified and inverted in its turn; it is Satan, and consequently vice or sin on every plane and not on that of morality alone.

Formal *Māyā* — which is not angelic and still less divine — brings into play a coagulating magic, separative and individualizing and thus possibly subversive; the reason for this is that it has become too remote from the Principle or the Substance, and gone too far towards nothingness which, however, is no more than a signpost or direction and not a concrete reality. In a way, nothingness is the one enigma of metaphysics by the fact that it is nothing and yet can be thought of and even tended towards; nothingness is, as it were, the "sin of *Māyā*," and this sin confers on *Māyā* an ambiguity that evokes the mystery "Eve-Mary," or the "Eternal Feminine" which both seduces and saves.

This ambiguity, which is quite relative and far from being symmetrical, cannot tarnish *Māyā;* "I am black, but beautiful," says the Song of Songs and also, "Thou art all fair, my love; there is no spot in thee"; the glory of Mary totally effaces the sin of Eve, which is to say that with regard to the total extent of Existence and above all with regard to its Divine Summit, there is no longer any ambiguity, and evil is not. Universal Existence, whose functioning is a boundless play of innumerable veilings and unveilings, is eternally virgin and pure, while being mother of all the reverberations of the One Substance.

*

* *

In the Catholic sign of the cross a ternary is superimposed on a quaternary; the content of the sign is in fact the Trinity, but the gesture itself consists of four stations; the fourth coincides with the word Amen. One could point out that this asymmetry or inconsistency is compensated by the fact that the word Amen betokens the prayer of the Church, and therefore the mystical body of Christ considered as prolongation of God; but it is equally possible to assert that this fourth station belongs to the Blessed Virgin as Spouse of the Holy Spirit and Co-Redemptress, that is, ultimately, as *Māyā* at once human and divine. This is moreover what is betokened by the Amen itself, for it expresses the *Fiat Voluntas Tua* of Mary.

The black color of the beloved in the Song of Songs, and of many images of the Blessed Virgin, expresses not so much the very relative ambiguity of Existence as its "self-effacement."[10] Relativity could not be personified in the Trinity because it is itself, in a way, the framework for the personifications; similarly in the Universe, *Māyā* is neither Radiation nor Image, but the principle of projection or its framework. On earth, we perceive things and changes; we do not directly perceive space and time. Even so, if Mary were not a kind of hypostasis,[11] she could be neither "Spouse" to God-Radiation nor "Mother" to God-Image.[12]

10. In the famous story of Laila and Majnun, in which Majnun sublimizes the beloved inwardly to the point of forgetting the earthly Laila, it is said that people reproached him for loving a woman of so dark a complexion; and this is certainly not devoid of meaning in the doctrinal context that concerns us here.

11. It is scarcely possible for theology to accept this mystery of Mary, because it can function only with simple notions, precisely defined and concretely useful; its philosophical dimension can refine this structure, but it cannot transcend it, although it may step outside this framework incidentally.

12. According to the revelations of Sister Mechthild of Magdeburg (13th century) the Blessed Virgin testified to her quality of Logos in the following words: "There I was the single betrothed of the Holy Trinity and mother of the Sages, and I took them before the eyes of God lest they fall, as so many others did. And as I was thus mother to many noble children, my breasts were filled with the pure and unmixed milk of true, sweet Mercy, in such wise that I nurtured the Prophets, and they prophesied before God (Christ) was born." (*Das fliessende Licht der Gottheit*, 1,22).

Ātmā-Māyā

"In the Name of the Father, and of the Son, and of the Holy Ghost, Amen"; this final word becomes a hypostasis by the very symmetry of the formula and by the gesture indicating it. Cosmic *Māyā* is identified metaphysically with the creative Word "Be!" and therefore with the creative Act, of which it is the effectuation and, consequently, the hypostatic prolongation. Now "God is Love" and He "created the World by Love"; He is Love in His bi-polarization into Radiation and Image — as an effect of *Māyā* — and He has created the world by Love, and therefore by *Māyā;* this latter is Love projected into the night of nothingness, or projected in illusory fashion "outside God" so that even nothingness might be somehow enfolded within Divine Reality.

Love, whether in God or in the Universe, comprises the poles of Goodness and Beauty; Beauty relates to Form, Image, Reverberation, and Goodness to Energy, Act, Radiation; all cosmic phenomena stem from this polarity whether directly or indirectly, positively or negatively, in a manner that imparts or deprives. It is not Divine *Māyā* that directly brings about the phenomena of deprivation, for which she weeps behind her veil; she weeps on account of the various modes of evil or the absurd, but cannot avoid these fissures since the creative radiation involves, in the final analysis and at its extreme limit, subversive and corrupting remoteness. Evil is the price paid for Relativity or Existence, but it is repaid in advance by Existence's victorious Divinity. Eve is infinitely forgiven and victorious in Mary.

According to an Islamic tradition, Eve lost her beauty after the expulsion from Paradise, whereas Mary is the very personification of Beauty; "And Her Lord . . . caused her to grow with a beauteous growing," says the Koran. But even without any recourse to the complementary relationship Eve-Mary, and applying the symbolism of the ambiguity of *Māyā* to Eve alone, we can discern in Eve on the one hand two blemishes: sin and the loss of beauty, and on the other hand two glories: reintegration into Perfection and the incorruptible beauty that this glory confers on the elect.[13]

*
* *

The basic problem of cosmology lies in the following chain of developments: the infinitude of the Divine Substance demands and brings about Relativity or Existence; Existence demands or brings about, or implies by definition, cosmic Manifestation; but it thereby implies or involves the mystery of remoteness from God, and thus incidentally of evil, since God alone is Absolute Good; to put it otherwise, the apparent contradiction of this Good cannot not occur at a certain stage, given that Divine Possibility knows no limits. Evil, if it is real within its boundaries which, however, are metaphysically illusory, is no more than a fragment of a greater good which compensates for it and, in a way, absorbs it; at its existential center, which surpasses its accidentality, evil ceases to be; it is reabsorbed into an ever pure substance in which it has never been.

God is the Absolute Good who desires relative good, that is, the relativity concomitant with His own Good; now the price of this relative good is evil. The argument that "good" is simply a moral idea and no more than a matter of human evaluation fails to take account of two factors: firstly, Good is a universal reality of which moral good is only one application among others; and secondly, to describe something as the product of human evaluation makes sense only if we bear in mind that man as such is

13. As Dante wrote: "The wound that Mary closed and salved, 'twas she at her feet who is so fair (*quella chè' tanto bella* = Eve) that opened it and soured it"; Eve recovered in Eternity her primordial beauty. It could also be pointed out that if Mary is *Māyā* in its immutable and inviolate reality, Eve represents *Māyā* under its aspect of ambiguity, but also of final victory, and therefore of fundamental goodness.

predisposed by definition towards making an adequate evaluation of things. Notions inherent in man are necessarily true, it is simply the individual who may err through his misapplication; that sentiment should feel satisfaction at the notion of good does not prove that this notion is inadequate or devoid of meaning, or created by wishful thinking; Good is not a value because man loves it, but man loves Good because it is a value. Or again, we do not call a value "good" for being loved by man; we call it good for being objectively lovable in virtue of its direct or indirect attributes of truth and happiness; now neither Truth nor Beatitude were invented by man, and the fact that man inclines towards them by his intellect, his will and his sentiment does not in any way invalidate their objective reality.

We have said that the price of relative good is evil. Now it is absurd for man to accept and desire relative good without at the same time accepting, not evil in a specific form, but the inevitability of evil. Every man, by definition, accepts and desires relative good in some form or other, and therefore he must accept the phenomenon of evil as a basis for finally rising above it. To be fully human is, on the one hand, to note and accept the inevitability of the absurd and, on the other hand, to liberate oneself from the absurd by discerning between accident and Substance, this victorious discernment that is precisely the very vocation of the human being. Earthly *Māyā* herself is liberated through man, for each particular liberation is something absolute and, from a certain viewpoint, realizes Liberation as such.

The Substance is not only Supreme Reality but, by being this is also, as we have said, Supreme Good; now "the good tends essentially to impart itself,"[14] and this ontological tend-

---

14. *Bonum est essentialiter diffusivum sui,* according to the Augustinian principle, which proves moreover that creation is not "an absolutely gratuitous act," and that Platonist emanationism in no way contradicts the intrinsic Liberty of God. — Likewise this *ḥadīth qudsī:* "I was a hidden treasure and I wished to be known; so I created the world."

ency provides an explanation not only for Relativity — or "Ex-sistence" — as hypostasis, and thus as radiation and reverberation in God Himself, but also for Cosmic Existence, itself also radiating and reverberating by definition, but "outside God." Thus it is that *Māyā* is not only an "illusion," as the Advaitists would have it, but also a necessary concomitance of the Goodness inherent in the Absolute Real; in other words, if Substance is good, it must project *Māyā;* and if God is good, He must create the world. It follows from this causality that *Māyā* is good; if it were not, it would have no place in God and could not proceed from Him. And if *Māyā* is good it is because, in a mysterious but not inconceivable fashion, it "is not other than God."

Māyā is the breath of *Ātmā; Ātmā* "breathes" through *Māyā.*[15] This breathing — apart from its inner or substantial prefigurations — is extrinsic, in the manner of our breathing here on earth, where a link is made between the inward, the living body, and the outward, the surrounding air. The Universe proceeds from God and returns to Him; hence the cosmic cycles governing the microcosm as well as the macrocosm. *Māyā* is the air breathed by *Ātmā,* and this air is a quality of His own Infinitude.[16]

15. In Medieval German, *ātem* still meant "spirit," whereas modern German retains only the meaning of "breath." In Old German the "Holy Spirit" was called *der heilige ātem.*

16. In the language of Sufism, the world proceeds from Goodness-Beauty, or from Beauty-Love, *Raḥmah;* this is what is called the "Breathing out of the Infinitely Good" *(nafas Ar-Raḥmān)* or the "Compassionate breathing out" *(nafas raḥmani),* and this breathing is Goodness, Beauty, Love, Mercy; *Raḥmah* is almost synonymous with *Māyā.*

The Human Margin

Christ, in rejecting certain rabbinical prescriptions as "human" and not "Divine," shows that according to God's scale of measurement there is a sector which, while being orthodox and traditional, is nonetheless human in a certain sense; this means that the Divine influence is total only for the Scriptures and for the essential consequences of the Revelation, and that it always leaves a "human margin" where it exerts no more than an indirect action, letting ethnic or cultural factors speak. It is to this sector or margin that many of the speculations of exoterism belong; orthodoxy is on the one hand homogeneous and indivisible, on the other hand it admits of degrees of absoluteness and relativity. We should not therefore be too scandalized at the anathemas which Dyophysites, Monophysites, Aphthartodocetae, Phartolatrae, Agnoetae, Akistetae and Ktistolatrae hurl at one another over the question of knowing whether Christ is of an incorruptible substance or whether, on the contrary, he was like other bodies, or whether there was a part of human ignorance in the soul of Christ, or whether the body of Christ is uncreated while being at the same time visible, or whether it was created, and so on.[1]

1. The following divergence may be noted with regard to the Blessed Virgin: Was Mary a priori delivered from the capacity for sin, or was she sinless through the superabundance of her virtue? In other

What is surprising in most cases though not always equally so, is the vehement desire to focus on questions which are not of crucial importance, and the incapacity to allow a certain latitude regarding things that the Revelation did not deem it indispensable to be precise about. It would have sufficed, both from the mystical and from the dogmatic point of view, to admit that Christ, as living form of God, had to show in his humanity supernatural prerogatives which it would be vain to seek to enumerate, but that inasmuch as he was incontestably man, he was bound to have certain limits, as is proved by the incident of the fig tree whose sterility he did not discern from afar. The question of the *filioque* is a clear example of this tendency to pointless precisions, and to a dogmatization producing a superfluity of divisions and anathemas.

In this connection, one is inevitably forced to conclude that fallen or post-edenic man is a kind of fragmentary being; one is therefore bound to acknowledge the obvious truth that a man's sanctity does not preclude the possibility of his being a poor logician with a mind more sentimental than intellectual, and that in spite of this he may feel a call to fulfill some teaching function, not of course through pretension, but through "zeal for the house of the Lord." Inspiration by the Holy Spirit cannot mean that the latter puts itself in the place of human intelligence

---

words, was she impeccable because of the absolute holiness of her nature, or was she holy as a result of the absolute impeccability of her intelligence and her will? Those who maintain the first thesis seek to avoid attributing to Mary an imperfection of substance; those of the second seek to avoid depriving her of the perfection of merit; but both sides seem to lose sight of the fact that at the degree of the Blessed Virgin the alternative loses all its meaning. The "immaculate conception" — attributed to Mary also by the Islamic tradition — admits of every meritorious attitude by its very nature, rather as a substance contains in synthesis all its possible accidents; and inversely, perfect impeccability — out of the question for the ordinary man — is *ipso facto* equivalent to the absence of "original sin."

and liberates it from all its natural limitations, for that would be Revelation; inspiration means solely that the Spirit guides man in accordance with the Divine intention and according to the capacities of the human receptacle. If this were not so, there would be no theological elaboration, nor would there be any divergences in orthodoxy, and the first Father of the Church would have written one single theological treatise which would have been exhaustive and definitive; there would never have been a Thomas Aquinas or a Gregory Palamas. There are moreover men who are inspired by the Holy Spirit because and to the extent that they are Saints, whereas there are others who are Saints because and to the extent that they are inspired by the Holy Spirit.

*

* *

The most ordinary examples of the human margin which Heaven concedes to traditions are to be found in the scissions within the intrinsically orthodox religions; and this has nothing to do with the question of heterodoxy, for intrinsic heresies lie precisely outside this margin. It is a fact that collective human thought is not good at conceiving the fluctuations between different points of view on the one hand, and the aspects to which they correspond on the other, or between different modes of the subjective and the objective; this leads to polarizations and scissions which, however inevitable and providential they may be, are nonetheless dangerous imperfections. Heaven allows man to be what he is, but this condescension or patience does not mean complete approval on the part of God.

As far as ecclesiology is concerned, the most ancient Christian texts sometimes uphold the Latin thesis and sometimes the Greek; the ideal, or rather the normal situation therefore, would be an Orthodox Church recognizing a Pope who was not totally autocratic but in spiritual communion with the whole body of bishops or patriarchs; this would be a Pope without *filioque,* but having nonetheless the right, in theology, liturgy and other domains, to certain particularities, which might be opportune or even necessary in a Latin or Germanic setting. The disorders — of a gravity without precedent — with which the Roman Church is now beset prove that the Latin conception of the Church is theologically narrow and judicially excessive; if it were not, these disorders would be inconceivable.[2] Moreover, there seems to be something tragically insoluble in the very structure of Christendom: give total supremacy to the Pontiff, and he will become a mundane, conquering Caeser; give supremacy to the Emperor, and he will make the Pontiff his pawn and tool.[3] But it must be admitted that we have here a vicious circle, the traces of which are to be found wherever there are men.

2. The coming of Protestantism, in the Latin West, affords the same proof. Psychologically — not doctrinally — Protestantism in fact re-edits, though of course in a much more extreme form, the protest of Arianism, which in spite of everything has in it a particle of truth and an element of equilibrium.

3. Most paradoxically, the one does not preclude the other. That is what has actually happened in the Latin West, where the Papacy has finally become the prey, not of the Emperor needless to say, but of politics and consequently of the democracy which determines them. Since the French Revolution, the Church has been so to speak substantially at the mercy of the laicist republics — including the pseudo-monarchies that in fact are republican — for it is their ideology that decides who is worthy of being a bishop; and thanks to a particularly favorable conglomeration of historical circumstances, politics has succeeded in pumping into the mold of the Church a human matter which is heterogeneous to the Church. The last Council was ideo-political, not theological: its irregularity springs from the fact that it was determined, not by concrete situations assessed on a theological basis, but by anti-theological, ideo-political abstractions, or more precisely by the democratism of the world monstrously setting itself up as Holy Spirit. "Humility" and "charity," ready to take on any shape, but henceforth limited to one direction only, are there to ensure the success of the enterprise.

The Human Margin

*

* *

The "unfathomable mystery" of the theologians is sometimes no more than a manifestation of metaphysical insufficiency; unless it refers to the unquestioned fathomlessness of the Divine Subjectivity which is as mysterious for objectivizing and separating thought as the optic nerve is for the sight; however, the impossibility of the eye's seeing the optic nerve is not in the least mysterious. Very often the thesis of "mystery" is either a gratuitous affirmation brought in to veil a theological contradiction or a truism pure and simple, seeing that we know what thought is and what its obvious limitations are.

All the drama of the theologies lies in the incompatibility between their simplifying sublimism and the idea of *Māyā* at the level of Divinity, or the idea of Divine Relativity; the theologies are therefore obliged to correct the deadlocks of their the deep-rooted voluntarism by means of philosophical expedients which are "providential" insofar as they are psychologically opportune for a particular collectivity. One of the great difficulties of Sufism is that the loftiest metaphysics finds itself inextricably mixed with a theology tarnishing it by its habitual confusions regarding "Omnipotence"; unless we admit that in this case, on the contrary, sapience deepens theology by infusing into it some liberating gleams of light.[4]

4. The deterioration in question is to be felt not only on the speculative plane but also on the operative plane where the volitive element too often confers on the method a somewhat violent aspect, as a substitute for a more intellectual alchemy; accidents of psychic rupture result from this, for the gates of Heaven cannot be forced by excesses without intelligence, however heroic these may be. There must be a balance between the quantitative and the qualitative, between the volitive and the intellective, and moralizing popularization turns a blind eye to this need. It is moreover this popularization that entails an imagery of extravagant prodigies and, by reaction, the equally unfortunate depreciation of the genuine miracles.

The theologies, by taking upon themselves the contradiction of being sentimental metaphysics, are condemned to square the circle; they are ignorant of the differentiation of things into aspects and standpoints and they have therefore to operate on the basis of arbitrarily rigid data, the antinomies of which can only be solved by going beyond that artificial rigidity; their working has moreover a sentimental slant, and this is described as "thinking piously."[5] In Christianity there is a desire to admit differentiation within the Divine Oneness and an equally imperious desire practically not to admit that there is a differentiation — the Hypostases being "merely relationships" — as if the three dimensions of space were to be willed into one dimension alone. In Islam, an obstinate unitarianism collides with the existence of the world and the diversities in it, whereas there would be no conflict if the unitarianism were metaphysical and therefore transparent and supple as its nature demands. In Christianity there is a certain dispersion in the object of worship: God, the Persons, Christ, the Eucharist, the Sacred Heart; in Islam there is on the contrary excessive centralization on a plane where it cannot be imposed, namely, a refusal to admit any cause except God or to be dependent on anything but Him alone, even in the face of immediate evidences, when in reality such evidences in no sense preclude everything from depending upon God, and when it suffices to be conscious of this to be on the side of truth. There is a zeal which is ever ready to replace thought by virtue, and truth by heroism; in saying this, we are very far from overlooking that a devotional attitude is normal to man and therefore normative, and that there is no balanced intellectuality without it; but everything must be put in its proper place, and this has become particularly difficult for the passional humanity of the "Iron Age."

5. The councils would sometimes degenerate into brawls, which is not very metaphysical but is always preferable to flabby indulgence with regard to manifest error, under pretext of "charity" or "humility."

What needs to be understood is that a soul filled with piety is capable of thinking with detachment, in perfect harmony with its piety and not despite it, the more so since the instinct to worship becomes deeper in exact proportion to its impregnation with truth.[6]

For extreme trinitarianism, God is of course One, but He is only so while being Three, and there is no One God except in and by the Trinity; the God who is One without Trinity, or independently of all hypostatic unfolding, is not the true God for, without this unfolding, Unity is meaningless. And it is here that the full gravity of trinitarianism comes to light: there are Christians who are incapable of seeing the slightest value in Islam — which, incidentally, is contrary to the opinion of most theologians; for them Islam and atheism are equivalent; if they do not level the same reproach at Judaism, it is simply because they project into it their own trinitarianism as an axiomatic implication. This justifies the Moslem reproach of "tritheism"; anyone who, owing to trinitarianism, is incapable of seeing that the Koran speaks of the God of Abraham — even supposing that it does so imperfectly — and that Moslems worship God and nothing else, really deserves the above reproach. Christ, in speaking of the supreme Commandment, or in teaching the Lord's Prayer, did not speak of the Trinity any more than did the God of Sinai, who deemed it sufficient to define Himself in these words: "Hear, O Israel: The Lord our God is one Lord."

As we have pointed out before on more than one occasion, trinitarianism is a concept of God determined by the mystery of Divine Manifestation; if we seek the prefiguration of this mystery in God, we discern the Trinity. Applied to any religion, monotheistic or not, the same idea calls for the following formulation: the Essence has be-

---

6. The Vedantic texts confirm this, and the monotheistic theologies themselves comprise, needless to say, sectors which bear witness to the same quality.

come form in order that form may become Essence; all Revelation is a humanization of the Divine for the sake of deification of the human.

*

* *

Judaism and Islam make the following objections to Trinitarianism: you say that the Son is begotten and that He is God; now God is not begotten, He is Absolute. You say that the Holy Ghost emanates and that he is delegated and that he is God; now God does not emanate from anything, nor is He sent. And you say that the Father is God and that He begets; now God creates, but He does not beget, otherwise there would be two Gods. Moreover, how can the Son and the Holy Ghost each be identical with God and not be identical with each other?

To these objections a Christian might reply that in Judaism and Islam Divine Mercy is not identical with Divine Vengeance but that both are identical with God; Jews and Moslems will reply that there is a serious nuance here, for while the Mercy and Vengeance are incontestably Divine, it would be false to affirm that God is to be reduced to one or the other.[7] The equation is only relative, and there lies the root of the problem: Judaism and Islam admit in a certain sense relativity *in divinis;* they distinguish between the Essence and the Attributes, whereas Christianity, at least at the theological level, seems to want to bring everything back to absoluteness, whence the problematic ellipses of trinitarian theology.

"I am in the Father, and the Father is in me": this is the identity of Essence. But "my Father is greater than I": this

---

7. Mercy is God, but God is not Mercy alone. Yet God is Mercy much more directly — the verb "to be" indicating here an identity of essence and not an equation pure and simple — than He is Vengeance, for the latter is extrinsic and conditional, whereas the former is intrinsic and therefore unconditional, without however being identical with Absoluteness as such.

is the difference of degree within the principial Reality, that is, at a level which is still uncreated or metacosmic. The sense of an absolute equation has been conferred on the first utterance, while relativizing the second; rather than combining both sayings and explaining each in the light of the other, the second utterance has been arbitrarily attributed to the human nature.

We have quoted the following argument: God creates but does not beget, otherwise there would be two Gods; we would specify that this is true unless one recognizes the notion of *Māyā*, which enables one to understand that the hiatus between Creator and creature is necessarily prefigured *in divinis,* by the differentiation between the Absolute as such and the Absolute relativized in view of a dimension of its Infinitude; but this difference, precisely, is real only from the standpoint of Relativity. For the Vedantists, the separation between the Absolute *(Paramātmā)* and the Relative *(Māyā = Ishwara)* is as rigorous as the separation between Creator and creature is for the Semites; but by compensation there is an aspect which admits the created and the Uncreated to be linked, since nothing that exists can be other than a manifestation of the Principle or an objectivization of the Self; "everything is *Ātmā.*"[8]

In other words: there is *Ātmā* and there is *Māyā;* but there is also *Ātmā* as *Māyā,* and this is the manifesting and acting Personal Divinity; and conversely, there is also *Māyā* as *Ātmā,* and this is the total Universe when seen as one polyvalent reality. The world will then be the Divine aspect termed "Universal Man" *(Vaishwānara)* or, in Sufism, "the Outward" *(az-Ẓāhir);* this is, incidentally, the deepest meaning of the Far Eastern *Yin-Yang.* And it is in

---

8. If philosophical pantheism had this aspect of things in view — which it has not, being ignorant of the degrees of reality and ignorant of transcendence — it would be legitimate as a synthetic or inclusive perspective. The polemics of the theologians readily confuse these two kinds of pantheism.

In the Face of the Absolute

the light of this doctrine that it has been possible to say that the *Avatāra* was "created before creation," which means that before creating the world, God has to "create Himself" *in divinis,* if one may say so, the word "create" having here a higher and transposed meaning which is precisely that of *Māyā*.[9]

The distinction between the human and divine natures reflects or symbolizes the distinction, within the Divine Nature, between inequality in relation to the Father and equality, or between relativity and absoluteness. On the other hand, this principial distinction also asserts itself on the plane of human nature, in which one dimension is marked by earthly contingence whereas the other is quasi-divine, whence the Monophysite interpretation. It is not surprising that this combination of three polarities — man and God, terrestrial man and divine man, hypostatic God and essential God — should have given rise by its complexity to the diverse opinions already alluded to, orthodox or heretical as the case may be; it is the basic polarity *Ātmā-Māyā* which repeats itself or reverberates in countless modalities, of which the most important for man is the confrontation between God and the world. The first verse of St. John enunciates this polarity, applied to Christ, by placing side by side two affirmations: *Et Verbum erat apud Deum, et Deus erat Verbum:* the dimension of subordination, then the dimension of equality or identity.

---

9. For Parmenides, pure Being coincides with pure Knowing; all the rest is "opinion," *doxa,* which is not unrelated to the notion of *Māyā,* with the reservation however that, in Vedantic terms, Being as conceived by Parmenides does not emerge absolutely from *Māyā* but is to be identified with its summit, *Ishwara.* Correlatively with their cult of Perfection, the Greeks have always had a certain fear of the Infinite, which is very visible even in their architecture: the Parthenon has real grandeur, but it expresses the religion of finite and rational Perfection which is opposed to virgin nature, in confusing the unlimited with the chaotic, the infinite with the irrational.

The whole of Arianism is to be explained by the urge — however unconscious — to take into consideration the principle of relativity *in divinis,* and therefore *Māyā:* Arius teaches that the Son, while not created "in time" like the entire creation (time having begun only with the creation), was nonetheless "drawn from nothingness," but that the Son is Divine inasmuch as he is the principle of cosmic creation, thus of creation properly so called; by this Arius means that the Word, while being Divine, has nonetheless an aspect of relativity. It is true that Arius spoils his thesis by some erroneous speculations on the person of Christ; but it must be recognized that there is in his doctrine a true and profound intuition, although clumsily formulated in terms of Semitic and creationist anthropomorphism. Instead of rejecting Arianism altogether, it would have been better to have adopted its positive theological intention, that of Divine Relativity as the prototype of cosmic limitation: the Word is neither totally other than the Absolute, as Arius would have it, nor totally — or in every respect — identical with the Absolute, as the Homousiasts would have it; if antinomism in metaphsyical dialectic ever has to be used, it is here. The very expansion and tenacity of Arianism, at a time so close to the origins of Christianity, proves that there was more to it than mere human error; the Nicene Council thus marks, not exactly the victory of truth, but the victory of the most important truth to the detriment of essential metaphysical shades of meaning. It is true that dogmatic theology has to simplify; but a unilateral or fragmentary outlook is what it is, and it cannot fail to bring about disequilibriums to the degree that its content calls for multidimensionality.

In any case, it must be admitted that the theological formulation of the Trinity constitutes, in a given milieu, a providential form destined not only to be the vehicle of the mystery while at the same time protecting it, but also to serve, by its very paradox, as a point of reference for the total and therefore necessarily multidimensional doctrine.

In the Face of the Absolute

*

* *

A distinction has to be made between metaphysical knowledge and the ability to express it. The Greeks and above all the Hindus have long possessed the instrument of dialectic, for it corresponds to their sense of objectivity,[10] whereas the primitive Semites — and therefore also Islam at its outset — were lacking in it; but it goes without saying that this has no bearing as regards the degree of wisdom of particular individuals, seeing that we find the profoundest metaphysics as it were condensed in certain Biblical and Koranic formulas or in certain utterances of Saints who were inspired by these formulas long before Hellenist influence could possibly have reached them. These remarks, and still more our previous considerations on the metaphysics underlying the various theologies, impel us to return to certain basic truths of the *sophia perennis* at the double risk of going outside the framework of our subject and repeating some of the things said already. At issue are always the notions of absoluteness and relativity, so important or so fateful in the context of the "human margin."

The Islamic Testification that "there is no divinity but the one Divinity" has first of all, metaphysically speaking, the objective meaning of a discernment, therefore of a separation, between the Real and the illusory or between the Absolute and the relative; there is also the subjective meaning of a spiritual distinction between the worldly out-

---

10. As to Far-Easterners, they are contemplatives, but symbolists, not logicians; they are above all "visual." The purely Mongol traditions are those of Fo-Hi with its Taoist and Confucianist branches, then Shinto, not to speak of the various Far-Eastern and Siberian Shamanisms. But the Mongol soul has also set its imprint on Buddhism which has thus become partially representative of the spiritual genius of the yellow race, particularly in the case of Zen and, more generally, in the whole field of sacred art.

76

ward and the Divine Inward: in this case the objective and transcendent Divinity appears as immanent hence subjective — taking the term "subjective" in a transpersonal sense, which is to say that the subject is not the human ego but the pure Intellect, the purified ego being no more than the path of access. In order to be total, the doctrine still has need of a unitive dimension, expressed in Islam by the second Testification: to say that "the Praised (Muhammad) is the Messenger of the (only) Divinity" means that the relative, inasmuch as it directly manifests the Absolute, is not other than the Absolute; and according to the subjective application, the outward, the world, is not other than the Inward, the Self.[11]

But if the relative can have this aspect of absoluteness which reintegrates it into the Absolute — since the Universe could not exist on the basis of an ultimate dualism — that is because relativity must be prefigured in the Absolute Itself; *Māyā* has its origin in *Ātmā,* otherwise the subsequent difference between God and the world would be inconceivable. That is why Creation as a whole, while being on the one hand separate from the Creator, is on the other hand a prolongation of Him and a "Divine aspect"; this is what the Divine Name "the Apparent" *(az̧-Z̧āhir)* expresses, as opposed to "the Hidden" *(al-Bāt̟in)* and this is what enables certain Sufis to affirm that "all is God," in conformity with the Koranic verse: "Wheresoever ye turn, there is the Face of God" (Sura "The Cow," 115). One particular manifestation of the relative reintegrated into the Absolute, or more precisely of the Absolute manifested as relative, is the Logos, the Prophet;

11. The fundamental Testimony, or the First *Shahādah,* has a negative part, which rejects false divinities, and a positive part, which affirms the True God: the former is the Negation, the *Nafy,* and the latter is the Affirmation, the *Ithbāt;* we have here the distinction between *Māyā* and *Ātmā.* The second *Shahādah,* that of the Prophet, adds that *Māyā* is not other than *Ātmā,* in its "not unreal" substance.

another is the Heart, the place of inward and transmuting theophany.

Quintessential Christianity expresses this relationship of identity as directly as can be: the Son is united with the Father; Christ is God. That man, who is relative, should be able to be identified with God presupposes that relativity has an aspect of absoluteness and that it is therefore prefigured *in divinis;* hence the doctrine of the Word. "God became man that man might become God": the Absolute comprises relativity and therefore relativity can be reintegrated into the Absolute; the Patristic formula we have just paraphrased thus means on the one hand that the human Logos directly manifests the Absolute, and on the other, that man can be reintegrated into the Absolute through being united with the human Logos, in and by which he virtually identifies with this Absolute.

The objection that Paradise is not the Absolute and that in no religion is man literally supposed to become God does not in any sense invalidate what has just been stated; for it is in fact a question not of a transmutation of the individual as such into the Divine Essence but, to begin with, of an "adoption" by God; man is then directly beneath the Divine axis, he is open to the Infinite in the innermost depth of his being, he "wears a crown of uncreated light." There is no common measure between his spiritual secret, the mystery of identity or absoluteness, and the existence — or the subsistence — of the individual form, but the one does not preclude the other; man remains man despite the reality of absoluteness which penetrates him. *Nirvāna* did not destroy the Buddha, it immortalized him; otherwise it would never be possible to speak of a human manifestation of the Logos. If God can "become man," this is because there can be no possible rivalry between the Divine and the human.

God and the world: each of the terms admits of polarization into absoluteness and relativity, and the two terms themselves represent this polarization. In God there are the Essence and the Attributes and their common Life; and in the world there is Heaven, standing for the Absolute, and earth, denoting the relative as such. Here, as *in divinis,* the Holy Spirit is the unifying Life.

The theological equation between the Uncreated and the Absolute on the one hand and between the created and the relative on the other is altogether insufficient. For if it is true that the created pertains by definition to relativity, it is false to admit that the Uncreated pertains in just the same way to absoluteness; only the Essence is pure Absolute, although the Divine Relativity clearly has the function of Absolute in relation to the created. The manifested Logos also has this aspect or function, but cannot be the "absolutely Absolute"; if Christ addresses a prayer to his Father, it is not solely by reason of his human nature, it is also by reason of the relativity of the uncreated Logos. If the Son were merely an abstract "relationship of origin," it would be impossible for him to take on a human nature.

The dogma of the Trinity existed before trinitarian theology; the latter pertains to the human margin, the former comes from Revelation. The dogma lays down metaphysical data; theology, by combining these data, westernizes them.

*
* *

A religion is not limited by what it includes but by what it excludes; since every religion is intrinsically a totality, this exclusion cannot impair the religion's deepest contents, but the exclusion takes its revenge all the more surely on the intermediary plane which we call the "human margin" and which is the arena of theological speculations and of moral and mystical fervors. It is certainly not pure metaphysics or esoterism that would oblige us to pretend that a flagrant contradiction is not a contradiction; all that wisdom allows — or rather obliges — us to do is to recognize that extrinsic contradictions can hide an intrin-

79

sic compatibility or identity, which amounts to saying that each of the contradictory theses contains a truth and thereby an aspect of the whole truth and a way of access to it.

When one religion places the human Logos of another religion in hell, or when one confession does the same with the Saints of another confession, it cannot really be maintained, on the pretext that the essential truth is one, that there is no flagrant contradiction or that this contradiction is not by definition a serious infirmity on its own plane; the only extenuating circumstance that can be adduced is to say that this plane is not essential for the tradition which is mistaken, and that therefore the essential spirituality is not necessarily impaired by the error in question, all the more so since contemplatives are not necessarily preoccupied by extrinsic anathemas of their religion; and it could be argued also that in these anathemas the persons aimed at become negative symbols, so that there is merely an error of attribution and not of idea, hence an error of fact, not of principle.

As regards the ordinary theological ostracisms — whether of the West or of the East — there lies a profound wisdom in the fables of Aesop and of Pilpay; the story of the fox and the grapes that were too high for him to reach and that he therefore declared to be sour repeats itself in all sectors of human existence. In the name of wisdom, one vilifies one's neighbor's wisdom to console oneself — or to take one's revenge — for not having found it oneself; eminent theologians have not hesitated to attribute the inner voice of Socrates to the devil and to declare diabolic all the wisdom of the Greeks — a pointless extravagance to say the least, seeing that Christianity, even in its Oriental branches, has not been able to renounce the help of that wisdom altogether.

In the closed space of theology there are two openings: gnosis and the liturgy. This quality of opening towards the Unlimited is immediately clear in the case of gnosis; but it is necessary to know that the formal language of the sacred, be it the language of sanctuaries or of nature, is, as it were, the complement or the prolongation of metaphysical wisdom. For beauty, like pure truth, is calm and generous; it is disinterested and is above passional suffocations and disputes about words; and one of the reasons for being of sacred art — however paradoxical this might seem — is that it speaks to the intelligence of the sage as well as to the imagination of the simple man, satisfying both sensibilities at one and the same time and nourishing them according to their needs.

*

*   *

There are dialectical excesses which are not to be found in Divine language; but human language does not shrink from these audacities, and it can only be concluded that man finds some purpose in them or that his zeal finds satisfaction in them. We have read in a Buddhist text: "Follow a master, even if he guides you to hell"; an analogous expression is to be found in Moslem texts: "Be happy in the Will of God, even if it destines you for the eternal fire." Literally, such expressions are contradictory, for the whole point of a master is that he should guide you to Heaven, and happiness in God and through Him coincides with salvation; nevertheless these expressions are meaningful, and obviously so, otherwise they would not exist in spiritual contexts. The point being made is the perfect detachment of the ego; the absurdity of the image guarantees the efficacy of the shock. We must act "as if the situation were such," although it cannot be such; and the purpose of this is to obtain a radical inward attitude, not easily obtainable by other means from the standpoint of sentimental voluntarism. This last specification provides the key to the enigma: voluntaristic mysticism readily resorts to biases, to catapulting arguments or surgical acts of violence, for the simple reason that at that level the truth pure and simple appears as an inoperative abstraction.

For the "gnostic" or the "pneumatic," the inverse takes place; while being insensitive to exaggerations and other means of pressure he is immediately receptive to the truth as such, because it is the truth and because the truth is what convinces and attracts him.

It is true, however, that there is no rigorous separation between the two languages; gnosis also may use absurd formulations, but it does so by way of ellipsis or catalysis, while presupposing intellectual intuition. Thus, when it is said that the sage "is Brahman," a powerfully striking image is put forward by isolating — in order to make it stand out — a relationship that is metaphysically essential and decisive humanly, but not exhaustive phenomenologically since there are other relationships.

The dialectic of the Sufis tends to be a "dance of the seven veils": it starts from the idea that nothing must be divulged which would risk being neglected, badly used, profaned and then despised, and that what is most important is the balance between doctrinal knowledge and methodic realization. This dialectic likes to wrap spiritual truths in abstruse complications; to accept them, or to accept their existence, we need only know the motive behind them.

A consideration which could be appropriate here is the following: it is necessary to react against the exaggerated opinion that attributes to sainthood as such — not to a particular kind of sainthood — all imaginable qualities and therefore also all possible wisdom; in this sense, the "wisdom of the saints" — any and all saints — has been set in opposition to metaphysics as such, which is considered as merely a matter of "natural intelligence." Now the phenomenon of sainthood consists of two things: on the one hand the exclusiveness, and on the other the intensity, of thought and will in view of the transcendent and the beyond, or of "God" and "Paradise." Sainthood in the most general sense is thus essentially a matter of exclusiveness and intensity on the basis of a religious creed; it is on these two qualities, supernaturally inspired, that the gift of miracles depends. In the case of wisdom, it is the depth and scope of intellective knowledge that determine the exclusiveness and the intensity of spiritual comportment, but both modes of perfection can meet or interpenetrate; there is no incompatibility or rigorous separation between them, for if on the one hand "the Spirit bloweth where it listeth," on the other hand man always remains man.

*
* *

The human margin is clearly not confined to the plane of doctrine or dialectic, and we have already alluded to this when speaking of rabbinical exaggerations stigmatized by Christ. In a similar vein, there are certain excessive practices, consecrated by tradition or tolerated by it, particularly in Hinduism, where certain opinions or attitudes, without being in general altogether unintelligible, are in any case disproportionate to the point of being actually superstitious. These things can be explained partly by the constant care taken to preserve the tradition in its original purity — certain abuses are then erected against existing abuses — and partly by a certain totalitarianism pertaining to human nature; the care for purity is obviously combined with the awareness that collectivities need formulations that are precise and therefore incisive and in practice excessive; otherwise the teachings would become blurred and vanish altogether.

But in some of these excesses there may be a realism which has the purpose of exhausting negative possibilities within the very framework of the tradition, in somewhat the same way that Holy Scriptures contain wisely providential imperfections, or that sacred art shows monsters side by side with divinities, and devils side by side with angels, in order to reduce to a minimum the inevitable reactions of the powers of darkness, by a kind of preventive and disciplined anticipation.

*

* *

If there are variations, or even divergences, which are spiritually and traditionally legitimate or admissible, this is ultimately because there are three basic human types together with their diverse combinations: the passional, the sentimental, the intellectual.[12] Every man is an "I" placed in the "world"; that world has "forms," and the "I" has "desires." Now the great question is to know how a man spontaneously reacts to or interprets, by his nature, these four data of human existence; for it is this spontaneous conception which is the mark of his spiritual type.

To the passional man, the contingent facts of existence, the world and the ego with their contents, men and things, good deeds and sins, appear practically as something absolute. God appears to him as a sort of abstraction, a background which is not self-evident to him a priori. Passion dominates him and plunges him deeply into the world of appearances;[13] his path is thus primarily a penitential one,

12. The trivialization of certain terms makes it necessary to state here that the words "sentimental" and "intellectual" are to be understood in their true sense, that is, neutrally, without giving "sentimental" the pejorative overtone and "intellectual" the platitudinous and profane overtone which common parlance bestows on them. "Sentimental" means pertaining to sentiment, be it low or lofty, foolish or intelligent, worldly or centered on the sacred; "intellectual" means pertaining to the intellect, be it doctrinal or methodic, discriminative or contemplative. The term "intellectual" has not in fact the same ambivalence as the term "sentimental," in that the faculty of sentiment is horizontal and ambiguous whereas the intellect — not just the intelligence nor mere reason — is by definition a vertical and ascending faculty.

13. It may be mentioned in passing that this is, moreover, the function of a large part of "culture" — to lure man into blind alleys of pernicious dreaming and mental passion, to draw him insidiously away from "the one thing necessary," to make him lose the taste for Heaven.

whether he redeems himself by a violent asceticism or whether he sacrifices himself in some holy war, or in a servitude dedicated to God. The passional man is incapable of being intellectual in the full sense of the word; the doctrine, as far as he is concerned, is made up of threats and promises, and of the metaphysical and eschatological minimum required by an intelligence that is mixed with passion.

For the man of the intellectual type, on the contrary, the contingent facts of existence are immediately apparent as such, they are as it were transparent; before asking, "What do I want?" he will ask, "What is the world?" and, "What am I?" which determines in advance a certain detachment with regard to forms and desires. It is true that he may have attachments in virtue of heavenly realities which shine through their earthly reflections; the most contemplative child can be strongly attached to things which, in the human desert with which destiny may have surrounded him, seem like reminders of a Paradise both lost and immanent. Be that as it may, it is the Invisible which is the reality for the fundamentally contemplative man, whereas "life is a dream" *(la vida es sueño);* in him the Platonic sense of beauty takes the place of brute passion.

The third type is the emotional man, who might be called the musical type; he is intermediate, for he may tend towards the passional as well as towards the intellectual type, and he is moreover reflected in each.[14] It is love and hope which constitute in him the dominant and operative element; and he will be inclined to put special stress

---

The great novels of the nineteenth century, for example, are there for that; we have in them the centrifugal and modern substitute for the Golden Legend and the romances of Chivalry.

14. The purely profane mode here is individualistic lyric poetry; this is in principle less harmful than the novel — on condition that it be authentic and natural and not decadent and subversive — firstly because it is brief in expression and then because it may take its inspiration from a cosmic beauty transcending the individuality of the poet; the case of music is analogous.

on devotional manifestations, with a predilection for musical liturgy; his is the spirituality of happiness, but it is also the spirituality of nostalgia.

All this amounts to saying that there are three fundamental ways of transcending terrestrial *Māyā:* firstly the penitential crushing of the ego; secondly the conversion of passional energy into celestial music; and thirdly intellectual penetration which reduces illusion to ashes, or which brings it back to its quintessence.

These three modes or these three human types necessarily give rise to diverse combinations, which are made still more complex by the intervention of ethnic, cultural and other factors; we must also take into consideration not only the three types inasmuch as they characterize different individuals but also their presence in one and the same individual and even, to a certain extent, in every individual.[15] However, what interests us here is not the complexity of the human being but the differences between men: it is the diversity of spiritual gifts and above all the fragmentation of primordial man, that necessitate the play of veiling and unveiling of which traditional thought is made up.

*
* *

It is a great temptation to attribute the apparent naiveties of the Holy Scriptures to the "human margin," which unfolds in the shadow of Divine inspiration; it goes without saying that there is no connection between the two, unless we take this margin in a transposed and altogether different way, as we will do later; but it is clearly no such

15. The types in question, which refer to the ternary "fear-love-knowledge," scarcely coincide with the three types as defined by Gnosticism: the hylic, the psychic and the pneumatic. The hylic is never a spiritual type; the passional is always a psychic, whereas the sentimental can be a pneumatic but is more commonly found in the psychic category.

transposition that modern critics have in view when they bring up as arguments against the sacred books the apparent scientific errors which they contain. Now the data — said to be naive — of Genesis for example, prove, not that the Bible is wrong, but that man ought not to know more, for the simple reason that he cannot cope with more. Needless to say, no knowledge is harmful in itself, and there are necessarily always men capable of spiritually integrating all possible knowledge; but the average man can only cope with the kinds of knowledge that come to him through elementary, universal, millenary and therefore normal experience, as the history of the last centuries clearly proves. It is a fact not only that scientific man — rough-cast by classical Greece and developed by the modern West — loses religion in proportion to his involvement with physical science, but also that the more he is thus involved, the more he closes himself to the infinite dimension of suprasensory knowledge — the very knowledge that gives life a meaning.

Paradise is described in the Scriptures as being "up above," "in heaven," because the celestial vault is the only height that can be empirically or sensorially grasped; and for an analogous reason, hell is "down below," "under the earth," in darkness, heaviness, imprisonment. Similarly, for the Asiatics, *samsāric* births — when they are neither celestial nor infernal — take place "on earth," that is, on the only plane that can be empirically grasped; what counts, for Revelation, is the efficacy of the symbolism and not the indefinite knowledge of meaningless facts. It is true that no fact is totally meaningless in itself, otherwise it would be nonexistent, but the innumerable facts which lie outside man's normal experience and which scientism accumulates in our consciousness and also in our life are spiritually intelligible only for those who have no need of them.

Ancient man was very sensitive to the intentions inherent in symbolic expressions, as is proved on the one hand by the efficacy of these expressions throughout the centuries, and on the other hand by the fact that ancient man was quite obviously a perfectly intelligent being; when he was told the story of Adam and Eve, he grasped so well what was meant — the truth of it is in fact dazzlingly clear — that he did not dream of wondering "why" or "how"; for we carry the story of Paradise and the Fall in our soul and in our very flesh. The same applies to all eschatological symbolism: the "eternity" of the hereafter signifies first of all a contrast in relation to the here-below, that is, a dimension of absoluteness as opposed to our world of fleeting and therefore "vain" contingencies; it is this and nothing else that matters here, and this is the divine intention that lies behind the image. In transmigrationist symbolisms, on the contrary, this "vanity" is extended also to the hereafter, at least in a certain measure and by reason of a profound difference of perspective; and here likewise there is no preoccupation with either "why" or "how," once the incisive intention of the symbol has been grasped as it were in one's own flesh.

In the man who is marked by scientism, intuition of the underlying intentions has vanished, and that is not all; modern science, axiomatically closed to the suprasensory dimensions of the Real, has endowed man with a crass ignorance and warped his imagination accordingly. The modernist mentality is bent on reducing angels, devils, miracles — in short all non-material phenomena which are inexplicable in material terms — to the domain of the "subjective" and the "psychological," when there is not the slightest connection between the two, except that the psychism itself is also made — but objectively — of a substance which lies beyond matter; a contemporary theologian, speaking of the Ascension, has gone so far as to ask slyly, "Where does this cosmic journey end?" which shows the extent of the self-satisfied imbecility of a certain mentality that wants to be "of our time." It would be easy to explain why Christ was "raised up" into the air and what the meaning of the "cloud" is which hid him from sight,[16] and also why it was said that Christ "will come in the same manner"; every detail corresponds to a precise reality, easily comprehensible in the light of the traditional cosmologies. The key lies in the fact that the passage from one cosmic degree to another is heralded in the lower degree according to "technically" necessary and symbolically meaningful modalities reflecting after their fashion the higher state, and this in the order of succession required by the nature of things.

In any case, the deficiency of modern science is essentially in respect to universal, hence transcendent causality. It will no doubt be objected that science cannot be blamed for this since it is not concerned with philosophical causality but with phenomena. But in fact Darwinist evolutionism is nothing other than a hypertrophy imagined in order to deny real causes, and this materialistic negation together with its evolutionist compensation pertains to philosophy — without the transcendent element precisely.

From an altogether different point of view, it must be admitted that the progressivists are not entirely wrong in thinking that there is something in religion which no longer works. In fact the individualistic and sentimental argumentation with which traditional piety operates has lost almost all its power to pierce consciences; the reason for this is not merely that modern man is irreligious but also that the usual religious arguments, through not probing sufficiently to the depths of things and not having had previously any need to do so, are psychologically somewhat outworn and fail to satisfy certain needs of causality.

---

16. Not a cloud made of oxygen and hydrogen, but an extra-material substance become visible in order to receive the body ready to penetrate into the upper cosmos. Elijah's "chariot of fire" has the same meaning, as also the "globe of light" seen at certain apparitions of the Virgin. All this has absolutely nothing to do with fairy tales, let alone with "depth psychology."

If on the one hand human societies degenerate with the passage of time, they on the other hand accumulate experiences in virtue of old age, however intermingled with errors these experience may be; this paradox is something that any pastoral teaching bent on efficacy should take into account, not by drawing new directives from the general error but on the contrary by using arguments of a higher order, intellectual rather than sentimental; as a result, some people at least would be saved — a greater number than one might be tempted to suppppose — whereas the demagogic, scientistic pastoralist preaching saves no one.

*

* *

The notion of the "human margin" can be understood in a higher sense which no longer has anything psychological or terrestrial about it, and in this case we enter into an altogether new dimension which one must be careful not to confuse with the vicissitudes of thought. We mean to say that this notion can also be applied to the Divine order and to the level of the Logos, inasmuch as certain human divergences are providentially prefigured in the Divine Intelligence; there is then no question of an excess of divergences such as spring in the main from human weakness, but of adaptations willed by the Divine Mercy. Doubtless there is no total difference of principle here, but there is an eminent difference of dimension, analogous to the differences between the square and the cube, or between whiteness and light.

When it is said that religious divergences are mere differences of formulation, this may be enough, provisionally, for those who are convinced in advance and in the abstract; but it is not enough when it is a question of entering concretely into details, for one also needs to know why these formulations are manifested as so many mutually incompatible affirmations, and not as simple differences of style. It is not enough to tell ourselves that the diverse traditional doctrines express "points of view" and therefore different "aspects" of the one Truth; we need to know that this is necessarily so, that it could not possibly be otherwise, because a means of expression cannot be exhaustive, though it provides a key which is perfectly sufficient for the total Truth. The same can be said of physical experience: it is impossible to describe a landscape so validly as to exclude all other descriptions, for no one can see the landscape in all its aspects at the same time, and no single view can prevent the existence and the validity of other equally possible views.

For man, the historical facts on which his religion is based prove its exclusive truth precisely because they are facts and therefore realities. For God, these same facts have merely the value of a demonstration that is at once made up of symbols and logical; they can therefore be replaced by other facts just as one demonstration or one symbol can be replaced — but not without a sufficient reason — by another demonstration or another symbol: the essential content is always the same Truth, celestial on the one hand and salvational on the other, but approached in diverse ways, since no angle of vision is the only one possible. This is what the contradictions contained in the Holy Scriptures indicate, and also, no doubt to a lesser degree, the divergences in the visions of the Saints.

All religious belief takes its stand on a point of view from which it alone appears sublime and irrefutable; not to share this opinion seems not only the worst of perversities, for it means opposing God, but also the worst of absurdities, for it means failing to see that two and two make four. Everyone in the West knows what grounds there are for feeling that Christianity is obviously true, but it is much less known why other religions decline to accept this feeling. It cannot be contested that Christianity, in its immediate and literal expression — not in its essence, which is necessarily universal and therefore polyvalent — addresses itself to sinners, to those who "have need of the physician"; its starting point is sin,[17] just as that of Buddhism is suffering. In Islam as in Hinduism — the oldest religion and the most recent religion paradoxically meet in certain features — the starting point is man himself; by comparison, the Christian perspective — still according to its literality which, outwardly speaking, is its "crowning proof" — will appear as limited to a single aspect of man and the human state, an aspect that is real, of course, but neither unique nor exhaustive.

But it is unanimity that matters, not separative diversity, and there would be small profit in talking about the second without thinking of the first. If by "science" one means a knowledge related to real things — whether or not they can be directly ascertained — and not exclusively a knowledge determined by some narrowly limited and philosophically defective programme and method, religion will be the science of the total hierarchy, of equilibrium and of rhythms on the cosmic scale; it takes account, at one and the same time, of God's exteriorizing Manifestation and of his interiorizing Attraction, and it is only religion that does this and that can do it a priori and spontaneously.

*

* *

There can be no doubt that the Epistles of the New Testament are divinely inspired, but it is inspiration in the secondary degree, that is, they are not direct Revelation like the words of Jesus and Mary or like the Psalms. It is this difference that accounts for a further difference of degree within this secondary inspiration, according to

17. Apart from the fact that the notion of sin is itself susceptible of being transposed to a higher plane — sin then being identified with that existential disequilibrium which is nothing else than the empirical ego or some aspect of it — the Gospel contains many sayings which go beyond the moral alternative, and whose universal bearing can easily be grasped; nevertheless the Christian religion as such has in practice its basis in the notion of sin in the ordinary sense.

whether the Spirit is speaking or whether it is almost entirely allowing man to be the speaker; now in this case, the man is a saint, but he is not the Holy Spirit. The apostle recognizes this himself when, in giving certain counsels, he specifies that he does so of himself and not under the inspiration of the Paraclete. "And unto the married I command, yet not I, but the Lord. . . ." Here it is clearly the Spirit that is speaking. "Now concerning virgins I have no commandment of the Lord: yet I give my judgement as one that hath obtained mercy of the Lord to be faithful. . . ." Here it is man who speaks. And likewise: "To the rest speak I, not the Lord. . . ." And again: "She is happier if she so abide, after my judgement: and I think also that I have the Spirit of God." (I Cor. 7:10 :25 :12 :40).

We are here in the presence of the "human margin," but it comprises yet another degree: following the apostle who gives his opinion, there come at a later date the Roman theologians who — not without unrealistic idealism and on the whole confusing asceticism with morality — deduce from this opinion celibacy for all priests,[18] a measure that goes hand in hand with too extrinsic a motive for the sacrament of marriage and with forgetting, in consequence, the spiritual aspects of sexuality.[19] The result of

18. The Orthodox, who are equally Christian, did not draw this conclusion. Until the tenth century, the majority of Catholic priests were married; Gregory VII, renewing the anathemas of Nicolas II and Alexander II, finally imposed priestly celibacy, after violent resistance which went as far as riots and the ill-treatment of bishops and pontifical legates.

19. "So that they shall no longer be two, but of one flesh," declares the Gospel, putting the emphasis on the mystery of union — symbolized in a certain fashion by the miracle of Cana — and not on the two Pauline motivations, namely physical relief and procreation, reserved for those who are incapable of abstaining. If it is right to avoid the pitfall of a moral automatism that is both prudish and hypocritical, it is even more necessary to reject the opposite pitfall, namely that of a facile, naturistic and vitalistic sexualism contrary to the spiritual dignity of man by its profaning casualness. Sexuality is sacred, or else it is subhuman.

this was, positively, the flowering of a sanctity of a certain type and, negatively, an accumulation of tensions responsible for all sorts of disequilibriums and culminating in the Renaissance and its sequels; not that the morally unrealistic and spiritually narrow pietism of a certain type of Christianity was the only cause of the subsequent naturalistic explosions, but it contributed strongly to this end and is suffering the consequences in its own flesh to this day.

In a general manner, when one considers simply the nature of things without underestimating theological intentions and mystical values, one gets the impression that Christianity, insofar as it is founded on the consciousness of sin and the sinful nature of man, has need of sin and even "creates" it, in a certain measure, by an appropriate moral theology, taking into consideration the fact that in this perspective sin is sexuality.[20] In other traditional perspectives, sexuality, in itself neutral, becomes intrinsically positive by a certain spiritual conditioning: obviously, sin is always the pernicious and prohibited act, whether sexual or not, but it is also, more fundamentally, profane distraction in itself, pleasure for the sake of pleasure, and thus forgetfulness of God and worldly exteriorization.[21] Piety, whether it excludes nature-as-sin or includes nature-as-sacrament, is not without a certain monotony; the guarantee of salvation lies essentially in the fixation of the heart in

20. Quintessentially, and not theologically speaking; the Church is not Manichean; she does bless marriage, but this is considered at one and the same time as a lesser good and as a lesser evil, which justifies — when one goes to the root of things — the association of ideas with the notion of "sin."

21. Some religious authorities who combine a complex of complicity as regards the Renaissance with an inferiority complex as regards the scientistic world, exhibit an astonishing indulgence for profane distractions which they qualify as "innocent." Scientific progress, and the irreversible maelstrom resulting from it, is all right provided one does not lose one's faith; jumping into the water is all right, provided one does not get wet.

the consciousness of God, with all that this implies according to the circumstances and vocations, whatever be the respective supports in the natural order.

It is well known that Judaism, which accords to David and Solomon hundreds of wives, and Islam, which accords nine to its Prophet, are far from sharing the Pauline perspective; in general, Christian theologians have no plausible explanation for Semitic polygamy — whereas unacceptable opinions are not lacking[22] — which shows that there is a dimension here which eludes, not every Westerner, needless to say, but the characteristic and therefore average perspective that has dominated the West for many centuries. This one-sided way of looking at natural things, although highly efficacious on its own plane, results in quite regrettable misinterpretaions as regards not only Islam — which in any case is not surprising — but also as regards the ancient Biblical world.

*

* *

The Mosaic law is given for all time, up to the end of the world; nothing can be added to it, and nothing taken away. This is the thesis of Judaism, and it is irrefutable. Nonetheless, Christianity has practically abolished the Law, since according to it "the spirit giveth life, the letter killeth"; this amounts to saying — since Christianity is intrinsically orthodox in its turn — that the thesis of Judaism has an unconditional application only within the dimension that Judaism represents, namely, religious legalism.[23] The negation, by Christians, of the esoteric di-

---

22. It is particularly inadmissible to attribute to the author of the Psalms an insurmountable weakness of the flesh and to attribute the opposite virtue to just any priest.

23. We have been assured that in Judaism there can be no question of mentally practicing the prescriptions that have become impractica-

mension, is strictly speaking inconsistent, since without the esoteric point of view Christianity is inconceivable; if there is no esoterism, the Jewish argument has an absolute application and Christianity is the transgression it appears to be from the Jewish point of view. Moreover, if the spirit gives life and the letter kills, that cannot concern Judaism alone: if the "letter" of Judaism can become quite relative from a certain spiritual point of view, then the "letter" of Christianity is subject to the same law, especially since the "spirit" which gives life "bloweth where it listeth," and this opens the door, not only to a Christian gnosis, but also to the acceptance in principle of the non-Christian religions. Christianity was born of the distinction between form, which by definition is relative, and essence, which alone is absolute; if it abolishes this distinction in favor of its own form, it robs itself as it were of its reason for being.

Without these subtle truths of principle, the Christian contradiction with regard to Judaism remains unintelligible, at least if one is aware, as one should be, of Judaism's argument. At the same time, these truths clearly do not express the whole concrete reality of Christianity; for it goes without saying that being a religion, it cannot possibly call into question its "letter" or its form without abolishing itself. What needs to be made clear is that the Christly message, as a perspective of inwardness or essentialization, is an esoterism; but this message nonetheless comprises an exoteric outer form owing to its voluntaristic, and thus de facto individualistic, character, and to the dogmatizing tendency resulting from its wish to expand, or from the necessity that it should expand.

If Christ is, on the one hand, the founder of a world religion, he is on the other hand a Jewish prophet sent to

ble, or of somehow compensating for them, or in a word, of interiorizing them, but that all the rules remain obligatory. It seems to us, however, that a religion cannot prescribe the impossible; the very fact that an observance is really impossible proves that it can be compensated for, quite apart from any question of esoterism.

Israel and speaking to it; in this second respect — which, by the way, the Koran points out — Jesus has the function of regenerator, he is the great prophet of inwardness, and in this respect he ought to have been accepted by Israel as Isaiah was;[24] however, this acceptance would have presupposed a spiritual flexibility that belongs more to India than to Judaea. In theory, Judaeo-Christianity ought to have perpetuated itself within the fold of Judaism — parallel to its function as a world religion — in the form of an esoteric community not unlike Essenism; in practice, various aspects of the "human margin" precluded what was possible in principle.

$$*$$

$$*\quad*$$

Genesis relates how God "repented" when he saw the corruption of mankind: "And it repented the Lord that He had made man on the earth and it grieved Him at His heart."[25] In an analogous manner there is something like a "Divine repentance" from one Revelation to another, in the sense that God manifests an aspect of the Truth which corrects, not the aspect manifested previously, but the human insistence on it, or which corrects the unilateral development given by the human receptacle to an aspect which in itself is much less limited.

The characteristic — and inevitable — misunderstanding of all exoterism, is to attribute to God a human subjectivity,

24. Christ, paraphrasing Isaiah, expresses himself thus: "This people honoreth me with their lips; but their heart is far from me. But in vain they do worship me, teaching for doctrines the commandments of men" (Matt. 15:8-9). And likewise: "Why do ye also transgress the commandment of God by your tradition?" *(ibid.*:3).

25. "If so be they will hearken, and turn every man from his evil way, that I may repent me of the evil which I purpose to do unto them because of the evil of their doings. . . ." (Jer. 26:3). Likewise: "And God repented of the evil that he had said that he would do unto them. . . ." (Jon. 3:10), and other passages of this kind.

and consequently to believe that every Divine manifestation is linked to one and the same Divine "I," and therefore to one and the same limitation. This is not to know that the Ego which in the Revelations speaks and gives a law, can only be a manifestation of the Divine Subject and not this Subject itself; one must distinguish in God — always from the standpoint of Revelation — firstly the one and essential Word, and then the manifestations or actualizations of this Word in view of particular human receptacles. The Divine "I" that speaks to men — and of necessity to "particular men" — could not possibly be the Divine Subject in a direct and absolute sense, but rather the adaptation of that Subject to a given human "container," and consequently assuming something of the nature of this container, failing which all contact between man and God would be impossible, and failing which it would be absurd to recognize that a Revelation, Hebrew, Arabic or any other is word-for-word of Divine origin.

Clearly, God cannot contradict himself; but this axiomatic truth concerns the essential, unlimited and formless Truth, the only one which counts *in divinis;* the relative enunciations may perfectly well contradict themselves from one Revelation to another — exactly as human subjects and material forms mutually exclude and contradict one another — providing that the essential Truth is safeguarded and made as efficacious as possible. The particular Divine "I" of a Revelation is not situated in the Divine Principle itself; it is the projection, or emanation, of the Absolute Subject and is identified with the "Spirit of God," that is, with the cosmic Center of which one might say that it is "neither divine nor non-divine." This revelation-giving "I" "is God" in virtue of the ray which attaches it directly to its Source, but it is not God in an absolute fashion, because it is impossible that the Absolute as such should speak a human language and say human things. This is the meaning of the doctrine of the "descent" of the Koran by successive stages, and this is what explains the discussions on the question of knowing whether the Koran is "created" or "uncreated," or in what manner and what respect it is one or the other; but this does not open the door to any naturalism or any humanism, for the earthly wording of a sacred scripture, while determined in a certain respect by human contingencies, remains Divine through its celestial origin and also through its so to speak theurgic substance.

*

* *

A particularly serious difficulty, in making an approach to Islam, is the accusation of "falsification of the Scriptures" leveled by Moslems against Jews and Christians; this accusation is aimed chiefly at what Islam considers to be a lack of receptivity with regard to total Revelation, which a priori is as if suspended between God and man and whose manifestation is determined by the human receptacle. Since from the point of view of Islam, the Jewish and Christian theologies contain restrictive crystallizations, Islam will present these restrictions of perspective as "falsifications," "Scripture" thus being implicitly conceived in its unmanifested and still celestial totality.

Islam would indeed accept the concepts "Chosen People" and "Man-God" in a compensatory metaphysical context that would re-establish the equilibrium of the total Truth, but the context in question, precisely, would appear to Jews and Christians as the annulment of their respective positions. Here it must be emphasized once again that every revealed and traditional symbolism is a key to the totality; but this does not nullify the distinction between spiritual forms opening more particularly onto a way, either of works, or of love or of gnosis, that is, fundamentally determined by one or the other of these elements — without these determinations having an exclusive character, however. In the economy of Revelation, spiritual opportunity requires limitations and consequently negations, in

99

accordance with the human receptacles; to be precise, it is sometimes necessary to deny things at the level of formal expression, without the essential Truth ever being in question.[26]

"Falsification of the Scriptures" — a reproach Islam levels at the two monotheisms preceding it — may also be reduced to a simple question of interpretation; thus Ibn Taymiyyah, Hanbalite protagonist of an extreme literalism, reproaches Jews and Christians for having falsified the meaning of several passages in their Scriptures — the meaning, and not the text itself. A given spiritual mentality may feel the need to fix dogmatically, and to develop theologically and liturgically, a given aspect of the truth to the detriment of another aspect possibly more important but not absolutely indispensable; we have in mind here the Talmudic speculations and the vicissitudes of trinitarian theology, and also the factors which provoked the Christian schisms and the rupture between Sunni and Shiite Islam.[27]

With these somewhat distant interpretations we do not intend to solve the whole problem of the divergences between the Bible and the Koran. Let us simply add that

---

26. Inter-religious ostracism is repeated within one and the same orthodoxy. When St. Benedict condemns outright the Sarabaite and Gyrovague monks, he does so above all in the name of a methodological and disciplinary perspective; for it is impossible to accept that the situations of these monks — the ones living in their own houses and the others wandering — did not correspond to real vocations, despite all the abuses which, at a later time, did in fact occur. Analogously, with regard to quietism — to quote only one example — the errors of certain seventeenth century quietists cannot be said to invalidate the principle of quietude.

27. The suppression of all gnosis, the condemnation of Origen, then the immense success of Arianism — not to speak of the excessive influence of that two-edged sword that was Aristotelianism — all in a relatively very young Christianity, prove how difficult assimilation was for a human receptacle that was at once too heteroclite and too narrow.

Moslems consider it strange that the Bible attributes the golden calf to Aaron without drawing the consequences from this, and that it seriously blames David and Solomon; or again, that it says that the hand of Moses became leprous when, as a sign, he withdrew it from his breast, whereas according to the Koran it became luminous "without any hurt."[28]

Certain religious theses with a polemical trend may seem unjust or crude, but it is by this very appearance of excess that they hide a Divine "point of view" which goes beyond dogmatism as such. The reproach of "falsification of the Scriptures" may moreover be caused by the liberty which Revelation sometimes takes with words. An example is the way in which certain passages of the Old Testament are reproduced in the New; there can be no doubt that in the eyes of the rabbis it is a question here of real falsifications,[29] whereas in reality, in cases of this kind, the

28. When one reads the predictions of Christ concerning the latter times, one is struck by the fact that they refer in part to the destruction of Jerusalem, but without the discourse distinguishing between the different applications; as the ancient prophesies foretelling Christ already indicate, it happens in fact that prophetic language accumulates two or more completely different, but obviously analogous, orders; now analogy is a certain mode of identity, metaphysically and "divinely" speaking. There are coincidences — or accumulations — of the same kind in the prophesies of Isaiah concerning Cyrus, the liberator of Israel (44:28, 45:1-6), if we apply them to the Prophet of Islam as do the Moslems, basing themselves on the fact that the name of Cyrus — *Koresh* in Hebrew — evokes the name of *Quraysh*, which is that of the tribe of Muhammad. It should be noted that in Persian the name Cyrus, *Kurush*, means "sun," while in Elamite *kurash* means "shepherd," a meaning taken up by Isaiah; now, the two meanings apply equally to the founder of Islam, who was originally a shepherd and later became a sun for a whole part of the world.

29. Nor is there any doubt that Christian theologians would be of the same opinion as the rabbis if it were a question of a non-Christian Scripture.

same idea is divinely "rethought" in function of a new human receptacle.[30]

*

* *

To return to the Moslem point of view, this is what is basically meant: if we take as our starting point the idea that "Scripture" is the "uncreated Koran" which, conserved in God, is none other than the Divine Word itself or the Logos, recipient of all truth, then the Revelations, which by definition are adapted in their expression to a given collective human receptacle — since "water takes on the color of its container," as Junayd said — are extrinsically restrictions with regard to the uncreated Word and consequently "falsify" it, in a certain way, if we may here employ this term in order to indicate an analogy; the "falsification" the Moslem reproach has in view is thus above all a restriction of perspective and a limitation from the point of view of totality and universality.

In Revelation one must distinguish three aspects, which are, firstly, the Eternal Word in God; secondly, its specification — on the archangelic level — for a particular human receptacle; thirdly, its manifestation on earth and in time to meet circumstances which, while being no doubt providential, are nevertheless human and terrestrial.[31] The second or intermediate degree presents two aspects, one essential and the other specific: thus the Koran, having descended to the seventh Heaven, remains on the one

30. The same can be said of the divergences between the Hebrew original and the Septuagint translation. According to St. Augustine, the Septuagint translators were touched in their turn by the breath of Revelation, and the divergences between their translation and the Hebrew text had in each case a meaning implicitly contained in the original text.

31. This doctrine is also to be found in the theory of the "three bodies of the Buddha": "terrestrial" *(nirmāna-kaya)*, "celestial" *(sambhoga-kaya)* and "divine" *(dharma-kaya)*.

hand the absolute and undifferentiated Divine Word, while on the other it becomes the specific Divine Order or particular Message. It is in the third degree that the Koran flows into human language and manifests its intentions of perspective, equilibrium and salvation by means of the human contingencies which determine a particular expression; the celestial Koran, and *a fortiori* the Divine Word in the absolute sense, does not speak of such and such a name or incident, but it contains the intention which, on earth, may be expressed by means of the most diverse human facts. To understand the nature of the Koran and the meaning of its discontinuities — not those which are due to simple contingencies of compilation — it is necessary always to keep in view these three degrees, intimately mingled in the verbal crystallization of the Book, but nevertheless recognizable by sudden changes of level.

It results from what we have just said, not only that the revealed Book essentially comprises three so to speak hypostatic degrees, but also that at the terrestrial degree it could be other than it is; the events and the words do not in themselves have anything absolute about them, otherwise contingency would not be contingency. One might compare the Logos in God to a formless and uncolored substance, and the Logos when it has "descended" into the archangelic world to a religious perspective that is still superhumanly unarticulated; terrestrial manifestation would then be comparable to the dispersion of a heavenly substance into terrestrial coagulations, shaped by the milieu and by circumstances but not affecting either the celestial substance or its divine essence. Or again: if we compare the eternal Word of God to gold as such, and a particular celestial specification of this Word to a particular mass of gold, it can be seen without difficulty that all forms that can be derived from this mass in no wise affect its weight or modify the nature of the metal.

This doctrine of the three hypostatic degrees of the Divine Word makes it possible to understand the principle of "abrogation" *(naskh),* which is manifested in every sacred Scripture at the level of language, even if one draws no practical consequence from it; if there were no "human margin," no abrogation would be possible.

Another principle connected with the same doctrine is that of "personal revelation," which is also directly divine, but given to a saint who has no prophetic mandate properly so called. It is true that every spiritual truth necessarily derives from the celestial prototype of the Book, but it does so in a way completely different from the descent of "personal revelation" which we have in view here, in which the literal wording is received, not by simple inspiration as in the case of certain writings of saints and sages, but by Revelation in the true sense, that is to say by virtue of a direct divine action. A celebrated case is that of the *(Bhagavadgītā,* which logically should be part of secondary inspiration *(Smriti)* since it belongs to the *Mahābhārata,* but which in fact is considered as an *Upanishad,* and thus as pertaining to directly celestial inspiration *(Shruti).* Another case, in Islam this time, is that of the chapter on Adam in the *Fuṣūṣ al-ḥikam* of Ibn 'Arabi which he declared to be divine revelation — like the Koran — and which in fact is a masterpiece as regards both form and content. The sage, as soon as he has become, by the effect of a very particular election, "his own prophet," is thereby "his own law"; this election is at the same time a "celestial adoption," manifested by objective signs, but of such a supereminent order that it would be vain to hope that the spiritual degree in question could be obtained through efforts and thanks to natural gifts. Be that as it may, it will be easily understood that the quality of "prophecy" *(nubuwwah)* could be attributed to certain Sufis — not "law-giving" prophecy in this case, but nevertheless "radiating" in one way or another:[32] objective and polyvalent Revelation re-

32. According to a *ḥadīth,* no woman was ever a prophet, but here it is a question exclusively of law-giving prophecy, which seems evident to

peating itself, as it were, in a given human microcosm, not in the sense of a general and obvious analogy — every intellection being a "revelation" — but in virtue of an entirely special possibility and a participation, outside time, in the "descent," or rather in the "reception," of the uncreated Book.

us; there is no reason for thinking, Islamically speaking, that the term "prophetess" *(nabiyyah)* could not fit the Virgin Maryam and should be replaced by such a phrase as "of prophetic nature" *(nabawiyyah)*, or that the eulogistic formula "on her be Peace" *('alayhā 's-salām)* should be replaced in her case by the formula, attributed to ordinary saints, "may God be satisfied with him (or her)" *(raḍiya 'Llāhu 'anhu* [or *'anhā]);* this is all the more obvious in that, from the point of view of cosmic manifestation, Mary eminently surpasses all the saints.

Part Two

Christianity

The Complexity of Dogmatism

Every confession of faith claims the guarantee of perpetual assistance of the Holy Spirit, and rightly so inasmuch as a confession of faith that is valid in itself — hence having the power to save, if not to lead to every mystical summit — could not contain an intrinsically false dogma or a totally inoperative rite; but this assistance is nonetheless always relative, given that Revelation itself is relative in relation to absolute Truth — the *Sophia Perennis* — otherwise there would not be different Revelations;[1] the assistance of the Holy Spirit is total only for the total Truth. One thing that should not be forgotten is that the purpose of religions is the divine wish to save men steeped in passion, and not to present an explanation of universal Principles and of the world; in consequence, the Holy Spirit claimed by Christianity is more a savior than it is a metaphysician, at least as regards its manifestation within the sphere of religion; it is more concerned with warding off that which, in connection with a particular mentality, is detrimental to salvation, than with rectifying doctrinal errors that are more or less a matter of indifference in this respect.[2]

---

1. Let us note, however, that archaic traditions do not have exclusivist dogmas; Hinduism in particular, combines a multiform symbolism with one of the most articulated and explicit metaphysical doctrines.

2. Thus it is illogical, to say the least, to wish to contrast the "wisdom of Christ," whose purpose is to save and not to explain, with the "wis-

Intrinsically "orthodox" dogmas, that is, those disposed in view of salvation, differ from one religion to another; consequently they cannot all be objectively true. However, all dogmas are symbolically true and subjectively efficacious, which is to say that their purpose is to create human attitudes that contribute in their way to the divine miracle of salvation. This, in practice, is the meaning of the Buddhist term *upāya*, "skillful means" or "spiritual stratagem," and it is thanks to this efficient intention — or this virtually liberating "truth" — that all dogmas are justified and are in the final analysis compatible despite their antagonisms. Thus the denial of purgatory by Protestants results, not from an exhaustive cosmology, to be sure, but from a psychological or mystical economy based upon the saving power of faith; obviously, faith does not save by itself, but does so in connection with the Divine Mercy which, in Evangelicalism, is crystallized in the unique Sacrifice of Christ. In such perspectives, the dogmatic concept does not contain its end within itself, that is, in its capacity to inform; it is merely a means in view of a result, and in this case it can be said without hesitation that "the end justifies the means"; this observation applies to all religious concepts that are objectively contestable, on condition, of course, that they issue from archetypal truths and pertain to intrinsically orthodox systems. The abrupt contrast between the dogmas of Christianity and Islam is, within the context of Semitic monotheism, the most salient example of these formal antinomies; it is clearly impossible for both parties to be right, or for them to be right in the same respect, but it is possible — and necessarily so — for each to be

dom of the world" — that of Plato for example — whose purpose is to explain and not to save; besides, the fact that the Platonic wisdom is not dictated by an intention to save does not imply that it is of "this world" or "of the flesh," or even that it does not contain any liberating virtue in the methodic context required by it.

right in its own way, from the point of view of the respective "saving psychology"; and thus by virtue of the results.

In eschatological logic, the Catholic dogma of purgatory results from the idea of justification through works, whereas the Protestant denial of purgatory results from the idea of justification through faith. On the Catholic side, it will be objected that the denial of purgatory entails lukewarmness and thus compromises salvation; on the Protestant side, it will be thought on the contrary that the idea of purgatory compromises saving trust (the *prapatti* of the Hindus) and leads to the excesses of penitentialism and the abuse of indulgences; in both cases the reproaches are unjust, even though each side contains an element of truth. Be that as it may, if the Protestant denial of purgatory leads to complaisance and unconcern, as the Catholics think, and if from the Protestant point of view the idea of purgatory leads to the cult of works to the detriment of faith, Hindus and Buddhists, with no less reason, could express analogous objections against the monotheistic idea of an eternal hell: they could make the point that this concept not only is absurd in itself since it abuses the notion of eternity, but also that it favors despair and in the final analysis unbelief and indifference. The transmigrationists will therefore think that the Protestant rejection of purgatory is neither worse nor better than the monotheistic rejection of transmigration, a concept that also, and necessarily, possesses psychological, moral and mystical virtues.

Thus it is proper to distinguish between "informative" dogmas, which have a direct import, and "functional" dogmas, whose import is indirect: the first communicate metaphysical, cosmological or eschatological information; the second determine moral and spiritual attitudes. Although purely functional dogmas, if taken literally, may possibly be erroneous, in the final analysis they rejoin truth by their fruits.

*

* *

It will be understood that all this does not mean that divergent dogmas are equivalent for the simple reason that they are justified in one way or another, for two contradictory theses cannot be right in the same respect; all we wish to point out here is the distinction between informative and functional dogmas, although the dividing line between them is not absolute. If the objection were raised that the denial of purgatory by the Protestants is false since purgatory exists, we would reply firstly that for the true "believer" — and for him alone — this denial means in practice that Paradise is accessible through the merits of Christ; secondly, the Orthodox also reject the idea of a place of expiation because, according to them, souls can no longer gain merit after death, even though they may benefit from the prayers of the Church, which adds an element of compensation; for the Orthodox, as for the Moslems, "purgatory" is the hell from which the Divine Mercy has removed particular souls.[3] Next, we would make the point that, if the Protestant rejection of purgatory is false — or to the extent that it is false — the Hindu and Buddhist idea of reincarnation, taken literally and not metaphysically, is also false; now the immense majority of Hindus and Buddhists take reincarnation quite literally, not in an arbitrary manner, but in accordance with the literal meaning of their Scriptures;[4] which is inadequate as

3. To the objection that their dogma is false, the Protestants would reply that they do not deny hell and that God always has the power to save whom He wills, which rejoins the opinion of the Orthodox Church and of Islam; moreover, certain Anglicans accept the idea of purgatory. Let us add that this idea, aside from other motivations, is justified because the sector in hell where the door remains open from above differs, necessarily, by that very fact, from the sector without such an opening, and this for quasi-metaphysical reasons.

4. Where there is a literal meaning, there is also a legitimate possibility of a literal interpretation: since the Law of Manu teaches that a given sin entails a given rebirth among animals, there are necessarily men who believe it, despite the cosmological transpositions of the sym-

regards cosmic reality, but not as regards spiritual psychology.[5] From the point of view of this psychology, the question is not that of knowing what some dogma includes or excludes, but what we draw from it.

Another materially inexact, but not functionally pointless, dogma is that of the reduction of animals to dust after the "resurrection of the body": our objection is that the subjectivity of a superior animal is far too personal to be reducible to nothingness: now "nothingness" here is in fact synonymous with "transmigration." Since transmigration is not admissible in Semitic monotheism, one replaces it by "nothingness," and thus rids oneself of a doctrinal responsibility that a monotheistic theology, having to remain centered upon man and the human, could not take on.

A classic example so to speak of a functional dogma is the denial in the Koran of the crucifixion of Christ; it is true that this denial has been interpreted by some Moslems as meaning simply that Christ was not vanquished, just as Abraham, thrown into the furnace, was not vanquished by the fire,[6] and as Daniel, in the lions' den, was not vanquished by the beasts; however, general feeling upholds the literal meaning of the passage.[7] Aside from

bolism made by others. This gives us an opportunity to insert the following remark: according to certain information, devotional Buddhism is said to teach that women have no access to the Paradise of *Amitābha* until after they undergo a masculine rebirth; this opinion is not only illogical within the framework of Amidism, but is also contrary to numerous accounts issuing from this school.

5. The idea of reincarnation is equivalent — not by its content but qualitatively — to the conviction that the earth is flat and that the sun circles the earth; in both cases there is "naivety" through lack of experience and also lack of imagination; but this "optical illusion" can nonetheless be utilized symbolically and psychologically.

6. "We *(Allāh)* said: O fire, be coolness and peace for Abraham!" (Sura "The Prophets," 69).

7. It should be noted that the idea that Christ was not crucified but was taken directly to Heaven existed already at the time of the apostles,

the fact that the denial of the Cross closes the door to the Christian perspective, which Islam quite evidently did not have to repeat, this denial contributes indirectly to the spiritual attitude pertaining to the Moslem perspective; the function here sanctifies the means, namely the symbolism.

*

* *

The naivety of certain concepts that have practically become dogmatic can be explained on the one hand by the natural symbolism of things and on the other by a wise concern for self-protection; for if the truth has, in the final analysis, the function of rendering man divine, it could not at the same time have the function of dehumanizing him. For example, it could not have the aim of having us experience the dreads of the infinitely great or the infinitely small, as modern science intends; to reach God, we have the right to remain children, and we even have no choice, given the limits of our nature.

A classic example of naive dogma is the Biblical story of creation, followed by that of the first human couple: if we are skeptical — therefore atrophied — we clash with the childishness of the literal meaning, but if we are intuitive — as every man ought to be — we are sensitive to the irrefutable truths of the images; we feel that we bear these images within ourselves, that they have a universal and timeless validity. The same observation applies to myths and even to fairy tales: while describing principles — or situations — concerning the universe, they describe at the same time psychological and spiritual realities of the soul; and in this sense it can be said that the symbolisms of religion or of popular tradition are common experiences for us, both on the surface and in depth.

which proves that the intentions behind this idea cannot be reduced to an exclusively Islamic function.

Christian Divergences

On the basis of what has been said in the preceding chapter, we may broach the question of the divergence between Catholicism and Evangelicalism, by showing firstly that it is improper to apply the logic of one confession to another; at least from the standpoint of intrinsic values, but not from the standpoint of a particular symbolism or a particular mode of efficacy.

Religious or confessional phenomena are ruled by two great principles, namely "apostolic succession" and "celestial mandate"; to the first pertains sacramental regularity, and to the second the extra-canonical intervention of Grace. "Celestial mandate" is a Confucian term, meaning that investiture, and consequently authority, descend directly from Above, without the intermediary of a sacramental means, by virtue of an archetypal reality that must manifest itself in a given world and in response to earthly conditions that call forth this descent. Such was the case of the emperors of China — it is in a way the Throne that created the emperor — and also, as Dante observed in his treatise on monarchy, that of the Roman, and later the Christian and Germanic, emperors; and quite paradoxically, the Papacy itself is an example of this kind of investiture, given that what creates a Pope is an election and not a sacrament.[1] In the framework of Christianity as a whole,

1. Let it be noted that baptism — *mutatis mutandis* — pertains partially to the same principle, since it does not necessarily require priest-

115

the Reformation, while appearing logically and technically as a heresy — but let us not forget that Rome and Byzantium anathematize each other — possesses in itself a justification and hence an efficacy which it draws from a spiritual archetype that was, if not entirely ignored by Rome, at least certainly "stifled."[2]

That is to say that the phenomenon of the Reformation, exactly as other analogous manifestations — notably in Hinduism and Buddhism — results from the principle of the "celestial mandate," hence from the providential intervention of the archetype of a spiritual possibility. On these grounds, this phenomenon is altogether independent of the rule of "apostolic succession" and "sacramental technicality," and this independence — the confessional or exoteric mentality being what it is — explains precisely the vehemence of the Lutheran and other denials. The sometimes naive character of the formulations plays no part here, for such is the general tone of exoteric ostracism; and it is symbolism, no more, no less.

*

* *

Protestants and Amidists — although still other examples could be cited — consider that it is faith that saves, not of itself, but by virtue of a Redemption, historical or mythological, according to case; and as they can neither admit that works add something to the Grace granted by Heaven, nor contest that moral effort is humanly indispensable, they see the motivation for this effort in our gratitude towards the saving Power. Now one of two things: either gratitude is necessary, in which case it is not

hood; nevertheless it is not unconnected to the initiatic sphere since it brings about the remission of original sin and thus transforms the primordial potentiality into virtuality.

2. Cf. *Christianity/Islam: Essays on Esoteric Ecumenicism,* the chapter "The Question of Evangelicalism."

faith alone that saves; or it is faith that saves, in which case gratitude is not necessary. But if one goes to the root of things, it will be perceived that "gratitude" and "sincerity" are synonymous here: that is, sincerity forms part of faith, thus it is only sincere faith — proved precisely by moral effort and works — that is faith as such in the eyes of God. In other words, sincerity necessarily manifests itself through our desire to please Heaven which, having saved us from evil, obviously expects us to practice good; and this consequentiality can be termed "gratitude."

It is known that the idea of Redemption, whatever its "mythical" expression, results from the idea of man's fundamental corruption; now this Augustinian and Lutheran concept, which implies the conclusion that man is totally incapable of righteousness in the eyes of God, is like the theological "caricature" of the very contingency of the human being, by virtue of which we can have no quality or power outside God. In Augustinism, what cuts the Gordian knot is grace combined with faith; metaphysically, what cuts it is also gnosis which participates in the Sovereign Good, or it is the Sovereign Good that is manifested in and by gnosis. And predestination is what we are, outside all temporal mechanism.

It is true that the anthropological pessimism of Saint Augustine did not apply to the first human couple before the fall, but to humanity marked by the fall. Adam and Eve, being creatures, were obviously contingent, not absolute; but the fall, precisely, derives from contingency and manifests it at an inferior level, that of illusion and sin. It is here that a divergence of perspective intervenes: according to some, fallen man always remains man, in him there is something inalienable, but for which he would cease to be human; according to others, fallen man is defined by the fall, which necessarily penetrates and corrupts all his initiatives, and this is the point of view of Saint Augustine, but to a less "totalitarian" degree than for Luther, for the Bishop of Hippo admits that under certain conditions we may be deserving of merit, whereas Luther denies this and instead substitutes the as it were impersonal mystery of faith. But aside from this difference in degree, the ancient Churches and the Reformation both make use — as does Amidism — of the idea of our fundamental helplessness as the springboard of a method founded upon saving faith.

*
* *

In this order of ideas, one has to distinguish between two ways of looking at things. According to the first it will be said: if man does not make efforts to transcend himself, he follows his passions and becomes lost; if he does not go towards his salvation, he drifts away from it, for he who does not advance, retreats; whence the obligation of sacrifice, asceticism and meritorious works. According to the second way, the contrary will be said: man is saved beforehand by religion, that is why religion exists; it suffices therefore to have faith and to observe the rules. In other words, every believer is by definition included in saving Grace, it suffices not to step out of it; that is, it suffices to keep one's faith while abstaining from vices and crimes; whence the obligation of moral equilibrium on the basis of faith.

The first of these perspectives, which is that of Catholicism for example, is dynamic so to speak: its symbol could be the star whose rays are either centripetal or centrifugal, according to whether man strives towards his salvation or on the contrary retreats from it. This dramatic alternative is addressed firstly to passional men — or to men insofar as they are passional — and then to those whose nature requires a mystical way that is combative and sublime, hence "heroic." The second of these two perspectives, which is among others that of Evangelicalism, is so to speak static and equilibrated: its symbol could be the circle which on the one hand includes and on the other excludes, according to whether man remains within the confines of salvation or on the contrary leaves them. This alternative, which in fact is reassuring, is addressed firstly to men given to trust in God, but trusting neither in their capacity to save themselves nor in priestly complications, and then, more particularly, to contemplatives of a calm type, who love simplicity and peace.

Both perspectives necessarily combine, despite their difference of accentuation; each of them gives rise to characteristic abuses: either to dramatism and to the cult of suffering in the first case, or to complacency and lukewarmness in the second.[3] Quite obviously, arguments against abuses can be used only in a very relative manner; there are no abuses possible in the archetypes.

In the same realm of ideas, we may note the following: the Reformers argue that the Redemption suffices to guarantee salvation to those baptized whose faith is sincere and consequently is accompanied by an impeccable morality; this in fact is all that is needed, in Christianity, to satisfy the requirements of what is minimally necessary. But when they reject monastic asceticism, which to them seems a useless luxury and even a lack of faith, they lose sight of the fact that asceticism stems not from the dimension of what is indispensable, but from that of love, and sometimes from that of fear; for on the one hand, it is necessary to love God with all our faculties, and on the other hand, it is better to go to Heaven and "that one of thy members should perish," than "that thy whole body should be cast into hell." The Reformers had in their favor at least two extenuating circumstances, one secondary

3. In authentic Evangelicalism complacency is excluded by intensity of faith and by the sense of duty, hence by that "categorical imperative" that is virtue and morality. In Catholicism, Thomistic intellectuality is capable of checking the excesses of "baroque sentimentalism"; moreover, medieval art, which is truly celestial, has in principle an analogous function, since it introduces an element of intellectuality and serenity into religious sentiment, for "those who have ears to hear."

and one essential, namely: firstly that the Catholics have attitudes the overaccentuations and narrownesses of which inevitably had to provoke reactions,[4] and secondly, that in the economy of the Evangelical perspective the love of God coincides with the active joy of gratitude; hence with the happiness that piety and virtue procure. Now this perspective is capable of a deepening that transcends ordinary measures and that pertains to the sphere of holy "peace," not holy "passion."

*

* *

After these generalities, some considerations concerning ritual divergences are called for. It is not exact to say that the Lutheran Communion is only a "remembrance," that it denies the ontological relation between Calvary and the rite; it is Zwingli and the liberal Protestants, not Luther, who thus minimize the eucharistic mystery; for the German Reformer believed in the Real Presence in both species. In denying transubstantiation — not inherence or consubstantiation — he refers moreover to Saint Paul, who speaks of the "bread that we break" (1 Cor. 10:16), and who says: ". . . so let him eat of that bread" (1 Cor. 11:28); that is to say, the Apostle speaks of "bread" and not of "appearance of bread." Even Calvin affirms that "Christ, with the plenitude of his gifts, is no less present, in Commun-

---

4. The confusion between the elementary requirements of what is strictly necessary and the feats of mystical heroism — the first dimension relating to salvation as such, and the second to the degrees of beatitude — is also found in the Moslem world, despite the sober and reassuring realism of the Koran and the Sunna, without which the Revelation would not be "good news" *(bushrā)*. The confusion in question seems to stem from an overly passional need for absoluteness, which instead of being qualitative becomes quantitative, and which in addition readily confuses legalism with virtue, and delights in exaggerations whose sole motive is to please God, as if He could, out of blindness, be biased favorably towards such things, *quod absit.*

ion, than if we were seeing Him with our eyes and touching Him with our hands." What actualizes the ontological relation between the Mass and Calvary is the Real Presence, independently of the question of transubstantiation; that one may conceive transubstantiation as a change of substance — an elliptical idea if ever there was one — is an entirely different question.

The Lutheran Communion pertains in the final analysis to the same ritual economy as the Moslem prayer; it is like a minimal fragment of the Catholic Mass from the point of view of content or grace, but it is something else from the point of view of the container or the form, so that the Catholic objections do not apply to it, except for the self-defense of Catholicism. The Catholic Eucharist offers graces commensurate with the spiritual possibilities of a Saint Bernard; the Lutheran Communion — given that there are "many rooms in my Father's mansion" — offers a viaticum commensurate with ordinary believers of good will — *et in terra pax hominibus bonae voluntatis* — exactly as is the case of the Moslem prayer — the only "sacrament" of exoteric Islam — which proves that it is eschatologically sufficient in its religious context. All Catholics must take Communion, but not all of them are Saint Bernard; and the very transcendence of the Eucharist entails terrible dangers, as Saint Paul attests. No doubt Luther closed a door, but he opened another; if he lessened the Eucharistic Grace, he nonetheless, by considerably simplifying and centralizing worship — too dispersed in Roman practice — opened the door to a particular spiritual climate which also possesses its mystical virtuality; on condition of being turned to account by a Christocentric fervor whose sap is faith, and thus by a comportment that is not "meritorious" or "heroic," but "normal" and "Biblical." For sanctity does not coincide purely and simply with "heroicalness of virtue," it also comprises modes akin to quietism where moral equilibrium, joined to contemplative union, plays a preponderant role.[5]

5. We were told this by a monk of the Eastern Church.

What matters in the Lutheran Communion, is the fact that the bread communicates Christ's will to save us, or the fact that He has saved us, which here amounts to the same thing; like certain Moslem theologians, Luther aims not at everywhere "dotting the i's" — which is the Roman tendency — but at believing in the literal wording of Scripture[6] and acknowledging that a given enigma is true "without asking oneself how" *(bilā kayfa);*[7] whence his refusal to accept transubstantiation, which in his opinion adds nothing to the Real Presence, any more than the Gnostic idea of an immaterial and merely "apparent" body adds something to the divinity of Christ.

Perhaps it is necessary to specify here that for the Lutherans there is only one saving Sacrifice, Calvary; Communion does not "renew" it, it is not a new sacrifice; it merely actualizes for believers the unique Sacrifice. For the Catholics however, each Mass is a new sacrifice, "bloodless" no doubt and "relative" in comparison with the blood Sacrifice, but nonetheless having a truly sacrificial character; Protestants see in this conception a multiplication of the Sacrifice — the multiple Masses being put in place of the one Sacrifice — whereas for the Catholics these Masses are precisely "relative," as we have just said; which does not satisfy the Protestants, given their archetypist insistence on the unicity of Christ and their horror of "secondary causes," as the Moslems would say. On the whole, the Catholic Mass is comparable to the image of the sun reflected in a mirror: without pretending to be the

---

6. *Alles geglaubt oder nichts geglaubt:* to believe all or nothing.

7. It is interesting to note that the problems of evil and of predestination, which are insoluble within monotheistic and theological logic, led Luther and others to perfectly Asharite reasonings, to Gordian knots which they could not cut except by means of that *deus ex machina* that is "faith," a movement that is a priori volitive and sentimental, yet in essence intuitive and, in privileged cases, capable of opening the door to gnosis.

sun, it "repeats" it in a certain fashion, and in practice the Catholics readily overemphasize this repetition, despite theological specifications which are not always kept in mind by the religious sensibility; whereas the Lutheran Communion is comparable — or aims at being comparable — not to the reflected image of the sun, but simply to its ray. The relentless Lutheran battle against the Mass is explainable by the idea that the Catholic rite becomes *de facto* too independent of its unique and indivisible prototype, to the point of seeming to substitute itself for it; obviously, the Catholics cannot accept this reproach, any more than the Islamic reproach of tritheism, but they could understand that at the basis of these grievances there lies an intention of method much more than of doctrine, of mystical attitude much more than of theological adequacy.

On the Catholic side — let us insist upon it again — it seems to have been forgotten that the majesty of the eucharistic sacrifice implies certain practical consequences concerning the handling of the rite. The concrete and demanding character of this majesty has been patently forgotten by submitting the sacrifice to all kinds of intentions, applications or modalities that are too contingent — we would almost say too casual — and thus profaning it in the final analysis;[8] it is as if the sense of the divine dignity of the rite were concentrated upon the eucharistic species only, particularly the host, which is exposed and worshipped in the monstrance but which is mistreated in being given to anybody and under ridiculous conditions. Be that as it may, the Lutherans reject the Masses on account of the historic and sacramental uniqueness of the Sacrifice, as the Asharites reject secondary causes on account of the

---

8. Experience proves that the "first communion" of children — obligatory for all and socially conventional — is a double-edged sword, for if on the one hand it benefits children who are really pious, on the other hand it exposes the sacrament to a profanation, which could not be in the interest of unworthy children, even if they are relatively innocent.

principial and efficient uniqueness of God; in both cases there is ostracism in virtue of an idea of absoluteness.

Before going further, it is perhaps necessary to recall the eucharistic theses of Catholicism and Orthodoxy; for the Catholics, the eucharistic presence of Christ is produced, not by "impanation" nor by "consubstantiation," but by "transubstantiation," meaning that the "substance of the bread no longer remains," which they justify — abusively in our view[9] — with the consecrating words of Christ; according to this theory, the "substantial form of the species no longer remains," not even their "raw material." The Orthodox, for their part, either do not admit transubstantiation, or they do not admit that it implies "a substance that changes and accidents that do not change"; their intention is to remain faithful — quite wisely — to the eucharistic teaching of St. John Damascene, according to whom "the Holy Ghost intervenes and does what transcends all word and all thought . . . . And if you enquire as to how this happens, let it suffice you to know that it happens through the Holy Ghost, . . . that the word of God is true, effective and all-powerful, the manner of it remaining unfathomable."[10]

*
* *

Catholicism is Catholicism, and Evangelicalism is Evangelicalism; by this truism we mean to say that a purely formal Protestantizing tendency has no organic connection with the archetype that motivated and brought about the Reformation, all the more so in that it is the archetype that

9. As regards pure doctrine, for we do not deny the possibility of a certain psychological opportuneness for a particular ethnic group. This kind of justification also obviously applies to the Reformation; in this case not in the sense of a quantity of superfluous "strategic" specifications, but on the contrary, in the name of simplicity and pious inarticulation.

10. *Exposé précis de la Foi orthodoxe*, IV, 13. The Reformers did not think otherwise.

chooses the man and not inversely; it is not enough to imitate or improvise gestures in order to be concretely in conformity to a spiritual archetype and consequently in harmony with the Divine Will. It is possible that Heaven could will a phenomenon such as the Lutheran Communion; but it is impossible that it could will the Lutheranization of the Catholic Mass, for God cannot contradict Himself on one and the same plane, the very one that would imply an intrinsic contradiction; the fact that God brings about the manifestation of the Islamic possibility in no way means that He wishes Christianity to be Islamized, any more than He desires that Islam be Christianized. The principle of the spiritual economy of archetypes means that one and the same form may be valid in a particular confessional context but not in another, except for an adaptation that stems from the archetype itself and not from a purely human enterprise.

According to Catholic logic, the Lutheran Communion is invalid, not only because the rite has been changed but also because the officiant is not a priest; whereas from the Lutheran — or general Protestant — point of view, the officiant is a priest thanks to the sacerdotal virtuality that man as such possesses by his deiform nature; Christ actualized this virtuality through the "celestial mandate" of which we have spoken above; this is to say that Heaven permits this Mandate to descend upon the officiant by virtue of his election by the Community, or by those whom the Community delegates, exactly as is the case — technically speaking — with the Roman pontiff.[11] Protestants reason that Tradition may well confirm this Mandate, but does not create it; the officiant is not a pastor *ex opere operato*. Doubtless, the Western Church never went so far

---

11. And for the ulemas, *mutatis mutandis*, whose authority is also derived from a delegation, in virtue of the sacerdotal potentiality of man. We have noted above that baptism, inasmuch as it can be conferred by a member of the laity, pertains to the same general principle.

as to deny the laity a kind of indirect sacerdotal function, but it has not granted it the same degree of recognition as the Eastern Church has; on the contrary it overly neglected it, the celibacy of priests helping to widen the gap between the tonsured and the laity, which, precisely, was avoided by the Orthodox.

*

* *

And this leads us to another problem: what is the meaning of the fact that the Reformation rejects Tradition and intends to base itself on Scripture alone? It means that it is a question of a religious possibility that is clearly marginal and not fundamental: the argument here is that Scripture alone is absolutely certain and stable, whereas Tradition occasionally calls for caution and is often diverse and variable, as is shown by the diversity — and in some cases the doubtful character — of the liturgies.[12] Catholics, Orthodox and Protestants are in agreement on the subject of Scripture, but not on that of Tradition; in Islam also, the abrupt divergences between Sunnites and Shiites have to do with Tradition and not with the Book. Quite obviously, the Catholics are right to maintain their point of view, which is fundamental, but that of the Protestants corresponds no less to a possibility in a particular theological, mystical and moral context, and not outside it. What Christ termed "precepts of men" certainly pertains to the element "Tradition"; the Talmud is incontestably "traditional." However the total absence of any tradition is impossible; even Lutheranism, Calvinism, and *a fortiori* High Church Anglicanism, are traditional in certain respects.

In this context, we cannot pass over in silence the following observation: on the Catholic side, there is a certain bureaucratization of the sacred, which goes hand in hand with a kind of militarization of sanctity, if one may be al-

12. Otherwise the Tridentine Mass would not have been necessary.

lowed to express oneself thus; in particular, there is the cult of the monastic "Rules" and that of the liturgical "rubrics." Protestantism intends to place itself in a more evangelical dimension, but it opposes Roman excesses with new excesses; only the Eastern Church maintains the Christic message in perfect equilibrium, all things considered. For the Eastern Church, Protestantism results from Catholicism, the one does not go without the other; they are the two poles of the Western disequilibrium.[13]

In other words: Tradition, considered in itself and outside any restrictive modality, is comparable to a tree; the root, the trunk, the branches and the fruits are what they must be, each part comes in its season and none of them wants to be another; this is what the Orthodox have understood perfectly, they who stop short at the Seventh Council and wish to hear no talk of any "institutionalized Pentecost," if we may use such an expression out of a desire for clarity. It is not that a Patriarch, with the agreement of other Patriarchs who are his equals, cannot undertake a particular secondary adaptation required by particular circumstances — the contrary would be opposed to the nature of things — but no Patriarch can make a decision regarding a substantial change such as the

---

13. One example, among others, of "Tradition" as a "precept of men," is the cardinalate: whereas bishops and patriarchs derive from the apostles, there is nothing in the New Testament that prefigures the cardinals. At the beginning of this papal institution, even the laity could obtain this dignity; after the 11th century, it was attributed only to the bishops, priests and deacons who surrounded the Pope; in the 13th century, every cardinal received the rank of bishop and the red hat; finally, in the 17th century, the cardinals received the title of "Eminence". All this has a more imperial than sacerdotal character and scarcely accords with the principle "everywhere, always, by everyone" *(quod ubique, quod semper, quod ab omnibus creditum est);* having said this, we do not contest that such an institution may be required by the Roman or Latin mentality any more than we contest the requirements of the play of Providence.

introduction of the *filioque* or the celibacy of priests, and
impose it upon all the Patriarchs who are his brothers.[14]
As a result of the unstable, adventurous and innovative
mentality of the Roman, German and Celtic Westerners,
the Catholic West has not been able to realize fully an
equilibrium between the principles of growth and conser-
vation, or in other words, it has needed an institution that
grants pre-eminence to the first principle over the second,[15] and which thus "traditionalizes" a possibility that in
itself is problematical. Thus, we admit that the Papacy —
for that is what is at issue — was a providential although
ambiguous necessity,[16] but the Protestant phenomenon
enjoys the same justification, at least in a secondary way;
which is to say that the very ambiguity of the Papacy necessarily gave rise to the Protestant reaction and to the de-
nominational scission of the Latin West.

*

* *

One of the great qualities of the Catholic Church —
which it shares with the Orthodox Church — is its sense of

14. The *filioque* could have found its place among the possible "theological opinions"; history proves that it was in no wise necessary to impose it tyranically upon the entire Church.

15. Let it be noted that the Mass of Pious V was not an innovation,
but a putting in order; the abuse lay in a preceding disorder, not in the
conservative measure of the Pope.

16. "But be not ye called Rabbi: for one is your Master, even Christ;
and all ye are brethren. And call no man your father upon the earth:
for one is your Father, which is in Heaven. Neither be ye called masters: for one is your Master, even Christ." (Matt. 23:8-12) — Now the
Pope is placed in a quasi-absolute fashion above the bishops, his brothers, and is called "Holy Father," and then there are the "Doctors of the
Church"; these facts clash singularly with the passage of the Gospel
quoted and offer — to say the least — extenuating circumstances for
the Orthodox and Lutheran protestation against the Papacy as it has in
fact presented itself. In a certain sense, the Papacy is a Trojan horse
which introduces the spirit of innovation into the Church.

the sacred, which is liturgically and aesthetically expressed by its solemn Masses; in Protestantism, this sense is concentrated uniquely on Scripture and prayer, which unquestionably entails a great impoverishment, not necessarily for the individual, but for the collectivity. It is true that the Anglican Church, the High Church in any case, has largely maintained the sense of the sacred, and Luther too was not insensitive to it, he who rejected all iconoclastic fanaticism; it is above all Calvinism that has put a rigid moralism in place of this sense, whereas liberal Protestantism — that typical product of the twentieth century — has in the final analysis squandered everything, which is also and even more thoroughly what Catholic modernism does. Be that as it may, authentic Evangelicalism has to a certain extent replaced the sense of the sacred by the sense of inwardness, with analogous psychological consequences; for he who sincerely, "in spirit and in truth," loves to stand before God is not far from the reverential disposition of which we are speaking.

*

* *

It has been said that the Protestant Reformation brought about an almost total destruction of sacred forms. Unquestionably it produced a certain void — although in Germanic countries there are temples that soberly prolong the Gothic forms — but is this void so much more deadly than the false plenitude of the Renaissance, and in particular the horrible profusion of the Baroque style?[17] In reality, the Protestant "destruction" goes hand in hand with a Catholic "destruction": on the one hand there is ne-

17. Which was the sentimentalist reaction to the pagan coldness of the Renaissance. The baroque style has been qualified by some as the "style of joy," whereas it is sad, owing to its dreamlike, hollow and pompous unrealism, that is, by its lies and its stupidity; the dress of the period attests to the same aberration.

gation and impoverishment, and on the other rejection and falsification.

The Roman, Byzantine and Gothic styles are not phases in an indefinite "evolution"; they are definitive crystallizations of modes of Christian art.[18] The center of the Western Christian world was the basilica of Constantine in Rome; now one fine day the Popes had the disastrous idea of destroying this venerable jewel of sacred art and replacing it by a gigantic, pagan and glacial imperial palace, as pretentious within as without, and of adorning it with naturalistic works expressing all the sensual and marmoreal megalomania of the time.[19] The art of the Renaissance entails as its consequence the obligation to admire it — no Pope has the power to destroy the work of Bramante and Michaelangelo — thus it has imposed a lack of discernment that does not stop short at the aesthetic plane, and the fruits of which are still being gathered today, indeed today more than ever before; the most general expression of this poisoning being what we may term "civilizationism," that is, the debasement of religion by means of the ideology of total and indefinite progress. Henceforth it is impossible to dissociate the Christian from the "civilized" man, in the narrow and somewhat ridiculous sense of this word; in this respect, the Christians of the East have been the victims of the Christians of the West, especially since Peter the Great. In any case, the Protestants cannot be held solely responsible for the modern deviation, even though it has been rightly pointed out that Calvinism has favored industrialism; but this takes nothing away from

18. There is, to be sure, "elaboration," but not "evolution": once the "idea" has been fully manifested, the style no longer has to change, in spite of a diversity that is always possible and even necessary. In sacred art, unlimited evolution is as nonexistent as in biology: growth stops the moment the idea — the specific type — is fully realized.

19. And since the price of this monstrous edifice was the sale of indulgences, one should have renounced building it; it is a question of a sense of proportions as well as of moral sense, or a sense of *barakah*.

the fact that everything began with the Renaissance, and that the Protestants had no part in that.[20] If we mention these things, it is not to enlarge upon a historical question that strictly speaking remains outside our subject matter, but it is to prevent a possible prejudice on the part of traditionalists who, sure of their principles — for which one cannot blame them — have had neither the idea nor the opportunity to verify some of their apparently plausible, but in fact inadequate, conclusions. In any case, no Church has ever opposed the acquisitions of the so-called "human genius" — artistic, literary, scientific, technical, even political. On the contrary, what has been sought is to attribute them to the "Christian genius," with a lack of discernment and imagination fraught with mystery.

All things considered, we still have to add the following observations: civilizationism is practically synonymous with industrialism, and the essence of industrialism is the machine; now the machine produces and kills at one and the same time; it produces objects and kills the soul,[21] not to mention its practical, and in the long run extremely serious, disadvantages that are only too well known. Religion has accepted and almost "Christianized" the machine, and it is dying from this — either through absurdity and hypocrisy, as in the past, or through capitulation and suicide, as today. It looks as if there were only two sins, unbelief and unchasteness; the machine is neither an unbeliever nor is it unchaste, therefore one may sprinkle it with holy water in good conscience.

20. Besides, the French Revolution took place in a Catholic country; and likewise, before it, the enterprise of the Encyclopediasts.

21. What distinguishes the traditional machine — such as the loom — from the modern machine, is that it combines intelligible simplicity and explicit and spiritually effective symbolism with an aesthetic quality, which for normal man is essential. The modern machine, on the contrary, does not have these qualities, and instead of serving man and contributing to his well-being, it enslaves and dehumanizes him.

It is in the climate of the Renaissance that the Reformation burst forth and spread with the force of a hurricane, and so it remains to this very day; and this allows us to apply the argument of Gamaliel to the Protestant phenomenon, namely that a religious movement that does not proceed from God will not last.[22] This argument of course loses all its value when it is applied to an intrinsically false religious ideology, and *a fortiori* to philosophical or political ideologies, for in such cases the reason for their success is something else altogether: it does not stem from the power of a spiritual archetype, but simply from the seduction of error and the weakness of men.

Protestantism encompasses almost a third of Christianity, consequently its importance in the Western world is immense, and it is impossible to pass over it in silence when one is considering religions, denominations and spiritualities. Let it be noted that without the Reformation there would have been no Council of Trent nor, consequently, the Catholic Counter-Reformation; now this necessary instrumentality of Protestantism speaks in its favor and indirectly proves the relative — not absolute, but confessionally sufficient — legitimacy of this powerful movement; without it, the Roman Church would perhaps not have found the necessary impetus to recover and rebuild.[23] The fact that this scission in the midst of Western Christianity created at the same time favorable conditions

22. The ostracism of Calvin — which contrasts with the generosity of Luther — is not an argument against the Reformation, for it is not Calvin who invented the Inquisition; in any case what is involved here is the exoteric, hence formalistic and intolerant, climate.

23. It is an interesting fact that the Fathers of the Council of Trent forwent condemning Luther in particular, which would have been required by conciliary usage; they preferred not to "close the door definitively to dialogue," which has a symbolical as well as a practical meaning.

for the final fall of the West, takes nothing away from the positive meaning of the Protestant phenomenon, but shows in any case how the meshing of the positive and the negative are part of the ambiguous and ingenious play of Providence. The same observation applies a priori to Catholicism, certain aspects of which have contributed to the origin of the modern world, which does not in the least take away from its quality as a great religious message and traditional civilization, hence its merits on the plane of intellectuality, sacred art and sanctity.

*

* *

Quite paradoxically, in Lutheranism there is at one and the same time an intention of esoterism and of exoterism, hence of interiorization and of exteriorization; on the one hand Luther aimed at bringing everything back to the inward — "But thou, when thou prayest, enter into thy closet,[24] and when thou hast shut thy door, pray to thy Father which is in secret" — and on the other hand, he aims at reducing everything to the "supernaturally natural" priesthood of man as such, hence of every man, or more precisely of every baptized man, for "all ye are brethren." With the first intention, the mystic of Wittenberg opens the door to certain esoteric possibilities, by the nature of things; with the second, he closes the door to a certain type of sanctity, founded upon the "chivalric" notion of "heroicalness of virtues," a notion which in itself is correct, but which becomes false when the aim is to reduce all possible sanctity to this type, while disparaging everything that relates to quietism and gnosis. Be that as it may: in being inspired by the injunction of Christ to the Samaritan — to worship neither on Mount Gerizim nor in the Temple, but "in spirit and in truth" — Luther wished to efface as much as possible the outward signs of worship — without being

24. That of the heart, according to the Hesychasts.

fanatical like Calvin — as if transcendence could not tolerate immanence; but at the same time he actualized a certain desire for esoterism, a paradox also manifested by Amidism and Shiism. The non-formal — or emptiness — is in fact a vehicle of the supraformal and of plenitude, as Saint Bernard understood quite well in emptying his chapels of all images and all adornments, and as the Zen monks understood no less well in making use of an art of bareness, hence of emptiness.

Not unconnected to this question of "exoterism tending towards esoterism" is the fact that the Reformation, which issued from an ascetical religion, "rediscovered" the spiritual potential of sexuality, exactly as was the case in Buddhism — also ascetical — when Shinran, monk that he was, married and introduced marriage into his sect, the *Jodo Shinshu*.[25] The intrinsically sacred character of sexuality was not unknown to Judaism or to Hinduism, from which the two ascetical religions just mentioned issued respectively; however, neither Judaism nor Hinduism was unaware of the value of asceticism, which obviously keeps all its rights in every religious climate.[26] Man is so made that he naturally slides towards the outward and has need of a wound to bring him closer to "the kingdom of God which is within you," and this notwithstanding the complementary fact that the contemplative — and he alone — perceives the traces of the divine in outward beauties, which amounts to saying that given his predisposition, these beauties have the capacity to interiorize him, in con-

25. Let us not lose sight of the fact that Catholicism witnessed the blossoming of the more or less "erotic" mysticism of the knights, the troubadours, and the *"Fedeli d'Amore"*; Tantric Buddhism exhibits analogous features, but with a very different emphasis.

26. Judaism gave birth to the ascetical sect of the Essenes; as for Hinduism, it is special in that its compartmentalized structure and metaphysical amplitude enable it to fully turn to account every spiritual possibility; fully, that is to say independently of every antagonistic religious context.

formity with the principle of Platonic anamnesis. This means that man's ambiguity is that of the world: everything manifests God — directly or indirectly or in both ways at the same time — but nothing is God; thus everything can either bring us closer to Him or take us further from Him. Each religion, or each confession, intends to offer its solution to this problem in conformity with a particular psychological, moral and spiritual economy.

*

* *

Someone has asked us[27] why Protestantism, since it manifests *grosso modo* the same archetype as Amidism, does not, like Amidism, possess a method of ejaculatory prayer; now this archetype does not of itself imply this mode of prayer any more than this mode of prayer implies that archetype; rather it implies the emphasis upon faith and the assiduous practice of prayer, and in fact we find both of these elements in authentic Evangelicalism.

Another question that we have been asked concerns the formal homogeneity that every intrinsically orthodox confession possesses; now if Protestantism on the whole does not possess this homogeneity, each of its great branches — Lutheranism, Calvinism, Anglicanism — possesses it. In the same way, each of the Ancient Churches is homogeneous, whereas Christianity as a whole is not, any more than are other religions, each of which comprises at least two more or less antagonistic denominations.

"When two or three gather in my Name, I am in their midst," Christ said. Among all the possible meanings of this saying, there may also be this one: the first two who assemble are Catholicism and Orthodoxy, and the third, which is mentioned apart, is Evangelicalism. In fact,

---

27. Referring to the Chapter "The Question of Evangelicalism" in our book, *Christianity/Islam: Essays on Esoteric Ecumenicism.*

Christ could have said: "When three gather", thereby placing the three confessions on the same level; but he said "two or three", which indicates a certain inequality, but always within the framework of religious legitimacy; inequality as regards completeness or plenitude, but at the same time legitimacy as regards the love of Christ and spiritual authenticity, hence underlying fraternity despite the differences.

Sedes Sapientiae

The Blessed Virgin is inseparable from the incarnated Word, as the Lotus is inseparable from the Buddha, and as the Heart is the predestined seat of immanent Wisdom. In Buddhism there is an entire mysticism of the Lotus, which communicates a celestial image of an unsurpassable beauty and eloquence; a beauty analogous to the monstrance containing the real Presence, and analogous above all to that incarnation of Divine Femininity that is the Virgin Mary. The Virgin, *Rosa Mystica,* is like the personification of the celestial Lotus; in a certain respect, she personifies the sense of the sacred, which is the indispensable introduction to the reception of the Sacrament.

*

* *

One of the names which the litany of Lorette gives to the Blessed Virgin is *Sedes Sapientiae,* "Throne of Wisdom"; and indeed, as was noted by Saint Peter Damien (11th century), the Blessed Virgin "is herself that wondrous throne referred to in the Book of Kings," namely, the Throne of Solomon the Prophet-King who, according to the Bible and rabbinical traditions, was the wise man *par excellence.*[1] If Mary is *Sedes Sapientiae,* this is first of all be-

---

1. If the Bible condemned his conduct, it was because of a difference of level — the Bible's point of view being a priori legalistic, and

cause she is the Mother of Christ who, being the Word, is the "Wisdom of God"; but it is also, quite obviously, because of her own nature, which results from her quality as "Spouse of the Holy Spirit," and "Co-Redemptress";[2] that is to say, Mary is herself an aspect of the Holy Spirit, its feminine counterpart, if one will, or its aspect of femininity; whence the feminization of the Divine Pneuma by the Gnostics. Being the Throne of Wisdom — the "Throne quickened by the Almighty," according to a Byzantine hymn — Mary is *ipso facto* identified with the Divine *Sophia*, as is attested by the Marian interpretation of some of the eulogies of Wisdom in the Bible.[3] Mary could not have been the locus of the Incarnation did she not bear in her very nature the Wisdom to be incarnated.

The Wisdom of Solomon — it is well to recall here — is at once encyclopedic, cosmological, metaphysical and also simply practical; in this last respect, it is political as well as moral and eschatological. That it is at the same time much more[4] emerges not only from certain passages of Proverbs

thus exoteric — and not because of an intrinsic wrong on his part. In Solomon there is manifested the mystery of "wine" and "intoxication," as is indicated on the one hand by his Song of Songs and, on the other, by the actions for which he is blamed in the Bible; but Solomon could have said, with his father David: "I have remembered thy Name, Yahweh, in the night, that I may keep thy Law." (Psalms 120:55).

2. Not losing sight of the fact that the body and blood of Christ are those of the Virgin-Mother, there being no human father.

3. "Yahweh created me in the beginning of his ways, before his works of old. I was set up from everlasting from the beginning, or ever the earth was. When there were no depths, I was brought forth; when there were no fountains abounding with water." (Proverbs, 8:22-24 and following verses).

4. This is what the majority of modern critics tend to dispute; however, if the wisdom of Solomon had been only practical and encyclopedic, the following sentences would be quite inexplicable: "I have not compared to it (to Wisdom) the most precious stone; for all the world's gold is but a piece of sand before it; beside it, silver is accounted as clay. I have loved it more than health and loveliness, I have pre-

and the Book of Wisdom, but also from the Song of Songs, a book particularly revered by the Kabbalists.

As for the Wisdom of the "Divine Mary," it is less diverse, because it does not embrace certain contingent orders; it could never be either encyclopedic or of "Aristotelian" tendency, if one may put it thus. The Blessed Virgin knows, and wishes to know, only that which concerns the nature of God and the condition of man; her science is of necessity metaphysical, mystical and eschatological, and thereby it contains in virtuality every possible science, as the one and colorless light contains the varied and colored hues of the rainbow.

One observation that should be made at this point is the following: if Mary is seated upon the Throne of Solomon and is even identified with that Throne[5] — with the authority it represents — this is not only by divine right but by human right as well, in the sense that, being descended from David, she is heiress and queen in the same way that

---

ferred it to the light, for its shining knoweth no resting point . . . All that is hidden, all that is to see, I have learned. In it there is, indeed, a spirit intelligent, holy; unique, manifold, subtle; lively, penetrant, without stain; clear, imperturbable, friend of the good, acute . . . which can do all things, surveyeth all things, entereth into intelligent, pure, most subtle minds . . . It is a breath of the Divine Power, a pure outpouring of the glory of the Almighty; also nothing that is soiled can enter into it. It is a gleam of the eternal light. . . . Being but one, yet it can do all things; without coming forth from itself, yet it reneweth all things. It extendeth itself throughout the ages in holy souls; it maketh of them friends of God and prophets . . . . Compared to the light, it is greater than light; for light giveth place to night, but against Wisdom naught can prevail." (The Book of Wisdom, 7:9-30). If the Wisdom of the Bible were only practical and encyclopedic, there would assuredly be no reason to identify it with the Blessed Virgin, or to identify her with Solomon's Throne.

5. Theologians — incidentally — do not seem to realize the immense "rehabilitation" that this association with the living *Sedes Sapientiae,* and thereby with the Word, implies for Solomon — an association which is either profound, or else utterly meaningless.

Christ, in like respect, is heir and king. One cannot but think of this when one sees the crowned Romanesque Virgins seated with the Child on a royal Throne; — those Virgins which all too often display considerable artistic crudeness and only a few of which are masterpieces,[6] but which then convey with all the greater hieratic eloquence the majesty and gentleness of Virginal Wisdom. Majesty and gentleness, but also rigor; the *Magnificat* bears witness to this when it affirms, with the accents of a martial Psalm, that *vincit omnia Veritas.*

According to the First Book of Kings (10:18-20) Solomon "made a great throne of ivory, and overlaid it with the best gold. The throne had six steps, and heads of bulls behind,[7] and arms on either side of the place of the seat; two lions stood beside the arms; and twelve lions stood on either side of the six steps; there was not the like made in any kingdom."[8] First of all, some observations on the symbolism of the animals: the lions represent, beyond any question, the radiant and victorious power of Truth, whereas the bulls may, correlatively, represent weighty

---

6. The Germanic peoples knew nothing of the plastic arts, the Greeks and Romans practiced only classical naturalism; Christian art, at least in the Latin world, had great difficulty in rising above this two-fold nothingness. In the Byzantine world, the art of icons was able to escape from such pitfalls.

7. Jewish translations and the Vulgate of Saint Jerome state that "the top of the throne was round behind"; they do not speak of "heads of bulls" as do some Christian translations, whose authors base themselves upon certain semantic factors and the fact that the Second Book of Chronicles (9:18) mentions a "golden lamb," in order — as they see it — to avoid an association of ideas with the pagan cult of the bull. It should be noted that the Jewish historian Josephus (reign of Vespasian) says: "In the place where this prince (Solomon) was seated, there were seen arms in relief which appeared to be receiving him, and at the place where he could support himself, the figure of a bullock was placed as if to support him."

8. This last phrase, applied to the Virgin, indicates her incomparability; her "avataric" uniqueness in the universe of the Semites.

and defensive power; on the one hand, power that looks ahead and, on the other, power that looks back, or imagination that creates and memory that conserves; invincibility and inviolability or again, alchemically speaking, sun and moon. But there is also the symbolism of the materials: ivory is substance and gold is radiation; or ivory, a material associated with life, is the "naked body" of Truth, whereas gold is the "raiment" which on the one hand veils the mystery and, on the other, communicates the glory.

The six steps of the throne refer to the very "texture" of Wisdom, one might say; six is the number of Solomon's seal. It is the number of total unfolding: the creation was completed in six days, and the fundamental metaphysical or mystical perspectives, the *darshanas*, are — and must be — six in number, according to Hindu tradition. This mystery of totality results from the combination of the numbers two and three which, the first being even and the second odd, initially summarize every numerical possibility,[9] — in the Pythagorean and not the quantitative sense. Spiritually speaking, the number two expresses the complementarity of "active perfection" and "passive perfection" as the Taoists would say; in its turn the number three indicates in this context the hierarchy of spiritual modes or degrees, namely "fear," "love" and "knowledge," each of these viewpoints containing, in fact, an active or dynamic aspect and a passive or static one.

The cosmic and human significances of the six directions of space — and the subjectivization of space is certainly not arbitrary — reveal the contents of Wisdom — its dimensions or "stations" so to speak. The North is Divine Purity and human renunciation, *vacare Deo;* the South is Life, Love, Goodness and, in human terms, trust

---

9. This is what space demonstrates: it has three dimensions, but the introduction of a more or less subjective principle of alternative or opposition gives it six directions; this structure retraces the totality of the Universe.

in God or hope; the East is Strength, Victory and, on the human side, spiritual combat; the West is Peace, Beatitude, Beauty and, in human terms, spiritual contentment, holy quietude. The Zenith is Truth, Loftiness, Transcendence, and thus also discernment, knowledge; the Nadir is the Heart, Depth, Immanence, and thus also union and holiness. This complexity brings us back to the cosmological and encyclopedic dimensions of Solomon's wisdom; it permits us to have a glimpse of the ramifications of the diverse orders of possibilities that unfold between the Nadir and the Zenith, that is to say, between the Alpha and the Omega of universal Possibility.

The foregoing considerations enable us to extend our analysis of the Solomonian number even further, at the risk of becoming involved in a digression that would raise fresh problems; but this does not matter, since further precisions may be useful. The axes of North-South, East-West and Zenith-Nadir correspond respectively to the complementarities "Negative-Positive," "Active-Passive" and "Objective-Subjective," which summarize the principal cosmic relationships and constitute the fundamental symbolism of the three dimensions of space: length, breadth and height. When looking towards the East, whence comes light, the East will be "in front," the West "behind," the South "on the right" and the North "on the left," whereas the Zenith and the Nadir remain immutable; these last two refer also to the pair Principle-Manifestation, the first term being for us "objective" by reason of its Transcendence, and the second term "subjective" because in the face of the Absolute the world is ourselves, and we are the world. But the Nadir may also represent "depth" or "inwardness" and thus the Divine Self, in which case the Zenith will take on an aspect of "projection," of limitless *Māyā*, and of unfolding and indefinite Possibility; in the same way, the root of a tree manifests and unfolds in and by the crown.

Space is defined likewise, and even a priori, by two principial elements, the point — subjectively the center —

142

and extension, which respectively express the two poles "absolute" and "infinite"; time, for its part, also comprises such elements, namely, the instant — subjectively the present — and duration, with the same significance.[10] In the number six, the implicit number three corresponds to the center or the present, and the number two to extension and duration; the center-present is expressed by the ternary, and not by unity, because unity is here envisaged in respect to its potentialities and thus in relation to its possibility of unfolding; the actualization of that unfolding is expressed precisely by the number two.[11] All this is a way of presenting the "Pythagorean" aspect of the number six and consequently this number's role in integral Wisdom.

"Fear," "love" and "knowledge," or rigor, gentleness and substance; then "active" and "passive" perfections, or dynamic and static ones; herein, as we have seen, lies the elementary spiritual message of the principial number six. This scheme expresses not only the modalities of human ascent, but also, and even primarily, the modalities of Divine Descent; it is by the six steps of the Throne that saving Grace comes down towards man, just as it is by these six steps that man ascends towards Grace. Wisdom is in practice the "art" of emerging from seducing and fettering illusion, of emerging first through the intelligence and then through the will; it consists firstly in knowledge of the "Sovereign Good" and then, by way of

10. From a quite different point of view, it can be pointed out that the number three refers more particularly to space, which has three dimensions, whereas the number two is concerned rather with time, whose "dimensions" are the past and the future, without speaking here of the cyclic quaternary contained in duration and which is no more than a development of duality.

11. The number three evokes in fact not absoluteness itself, as does the number one, but the potentiality or virtuality which the Absolute necessarily comprises.

consequence, in the adaptation of the will to this knowledge; the two things being inseparable from Grace.

The Divine *Māyā* — Femininity *in divinis* — is not only that which projects and creates; it is also that which attracts and liberates. The Blessed Virgin as *Sedes Sapientiae* personifies this merciful Wisdom which descends towards us and which we too, whether we know it or not, bear in our very essence; and it is precisely by virtue of this potentiality or virtuality that Wisdom comes down upon us. The immanent seat of Wisdom is the heart of man.

Part Three

Islam

Islam and
Consciousness of the Absolute

In order to introduce our subject, we must once again formulate the following doctrine:[1] the Supreme Principle is both Necessary Being and the Sovereign Good; it is Being with respect to its Reality, and Good with respect to its Positivity — or its Qualitative Potentiality — for on the one hand, "I am that I am," and on the other, "God alone is good." From "Necessary" Being is derived "possible" being — which may be or may not be — that is, existence; and all manifested qualities are derived from the Sovereign Good which is their only cause or essence.

On the one hand the Sovereign Good is the Absolute, and being the Absolute, it is *ipso facto* the Infinite; on the other hand it is hypostasized — if one may put it thus — into three "divine modes": Intelligence, Power and Goodness; Goodness coinciding with Beauty and Beatitude. Each of these modes participates in Absoluteness and Infinitude, for each is linked to the Sovereign Good or Necessary Being.

Evil cannot be absolute, it always depends upon some good which it misuses or perverts; the quality of Absoluteness can belong to good alone. To say "good" is therefore

1. We have spoken of it in several works, including this one in the chapter "The Problems of Evil and Predestination."

147

to say "absolute," and conversely: for good results from Being itself, which it reflects and whose potentialities it unfolds.

We have alluded more than once to the Augustinian notion that it is in the nature of the good to communicate itself, hence to radiate; to project itself and thereby to become differentiated. This is the Infinitude proper to absolute Reality; the Infinite is none other than the Absolute *qua* Possibility, it is both intrinsic and extrinsic since it is first of all Divine Life and then Cosmic Radiation.

As pure Potentiality or Possibility as such, the Infinite gives rise, in the order of cosmic gradation, to the veil of *Māyā* and thus to the unfolding of universal Manifestation, the content of which is still Necessary Being, hence the Sovereign Good, but in relative and differentiated mode, in conformity with the simultaneously exteriorizing and diversifying tendency of Possibility. Moreover, the pole "Infinite," in combining with the pole "Absolute," becomes mirrored in the space of *Māyā:* if the existential categories[2] and the indefinite diversity of things — in short, all modes of extension — stem from the Infinite, the pure and simple existence of things stems from the Absolute, and the qualities of things testify to the Sovereign Good as such.

The existence of things refers to the Absolute by analogy — and analogy necessarily indicates an ontological link — namely in respect to "abstraction," "contractivity" and "explosivity," if such images are permissible in this domain; for the unexpected miracle of existence — this affirmation of all in the face of nothing — is something absolute and consequently must refer to That which is all and which alone is.

The principle of differentiation does not stem solely from the Infinite insofar as the Infinite unfolds the poten-

2. Space, time, form, number, matter, extending the meaning of these categories to all levels of the cosmos; in which case the notions become no more than symbols.

tialities of the Good, it results also from the Good itself inasmuch as the Good bears these inexhaustible potentialities within itself; their foundation being the ternary Intelligence, Power and Goodness-Beauty-Beatitude. All the cosmic qualities, including the faculties of creatures, derive ontologically from these archetypes *in divinis.*

*
* *

Totality of intelligence, freedom of will, disinterestedness of love, hence capacity for generosity, compassion, transcending of self, in short, capacity for integral objectivity: these characteristics of man prove that his reason for being is his relationship with the Absolute. This is to say that only man's faculties are commensurate with this relationship, and moreover this is why the posture of his body is vertical and why he possesses the gifts of reason and speech; man is so made that he can conceive, will and love that which transcends him infinitely. He can be a metaphysician and can practice a spiritual method; he can find his happiness therein and prove it by his virtues.

It is this nature of man, thus this fundamental disposition — or specific capacity — to know God and to go towards Him, that every religion necessarily takes for granted; not every religion, however, necessarily bases itself upon the saving power inherent in man's deiformity. Theravadin Buddhism and Zen have as their starting point this power to the point of excluding from their perspective all that seems to serve as an objective Divinity; Christianity on the contrary puts the entire emphasis upon the humanly irremediable fall of our nature and upon the absolute necessity of a divine intervention, hence coming from outside the human being. The position of Islam is intermediate: man is saved both by virtue of his unalterable deiform characteristics — for fallen man is still man — and by virtue of a divine intervention which turns them to account. What in Islam is human na-

149

ture turned to account by Revelation will, in Christianity, be represented by Christ: it is He, "true man and true God," who restores man's nature; fallen man — the "sinner" — is regenerated in and by the Redeemer.[3] This amounts to saying that Christianity is not directly linked to the Absolute as such, but to the Good inasmuch as it manifests its reintegrating function of Mercy; this relativization corresponds to the *de facto* reduction of human nature to a "historical" or cosmic accident, but it goes without saying that in Christianity — as in every religion — there is also a key to the Absolute as such. In Islam, and in analogous perspectives, what corresponds to the "Christly" principle will be the "heart," sometimes compared to a tarnished mirror; the purpose of Revelation is to restore to this mirror its primordial luminosity. Islam, founded on Unity and Transcendence, necessarily accentuates in its expressions and attitudes the essential aspects of the One, aspects which we spoke of at the beginning of this chapter; it is true that the same accentuations may, or even must, necessarily be found everywhere in one form or another, so that our exposition allows for appropriate applications to the most varied perspectives; but what we are concerned with here is the concrete case of Islam.

Infinitude, as we have said, is the radiation, both intrinsic and extrinsic, of the Absolute: a priori it is internal Bliss, if one may say so; in becoming relative a posteriori, it becomes hypostatic and creative as well as saving *Māyā;* these two aspects, the Absolute as such and its radiating *Shakti* — Infinitude at once substantial and unfold-

---

3. We have often had occasion to cite this patristic formula: "God became man that man might become God." In Lutheran mysticism, the relationship between God and man gives rise to this reciprocity: in making our sin His sin, Christ makes His justice our justice; that is, Christ takes the chastisement upon Himself and from us requires faith alone, and also, as a consequence of faith, the accomplishment of our duty and the sincere intention not to sin; sincerity here being the key to efficacy, and the support for the justice which Heaven grants us.

ing — determine the most characteristic manifestations of Islam. They are prefigured phonetically in the very Name of the Divinity, *Allāh;* the first syllable, which is contractive, seems to refer to the rigor of the Absolute, whereas the second syllable, which is expansive, evokes the gentleness of Infinitude.

In conformity with these two poles, the characteristic manifestations of Islam can be divided into two categories: one which evokes implacable Truth *(Ḥaqq)* and the Holy War *(jihād)* associated with it, and one which evokes generous Peace *(Salām)* and moral and spiritual resignation *(islām).* And similarly: the mystery of the Absolute is linked to the idea of the Lord *(Rabb)* before whom man can only be a slave *('abd),* and the mystery of the Infinite is linked to the idea of the Clement *(Raḥmān)* who encompasses everything; Rigor and the Law are related to the Absolute, and Gentleness and Pardon are related to the Infinite; this is the complementarity between "Majesty" *(Jalāl)* and "Beauty" *(Jamāl).*

*

* *

To the objective reality of the Absolute there responds the subjective reality of certitude; certitude gives rise to a characteristic feature of the Moslem mentality, because the entire faith of Moslems is based upon the simple and irrefutable idea of "Necessary Being" *(Wujūd wājib)* or "Absolute Being" *(Wujūd muṭlaq);* the necessary is that which cannot not be, whereas the possible *(mumkin)* or the contingent is that which may or may not be. Not that certitude is lacking in the other forms of religious faith; but in Islam it has a crystalline and implacable quality stemming precisely from the metaphysical self-evidence of its fundamental content; assuredly, not every Moslem is a metaphysician, but the self-evidence of the Absolute is in the very air that he breathes. Thus the Moslem has the reputation for being "unconvertible," and this inflexibility

151

is all the more understandable in that, in a certain respect, the simplest truth is the surest.

The sense of the Absolute has produced in Moslem theology a curious over-emphasis on the confrontation "Lord-servant" or "Master-slave": one piously imagines that God has the right to anything, even the right to commit what, for us, is an injustice and an absurdity;[4] thus one forgets that the personal God, being perfect, cannot have the imperfection of laying claim to all possible rights, and that it is only the impersonal Divine Essence which, as All-Possibility, has "all rights" in the sense that, given its limitlessness, it manifests the negative as well as the positive possibilities; but this Essence, precisely, asks nothing of man. Being perfect, God cannot be inconsequential: He could not create a being with the aim of having an interlocutor without thereby assuming certain limitations; for reciprocity is not conceivable without certain sacrifices on the part of both partners, intrinsically incommensurable though they may be. Once God turns to man, He situates Himself in *Māyā*, and assumes all the consequences.

One could also say, in this order of ideas, that the notion of right implies that of duty, logically and ontologically; the just man who does not wish to assume a particular duty renounces *ipso facto* a particular right. To say that the pure Absolute[5] has no duty means that It cannot lay claim to any right, for It has no interlocutor.

4. The Koranic formula "do not impose upon us that which we have not the strength to bear" concerns a relative, not an absolute situation; a factual difficulty, not a principial one, and thus a situation with indeterminate boundaries. This formula seems to allude to the ancient Hebrews, whose prescriptions were realizable, but which in fact the Hebrews frequently violated either by reason of shortcomings — obviously relative — in their mentality, or because of the seductiveness of the pagan ambience.
5. We have alluded more than once to the seemingly contradictory, but metaphysically useful and even indispensable, idea of the "relatively absolute," which is absolute in relation to what it rules, while pertaining to relativity in relation to the "Pure Absolute."

The Law exists for man, not man for the Law;[6] in other words: the personal God is by definition a moral Person; it is true that the divine Essence is "amoral," if one will, but it does not follow from this that the divine Person is immoral, *quod absit;* to maintain that He is so, even in an indirect way and through the use of pious euphemisms, amounts to confusing the impersonal subjectivity of All-Possibility with the personal subjectivity of God as Legislator and Savior.[7]

In an altogether general manner, the Moslem tendency to abrupt simplifications, trenchant alternatives and peremptory gestures (of which the reputedly rough and ready justice meted out by the *qādis* is at least a symbolic example, for in fact Moslem law is not so simple as that) stems, in the final analysis, from a voluntaristic distortion of the sense of the Absolute. By vulgarizing the idea of the Absolute in the moral climate of an Imrulqais, of a Tarafa and of an Antara,* there is a considerable risk of ending with the logic of the drawn sword.

*

* *

6. Exoterically, one submits to the Law in order to please God and escape chastisement, not to mention the practical or moral value of the Commandment, to which every man should be sensitive; esoterically, one submits to the Law taking into account its intentions, and knowing that God does not require anything more, as He sees the nature of things and the "spirit," rather than the "letter."

7. In the climate of Christianity, we have encountered an analogous opinion: it appears that God has the "right" to impose what is nonsensical on the human mind, since He is "above logic"; but this too is impossible, for having created human intelligence "in His own image," God could not possibly wish to impose upon it contents incompatible with the ontological relationship between the mind and the truth, and therefore contents which are necessarily false. *Credo quia absurdum* quite clearly has in view apparent illogicalities only — ellipses touching on things that escape our earthly experiences or fragmentary reasonings.

*Famous pre-Islamic poets of the 6th century. (Translator's note)

153

To repeat, the point to bear in mind is that the two mental or moral attitudes that typify Islam *de facto*, namely certitude and serenity — which, when exaggerated, become fanaticism and fatalism — derive in the final analysis from the mystery of Unity as it becomes polarized into Absolute and Infinite. As regards the consciousness of Infinitude, the importance of the idea of Peace in Islam is well known; it is this which inspires resignation and generosity, the two key-virtues of Moslem piety. And it is again this same element that is outwardly manifested in such liturgical phenomena as the call to prayer from the height of the minarets, or in such cultural phenomena as the monotonous whiteness of Arab clothing and towns;[8] this climate of peace is prefigured in the desert which is inseparable from the Arab world — ancestrally the world of Hagar and Ishmael — and consequently from the Islamic world. In the Moslem Paradise, the chosen "say only Peace, Peace" *(illā qīlan salāman salāma);* and "God calleth to the abode of Peace" *(ilā dār as-salām);* the same fundamental idea is moreover contained in the word *islām,* which means "abandonment" to the Will of Him Who, being the One *(Aḥad),* is the "Absolutely Real" *(Wujūd muṭlaq).*[9]

Certitude and serenity: with these two attitudes are associated respectively combativeness and resignation. It is well known how important in the Path *(ṭarīqah)* are on the one hand spiritual "combat" *(jihād)* — prayer in all its forms *(dhikr)* being the weapon against the still untamed soul — and on the other hand "poverty" *(faqr)* "for the

---

8. Leaving aside, of course, Turkish and Persian influences.

9. There is no point in objecting here that the personal God is not, strictly speaking, the Absolute since by definition He is already situated — He first of all — within universal Relativity; for He represents Absoluteness for all the subsequent contents of this Relativity. Similarly, when we speak of "Necessary Being," we simply mean transcendent Reality and not the creating and personal Principle only; the word "Being" has in fact two different meanings, namely "Reality" and "ontological Principle."

sake of God" *(ilā 'Llāh)*, which make us independent of both the seductive world and the seducible soul. The Sufi is both *mujāhid*, "combatant," and *faqīr*, "poor"; he is always on a battlefield and, in another respect, in a desert.

The Testimony of Faith of Islam, according to which "there is no divinity except the one Divinity" is both sword and shroud: on the one hand it is a lightning-bolt in its fulgurating unicity, and on the other hand a sand dune or a blanket of snow in its peace-giving totality; and these two messages refer respectively, not only to the mysteries of Absoluteness and Infinitude, but also — in a certain fashion — to those of Transcendence and Immanence. Moreover, Immanence would be inconceivable without the Infinite: it is thanks to the Infinite that there is a cosmic projection enabling the Sovereign Good to be immanent; and it is starting from this projection that we can have the presentiment that all values and qualities have their roots in — and open out onto — Necessary Being, which is the Good as such.[10]

10. If the first Testimony of Faith, which testifies to the Unity of God, is linked to Transcendence, the second Testimony, that of the Prophet or of the Logos, is in the final analysis the formula of Immanence.

Observations on
Dialectical Antinomism

There is a dialectical antinomism just as there is a moral antinomism; the latter is synonymous with "amorality" — not necessarily with "immorality" — whereas the former consists in bringing out two opposing principles, not in order to choose between them, but to point out an intermediary term which justifies them both, so that both become points of reference — each admissible by itself under certain conditions — serving to disclose an underlying truth which abolishes the contradiction. Thus one speaks of an "antinomic" theology[1] which consists in confronting two contradictory affirmations concerning God in view of a superior, possibly ineffable, truth, but without intending to negate either of the two affirmations; for the purpose is to confront, not a truth and an error, since that would not lead to a new conclusion, but two truths, each of which is valid in itself but insufficient in respect to their antinomy.

The prototype of antinomic dialectic is furnished by the diversity of religions: apparently false in relation to one another, each is true in itself, and in addition each hides — and provokes — a common and unifying truth which pertains to the plane of primordial and perennial wisdom.

1. We have come across this expression in a book on Palamite theology, if our memory is correct.

But the absolute archetype of dialectical antinomism is not situated on the plane of doctrine; it is found in the very nature of relative or contingent subjectivity, namely in the phenomenon of individuality, which is both evident and contradictory: evident because the "I" exists unquestionably — *cogito ergo sum* — and contradictory because, while the "I" is unique by definition, it is nonetheless repeated; because there are "I's" which empirically are not "me," or rather, because no other "I" is "me."

Thus when a Moslem — and a priori an Arab — passes from one aspect of the real to another, he changes egos so to speak: either he sees only the Divine Rigor, or he sees only the Gentleness; he is capable of loving one or more women while trembling at the idea of the Last Judgement — something which the Westerner is incapable of doing. When a Westerner trembles at the idea of Judgement he enters a convent or becomes a hermit; when he thinks he has the right to love a creature in the face of God, he does not tremble; trust then takes precedence over terror, once and for all.

Extreme fear and extreme trust: the underlying coherence of these opposite positions resides in the spiritual temperament of the Oriental, namely in a desire to go the root of things, a desire for total commitment; in short, it is to perceive the data of the Revelation and the Sunna, not according to their logical continuity and overall equilibrium, but according to a discontinuity that seeks to isolate each datum in order to grasp it in depth; the apparent incoherence may result from the fact that two different subjects are involved — in which case we would speak of a vocational disparity — but it may also be situated in one and the same subject. In the first case, the enigma lies in the religion which permits taking such divergent and abrupt positions; in the second case, it lies in the mentality of the individual who changes egos, so to speak, according to his perception or state.

*

* *

This question of the antinomy between fear and trust, or between Rigor and Clemency, leads us to the following consideration. According to the Koran, "God forgives whom He wills and punishes whom He wills": which for some people means that Justice depends upon the Divine Will, whereas in reality it is the Divine Will that is governed by Justice, for Being "precedes" Willing; otherwise the Divine Name "The Just" *(Al-Ḥakīm)* would be meaningless. The Koranic verse we have just quoted could only mean: God forgives some people who, according to human measures, do not seem to deserve forgiveness, and He refrains from punishing some who, according to the same measures, seem to deserve punishment; and He acts in this way not solely because "He wants to" — which precisely would not be a reason — but for reasons we may have no knowledge of, since we do not dispose of God's measures; the apparent voluntarism of the Koran is therefore a dismissal of the case. Clearly, it is absurd to say that something is good simply because God does it, without understanding that God, being the Sovereign Good, does it because it is good, just as He is Good; because it manifests the Divine Goodness or some aspect of it. God's Qualities precede His Willings, and not conversely; His Willings are inconceivable without His Qualities; "there is no divinity except God," and not: "except God's Will." If, Koranically speaking, "God doeth what He wills," it is because metaphysically He does what He is.

In this connection, we would point out that, in speaking of God, the exegetists distinguish between "Desire" *(Irādah)* — or "Commandment" *('Amr)* — and "Will" *(Mashī'ah):* God "wills" good and evil, but He "desires" or "orders" only good; now this point of distinction does not suffice to take us out of the vicious circle of a voluntarism which lends an almost human subjectivity to All-Possibility and which for that reason becomes morally unintelligible. It is true that Ghazali alludes to "mysteries whose divulgence is forbidden," and doubtless he means the complexity of the Divine Nature, thus the degrees of principial Subjectivity, in short, all that could open the door both to polytheism and pantheism. Still, the Sufis, who are supposed to know these mysteries, have too often given their support to anthropomorphist voluntarism as well as to legalistic moralism, thereby assuming responsibility for all the pitfalls inherent in exoteric simplifications.

To be clearer, we must summarize here what may be termed — rightly or wrongly according to case — the doctrine of the "Divine Will." The Supreme Principle is the Absolute, and in the final analysis it is from this quality that the existence of things derives; being the Absolute, the Principle is *ipso facto* the Infinite: hence All-Possibility, the suprapersonal Divine "Will," from which is derived the diversity of things, of creatures, of events, in short, of all that is possible. Being the Absolute and the Infinite, the Principle is also the Sovereign Good, and the positive qualities of things on the one hand, and the regulating, legislating and saving Will of God on the other derive from this aspect. But this is not to say that the same logical and moral subjectivity "wills" at one and the same time existence and the division into good and evil, and the realization of the good; the will that wants the good "superimposes" itself upon the ontological functions that "precede" it, which amounts to saying that this will is not the fundamental hypostasis of the Divine Order, although it manifests its essence, otherwise it could not be the will of the Good.

If the hypostasis that most directly touches upon the human order is this will of the Good — thus the personal God who reveals and saves — it is precisely because the Divine Essence, namely the Absolute with its aspect of Infinitude, is a priori the Sovereign Good; and this is so notwithstanding functional and transitory appearances to the contrary resulting from the limitlessness of Possibility.

*
* *

160

According to Moslems, God owes man nothing, but keeps His promises because He cannot lie. The key to this mystery is the combination — or parallelism — between two antinomic truths: firstly, God in Himself can owe nothing to man, for the Absolute can owe nothing to the contingent, and this is the relationship of incommensurability; secondly, God as Creator "wishes to owe" something to man, otherwise He would not have created him intelligent, free and responsible, and this is the relationship of reciprocity. In ignoring the first relationship, man sins through irreverence, through lack of fear; in ignoring the second, he attributes to God a tyranny and arbitrariness that are contrary to the Divine Perfection, and this borders on blasphemy; but depending on milieu or circumstances, it may be opportune to stress one of these relationships more than the other. Monotheism, to the extent that it is "totalitarian," has the tendency to reduce divergent realities to a single relationship, that of the "will" of God.

In an analogous manner: on the one hand, man possesses intelligence, thus he has the right to think and cannot help doing so; on the other hand, God alone is omniscient, thus man cannot know more than God, nor understand better than God; he can know and understand only through God. Wisdom consists in being aware of both relationships.

Let us return now to the abrupt juxtaposition between fear and trust: the first is motivated by the idea of Judgement, and the second finds, upon the whole, its immediate expression in the integration of sexual pleasure in the Way. The Islamic insistence on the religious value of sexuality is easily explained: according to the Prophet, marriage is a school of generosity and patience, apart from the concern of procreation; it comprises a mystical function because, again according to Tradition, sexual union prefigures celestial beatitude and, we may add, contributes to the sense of the Infinite to the extent that man is contemplative, which he is supposed to be. Besides, when a

Junayd says that he needs to unite with woman as he needs to eat — an illogical comparison, objectively, since man can live without woman but not without food — he has in mind the experience of sexual *barakah* and not a biological necessity; this experience, thanks to its affinity with the mysteries of Infinitude and Extinction, had become for him as necessary as daily bread. What takes precedence here is the association of ideas which forces itself upon the contemplative, and not a concern for logic; the ill-sounding character of the expression proves the implausibility of its literal meaning — in accordance with the principle *credo quia absurdum* — given that a saint is involved.

A marginal note may be useful in this order of ideas, by way of forestalling difficulties that could arise when reading certain texts: according to Ghazali and others, one of the advantages of marriage is that it allows one to "vanquish" the goad of the flesh; now by "victory" is meant simply appeasement inasmuch as it enables one, by the absence of bodily desire, to draw closer to God by direct and positive spiritual means which compensate for what might seem to be a defeat, and which it would be without said compensation. Another element of "victory" lies moreover in the sexual experience itself: the extinction and unifying consciousness of the metaphysical or mystical transparency of the sensible phenomenon.

But the great enigma of the average Sufic mentality is not the accentuation of sexuality and thereby of the perspective of trust or hope, it is the excessive accentuation — even though only incidentally — of the perspective of fear and thus of legal scrupulousness.[2] It must be said that the ideas of sin, Judgement, hell and predestination were unknown to the pagan Arabs, or were known to them only as "tales of the men of old" *(asātīr al-awwalīn);* the new, insistent and incisive presentation gripped their imagination all the more

2. Cf. *Sufism: Veil and Quintessence,* the chapter "Paradoxes of an Exoterism."

powerfully. But even so, the overaccentuations — examples of which are given by Ghazali — logically lead to despair, and are compatible neither with the "good news" *(bushrā)* which is the purpose of Revelation, nor with the spiritual quality and right to hope of those who make themselves the spokesmen of these excesses; for, after all, when a man who is supposed to be a great saint declares that when he thinks of the Judgement he would rather be a wisp of straw than a human being, one is tempted to think that under such conditions religion has scarcely any meaning — despite Pascal's wager — even though one may be able to guess, in such a case, that what is involved is a subjective experience that eludes the laws of logic or language. As for the limits — by right or in fact — of symbolism, metaphors and hyperboles, they are rather inexact, above all in the Oriental climate.[3]

No doubt, there is a blind fideism which abolishes intelligence, as there is a pedantic legalism which ruins the moral sense, but it would be imprudent, to say the least, to attribute such aberrations to all those whose language and comportment err on the side of excess. For evidently, we are in the climate of *bhakti* and *karma yoga* — to speak in Hindu terms — and certainly not in that of *jnāna;*[4] and we are thus, in any case, in the climate of mystical individualism, not of liberating knowledge. The expressly anti-intellectual tendency of a certain bhaktism, infatuated more with efficacy than with truth, can moreover explain many

3. In *Mahāyāna* Buddhism, the desire to deliver the last blade of grass is absurd in many respects when taken literally, but it expresses an intention of generous impersonality and in the final analysis refers to the Apocatastasis.

4. It would be a naive illusion to believe that at the beginning of a religion all the apostolic personages had to be *jnānis; jnāna* — gnosis — possesses the deepening and transforming virtue resulting from its very nature, which is both intellective and unitive; but it does not for that reason have the expansive impetus required by a newborn religion.

paradoxical and disappointing phenomena, on the practical as well as theoretical planes.

*

* *

We must return once again to the case of the saint who wishes, through excess of fear, to be a wisp of straw rather than a man: from the symbolist point of view, we may assume that subjective expressions have here an objective meaning, as if one were saying, "If you knew what the Judgement is, you would want to be wisps of straw" — but the books do not make this intention clear; in any case, what seems to be preferred is a nonsensical utterance, which is supposed to have a catalyzing effect. Apart from the matter of symbolism, we may surmise that the expressions in question have been uttered under the sway of a mystical state or during a particular period; thus this argument is not used except in the case of theopathic exclamations — such as, "I am the Truth" or "Glory be to me" — which run the risk of disturbing the believers' faith, whereas edifying extravagances are supposed to stimulate it, even though they defy common sense.[5]

Keeping to the image of the wisp of straw and analogous images and sayings, there is also this hypothesis to be considered: according to Ghazali, men have to be whipped into Paradise, and that is why the Koran contains threats; now this reasoning, plausible in itself, opens the

5. One has to know that the Koran contains nothing that authorizes eschatological terror on the part of pious men, and still less on the part of the Companions of the Prophet: "Surely God's saints — no fear shall be on them, neither shall they sorrow. Those who believe and who fear Him — for them are good tidings in this life and in the next. There is no changing in the words of God: that is the supreme happiness." (Sura "Jonah," 63-65). "Who believe and who fear Him": these are those who on the one hand accept the Truth and on the other respect the Law, which has no connection with a "totalitarian" mysticism of fear, or rather of dread.

door to every exaggeration, including the most implausible and scandalous. But this is not all: in order to endow the threat with a maximum of authority, it is placed in the mouth of a great saint; it is believed that a maximum of persuasive force is achieved thereby, whereas one simply falls into absurdity. In other words, attributing the saying of the straw to a saint to whom it could not possibly apply might be a pious fraud; in fact, it does seem impossible to rule out this hypothesis completely, even though it would throw into discredit many traditional sayings;[6] by compensation it has the merit of avoiding perplexing men who are aware that wholesome logic is a gift of the Holy Spirit.[7] Now, we do not deny that symbolism has its rights, even when the symbolism is outrageous to the point of absurdity, although sufficient in many cases; yet pious frauds exist nonetheless.

To return to the "whippings" of Ghazali: when the Koran specifies that in hell sufferings "shall not be lightened," one is tempted to think that this is metaphysically impossible since all duration comprises cycles, hence alternations, and that an absolutely "compact" punishment is inconceivable;[8] but it is not this cosmic law that the Koranic passage has in view, the explanation being much more simple: it is solely a question of forestalling the irritating tendency to imagine escapes that could neutralize

---

6. A "sincere fraud," sincere since it is founded — as Massignon rightly or wrongly supposes for certain *aḥadīth* — on a mystical "mediumship" which, even if it is not illusory, has in any case nothing to do with historical truth.

7. "Wholesome logic": that which operates starting from intellection and with certain and sufficient data — which rationalism does not do.

8. The same is true — but inversely — for paradisiacal bliss, with the difference that there is no symmetry between Paradise and hell, and that the shadows in Heaven have nothing to do with punishment. Let us note that Buddhism insists on the omnipresence of Mercy; this idea also follows from the Koran, for the divine *Raḥmah* "encompasseth everything."

the threats of the Scriptures. Similarly, when the Koran rejects the opinion of unbelievers that in the fire "their days will be numbered"; which is metaphysically true but morally false, if one may express it thus, all the more so in that unbelievers who put forth the argument are certainly not metaphysicians.

An example of symbolism which is arbitrary and excessive at first glance, but plausible in the final analysis, is the *ḥadīth* that dooms painters and sculptors to the depths of hell. It will of course be objected that the plastic arts are natural to man, that they exist everywhere and that they can have a sacral function — that this is even their deepest reason for being — which is true, but misses the essential intention of the *ḥadīth*. For the literal meaning of the saying, by its very violence, represents a "preventive war" against the ultimate abuse of human intelligence, namely naturalism in all its forms: artistic naturalism on the one hand and philosophical and scientistic naturalism on the other; hence the exact, exteriorizing and "accidentalizing" imitation of appearances, and recourse to logic alone, to reason alone, cut off from its roots. Man is *homo sapiens* and *homo faber:* he is a thinker and therefore also a producer, an artisan, an artist; now there is a final phase of these developments that is forbidden to him — it is prefigured by the forbidden fruit of Paradise — a phase therefore that he must never reach, just as man may make himself king or emperor but not God; in anathematizing the creators of images, the Prophet intended to prevent the final subversion. According to the Moslem conception, there is only one sin that leads to the depths of hell — that is to say, which will never be forgiven — and that is the fact of associating other divinities with the one Divinity. If Islam places such creators in Gehennah, it is because it seems, quite paradoxically, to assimilate the plastic arts with the same mortal sin, and this disproportion proves precisely that it has in view, not the arts in their normal state — even though it assuredly forbids them — but the reason why it forbids them; namely the naturalistic sub-version of which the plastic arts are, for the Semitic sensibility, the symbols and prefigurations.[9]

This example, at which we have paused to some extent, shows how excessive formulations can be the vehicle of correspondingly profound intentions, which leads us once again to the principle *credo quia absurdum.*

*

* *

In order to properly situate the problem of man's sentiments in the face of God, it is important to specify that fear refers to the relationship "Lord-servant," and to the Law; Christ, who insisted upon love and inwardness, advocated the relationship "Father-son," which, being necessarily in the nature of things, must also find a place in Islam, a posteriori at least; not on the plane of legalism, but on the plane of gnosis and of love.

Still on the subject of fear and referring to the Gnostic* terminology, one could also put forth the argument that for the "hylic" or "somatic" type, it is primarily threats that determine the will; for the "psychic" it is primarily all of the promises or the imagery of religion in general; whereas for the "pneumatic," it is the metaphysical idea. But as man is not an absolute unity, we may also speak of man "inasmuch as" he is this or that, in order to avoid the idea that threats concern the "hylic" exclusively, or that the "psychic" — always in connection with volitive assimi-

9. In condemning images, Islam — blessedly "sterile" — at the same time refuses "culturism" — the plague of the West — with its torrents of artistic and literary creations, which puff up souls and distract them from the "one thing necessary."

*One must not confuse gnosis and Gnosticism; the latter is a heterogeneous counterfeit of the Perennial Wisdom, while containing certain truths and symbolisms that are valid in themselves, such as the above ternary. (Translator's note)

lation — is necessarily inaccessible to the language of universal principles.

*

* *

Dialectical antinomism is characteristic of Sufism because it springs from the very character of the Arabs, which — as we have suggested above — tends to enclose the mind in a particular aspect of things to the detriment of the homogeneity of the overall vision of the real; negatively, this is to be incoherent; but positively, it is to do nothing by halves.[10] Thus the ancient Arab was wholehearted in everything, which explains his propulsive force — not capable of miracles by itself, but when turned to account by supernatural factors.

But there is something else. A language that is both abstract and logical is an acquisition resulting from long experience; originally, language is concrete, allusive and associative: concrete because it expresses principles through images, and allusive or associative because instead of logical concatenation it makes use of associations of ideas or of analogies; it readily replaces complex demonstrations by percussive images, of which a classical symbol is Alexander cutting the Gordian knot. An example of this manner of proceeding — common in Islam on account of its almost Bedouin origin — is this saying of Ibn Abbas: "The best of Moslems is he who has the most wives"; now, in order not to be scandalized,[11] one has to

---

10. Someone has told us the story that one day Saint Therese of Avila had prepared a turkey for dinner, and that one of the nuns was astonished at it; the saint is said to have replied: "When I fast, I fast, and when I eat, I eat." This is what is called doing things wholeheartedly, whatever one does; but without exaggeration.

11. David and Solomon would not have been able to disapprove this opinion. It is a question of the spiritual significance of polygamy, which we do not have to analyze here, particularly since we have done so elsewhere. We are forced to admit that human possibility is diverse.

168

know the Arab-Islamic implications, which are at once practical, psychological, moral and contemplative. We are here in the presence of a dialectical procedure which consists in suggesting what is most substantial by what is most accidental; a two-edged sword if ever there was one, yet it is an efficacious language for a mentality used to elliptical, implicit and multidimensional symbolism; the scandal of a crude and at times quantitative image has here the function of a catalyst, something which is met with in all mythologies.

To be sure, there would be no need to speak of antinomic dialectic if it were merely a question of exaggeration in one subject only; but what allows us to speak of antinomism is precisely the fact that exclusive overemphasis is repeated in relation to different and contradictory subjects, and all within the same mind. It is this fact, and not some isolated exaggeration, that places us before a phenomenon a priori unintelligible and exasperating; logically unacceptable, it is psychologically decipherable in the final analysis, and instructive in the sense that it teaches us about one more modality in the range of indefinitely diverse possibilities of the soul and the spirit.

Unquestionably, in antinomic dialectic — in this curious capacity to change egos according to the trajectory of a thought — there intervenes a passional element, and this element also explains another tendency, that of gratuitous argumentation: some truth is conceived perfectly, and it is believed that one owes it a proof, but this proof will be anything, and this anything — in the mind of the thinker — is justified by the truth; the proof is good since the thing to be proved is true.[12] Many defective and disappointing

12. An example of this procedure is, in Sufism, the subjectification of evil with the intention of showing that God wills only the good. One encounters analogous reasonings — as regards their gratuitousness — in Christian climates, for example, in order to prove that God cannot but comprise three Persons.

reasonings of theologians, metaphysicians and mystics are explained by this pious intention to fly to the rescue of a truth that often has no need of this solicitude and that in any case would deserve being supported by serious arguments. It could be said that it is a matter less of furnishing an objective proof than of creating a mental satisfaction; from such a point of view, a proof and a semblance of proof are equivalent, for in any case, the truth is what it is.

A particularly misleading aspect of a mentality too unilaterally symbolist is the omission of necessary information: something is affirmed that is not understandable or plausible unless one knows in what connection it is being considered, but this connection is not expressed; such dialectical deficiencies evidently presuppose a reader who has an intuition of the unarticulated intentions, and then this lack of articulation is not supposed to be a problem in the framework of the ethnic mentality in which the phenomenon is produced; a mentality that combines allusive language with a need for absoluteness, and the elliptical with the explosive.[13]

In addition, as we have already mentioned, mental and moral antinomism in the Arabs and other peoples — especially those who are Arabized — is not unrelated to the symbolist mentality for which the symbol takes precedence over the fact, either relatively or absolutely: rightly so in the first case, and mistakenly in the second. This does not mean that the second case cannot be legitimate in its turn, particularly when the denied fact is without importance from the point of view of the symbolism affirmed, as is often the case in religious dogmatisms.

Be that as it may, there are *grosso modo* two kinds of symbolist thought: one respectful of facts and at the same time careful to preserve the homogeneity of the overall

13. Aside from tautology and platitude, born of the need to depict things, to have them enter the imagination; to contemplate them, as it were.

view of the real, and the other infatuated with the essence of the symbol — infatuated with the absolute within the limits of a given symbolism — to the point of neglecting the exactitude of facts and, in addition, isolating the symbolism by cutting it off from all other aspects of reality. It is in fact a certain need for absoluteness that explains, in the Arab, the tendency on the one hand to isolate an idea or an image from every compensatory context, and on the other to exaggerate the specific coloration of the image, making of it an absolute, precisely; which is yet another way of "doing nothing by halves" and of "doing everything with the heart." If on the one hand this predisposition gives rise to a curiously dynamic thinking — at least on the plane of religion and aside from the influence of the Greeks — on the other it opens the way to a unitive mysticism that goes straight to the mark, with the simplicity of the forces of nature.

171

Diversity of Paths

One of the chief distinctions in Sufic methodology is that between the path of "stations" *(maqāmāt)* and the path of "attraction" *(jadhb);* the first is systematic and proceeds from stage to stage under the vigilant eye of a master *(murshid)* — there may be several of them — whereas the second is subject to no rule other than the spiritual intuition of the mystic *(dhawq)* and the Divine aid *(tawfīq)* or Grace *(Raḥmah)* that answers it and at the same time provokes it. The difference of principle between the two paths could not exclude combinations that are possible by the nature of things, since man is one, and above all, because God is one; hence there could be no absolute boundaries between these two paths, despite the rigor of certain conditions.

The first path, which is initiatory in the proper sense, and thus methodical, is based essentially on the idea that in the human soul there are blemishes which have become natural owing to the loss of the earthly Paradise, and that the "Path" *(Ṭarīqah)* or the "Journey" *(Sulūk)* consists in eliminating them successively; and this explains the need for a master who must define these obstacles, point out the remedies, validate the cure, and then take necessary or useful measures to prevent the victory — by becoming too individualized — from turning into a defeat, and even the most serious defeat of all.

173

The main obstacle, it is said, is the unconscious attachment to "secondary causes" *(sabab,* pl. *asbāb);* by this term two things are meant: firstly, natural, verifiable causes, and secondly, human causations, particularly the means of sustenance; work, for example, is a "cause" *(sabab)* of our gain as the sun is the "cause" of heat. All "secondary causes" are "veils" *(ḥijāb,* pl. *ḥujub)* hiding the "First Cause" (Tustari: *as-Sabab al-Awwal),*[1] the only one that is; the path consists in overcoming the optical illusion of relative and multiple causes, in order to allow for the final perception of the only Cause in all things, including our own acts, which "veil" the true Agent; not "such and such an agent" but the "Agent as such."

1. Let us note here — since we are on the topic of Sufism — that it is aberrant to have the esoterism of Islam coincide with Shiite "imamology" and "gnoseology," as Corbin would have it; then to reduce metaphysics to an inspirationist exegesis, as if intellection — which is also supernatural — did not exist or had no role to play. Authentic esoterism stems from the nature of things and not from a dynastic institution; its seeds are everywhere present, sparks can flash from every flint; to make esoterism result from a religious program and a theological argument is a contradiction in terms. Of course, fundamental truths were expressed initially by those whom the Shiites consider to be imams; however, Sunnite Sufism refers to these sages, not insofar as they are supposed to be imams in the theological sense of Shiism, but insofar as they are "poles" *(quṭb,* pl. *aqṭāb)* of Islam as such, outside all confessional interpretation or annexation; *Spiritus autem ubi vult spirat.* Nevertheless, it could be admitted that the Persians, being Aryans, are a priori more apt for metaphysical speculation or formulation than the Arabs, who are Semites; but the Arabs having assimilated the Greek influence — like the Hellenized Jews — did not need the Persians to have a posteriori the aptitude in question. What the Iranian spirit was able to confer upon the Shiites, the Greek spirit was able to confer upon both the Sunnites and the Shiites; this may be said without forgetting that many of the greatest Sunnites were Iranians, and that the indirect, or direct, founders of Shiism were Arabs. Let us also specify that the general tone of Moslem philosophy allows us to include it in the religious thought — in the widest sense — of Islam; with some reservations, according to case.

Diversity of Paths

The "Remembrance of God" *(dhikru 'Llāh)*, of which the Koran says that it is "greater" than the prescribed prayer, or that it is the "greatest thing of all," is basically a spontaneous act of awareness of the divine causality, in ourselves as well as around us. Every moral defect, and even every innocently individualistic attitude, is a forgetting of God, whether naively habitual or perverse; this is the "forgetfulness" *(ghaflah)* mentioned by the Koran and spoken of by the Sufis; conversely, each moral quality coincides with a way of remembering the Divine Cause, which is the Good and the Norm. And that is why, to conquer the superstition — or the idolatry — of secondary causes amounts to acquiring the virtues; it is also to render the natural virtues supernatural. Superstition or idolatry; but we could also say: "association" *(shirk)* of something with God — of a second reality with the one and only Reality — for therein lies, in the Koranic perspective wherein everything converges on Unity, the sin of sins, together with "unbelief" *(kufr)*, which implies the idea of ingratitude and blasphemy.

Thus, in order to obtain the spiritual cure, the disciple *(murīd)* or the traveler *(sālik)* must detach himself from "secondary causes" as far as possible in practical life, for awareness ought to be concrete and thorough: for example — although this is only a symbol of attitudes exhibiting the greatest variety and, at times, the greatest subtlety — the disciple will refuse alms because "God alone provides," or he will refuse a remedy because "God alone cures." This is the virtue of "trust" *(tawakkul)*, which is crucial, but which in fact gives rise to many abuses; doubtless it is better to be absurd than to be impious, and it is better to exaggerate than to stop halfway; nonetheless, overreacting is a double-edged sword. However, if the realists of spirituality are right in thinking that a philosophical awareness of divine causality is insufficient, and strictly speaking that it amounts to "hypocrisy" *(nifāq)* — for the usual behavior of the mere "thinker" hardly corroborates his sublime con-

175

victions — they are all too often wrong in forgetting the "supernaturally natural," and in principle efficacious, role of intelligence; a forgetfulness that can be explained primarily by the fact that they address themselves to the average — even though normally endowed — man and not to the "pneumatic," and do so in accordance with the voluntaristic and a priori anthropomorphic perspective of the common religion. In Sufism, extreme vulgarization and initiatory elitism go hand in hand; each has its place but there are also paradoxical and problematic minglings. The excuse could be made that not only profane or passional men are addressed, but the profane or passional aspect of man as such; in which case everything comes down to the question of proportion and opportuneness.

An objection that could be raised against this therapy consisting in eliminating "secondary causes" is the following: if it is not the sun that illumines, fire that burns, food that nourishes, medicine that cures — on the "pretext" that God alone does it all — the object of the operation should also be placed in the Divine Order, because the sufficient reason for physical causes is that God contacts the physical domain only through them — except in the case of miracles — and He does this precisely because the causes are physical.[2] Consequently, the evil to overcome is not the fact that man attributes earthly effects to earthly causes, but that he does not perceive in the depth of these causes the immanent Divine Cause, as he ought to perceive, in the final analysis, the Divine Self in the depth of his own spirit.

The idea of divine intervention in natural causality leads us to the following considerations: if on the one hand God does not "enter" the physical order except in the case of a miracle, on the other hand He does not "leave" the Divine Order except in the case of creation;

---

2. In the Aristotelian sense of the word, embracing the entire order of "nature," at least logically and *de jure*.

He "enters" without leaving Himself, and He "leaves" without entering into what is other than Himself; the first miracle being Revelation, and the first creation being the Logos. Or again: if we say that divine "causes" do not enter directly into the created order, except in cases of miraculous intervention, we could also say correlatively that the "effects" of these causes are situated, like the causes themselves, in the Divine Order, except in the case of creative projection.[3] From still another standpoint, we may say that if the Uncreated does not "enter" into the created except through theophany, conversely the created does not "enter" into the Uncreated except through the Apocatastasis; both "entries" being only apparent, quite evidently, for the Principle and manifestation cannot mingle; we are here at the limit of what is expressible.

*
* *

The distinction between the path of methodical "progression" *(sulūk)* and that of mystical "attraction" *(jadhb* or *jadhbah)* means, not that there are only these two paths in Sunnite Islam, but that each of them is a category encompassing an almost indeterminate number of possible paths; according to a Sufi adage, "There are as many paths towards God as there are human souls." An example of this diversity is the difference, on the plane of the "stations," between a positive method, that of a Qushayri, and a negative method, that of an Ibn al-'Arif. In the first case, one is expected to overcome the illusion of "secondary causes" by means of the corresponding and corrective virtues; whereas in the second case virtue itself is consid-

---

3. Which is to say that *in divinis* the relationship of cause to effect and the nature of the two poles appear quite differently than they do in the physical order, the metacosmic archetype of all causality being the relationship — in Sanskrit terms — between *Brahma* and *Ishvara,* and then between *Purusha* and *Prakrti.*

177

ered as an attachment to such a "cause," and it must be overcome by an "extinction" that puts God in place of the virtue, or more exactly, by an "extinction" having the effect of rendering God present where the "vulgar" *(awwām)* places his virtue or, what amounts to the same, his "station." Our intention here is not to comment on this point of view which is characteristic of the Sufic tendency towards subtle eliminations and "unveilings," but simply to take account of the complexity of the paths or of the Path.

Concerning the fact of replacing the superstition of secondary causes with the awareness of divine causes or with God-as-Cause: the main pitfall of this alchemy is the definition of the Divine Will on the one hand, and of the object of this Will on the other; in other words, the idea — elliptical, to say the least — that God is the only cause of cosmic or natural effects leads us immediately to the question of evil as object of the Will of God.

We have often said, and doubtless will repeat, that God could not will evil as evil, that He wills it only in one respect where, precisely, evil ceases to be evil. A phenomenon which, at its own level and in our experience, is an evil, is not linked to the Divine Will except as a fragment or phase of a good, and not taken separately; the possibility of what at its own level is an evil stems not from the Will of God as a Person who creates, legislates and metes out justice, but from the Divine All-Possibility, which is evidently impersonal since it pertains to the Divine Essence. Or again, if it is affirmed that God is the only agent of every act, it ought to be specified that He is, in every act, the Agent of the act as such, but not of a particular act.

Be that as it may, in pure theosophy there is no question of wishing to take away from God His mysteries by means of unveilings and delimitations; for however acute our discernments, the divine mystery remains complete by reason of the Infinitude of the Real.

*
* *

Whatever the ideological or moral excesses that the disciple may find useful to adopt in the course of his way, the method consists, as we have seen, in divesting oneself progressively of profane prejudices that are so many forgettings of God — this being the well known "breaking of habits" — and in realizing "sincerity" *(ṣidq)* of faith in the One; each divestment being a "disappearance" *(fanā')* before the real Cause — or in other words, an "extinction." But it is here, according to Ibn 'Arabi, that the major temptation of the Path intervenes: having obtained the awareness of a given aspect of divine causality, man, in accordance with his individualism or inveterate egoism, risks appropriating this victory for himself, and forgetting that the subject as well as the object of the victory is God; now "pride" *(kibar, istikbār)* kills all the other virtues. Thus it is a question not only of eliminating the superstition of a given secondary cause — of a given causality lived outside God — but also of uprooting all temptation to luciferianism on the part of the subject who risks wishing, with a spiritually paralyzing satisfaction, to settle into a given "station" *(maqām)*, the awareness of which he individualizes; therein lies the whole danger of spiritual narcissism. Symbolically, it will be said that each station tempts the "traveler" with a particular treasure which he must refuse if he does not wish to lose everything; numerous initiatory stories — from myths to fairy tales — take account of this spiritual drama, and this is also one of the meanings of the "extinction of extinction" *(fanā'u 'l-fanā')*, although this term applies primarily to an extrinsic aspect of the supreme goal.

Some precisions are necessary here, for one should not fall into disproportionate fears or into a blind humilitarianism refractory to all objectivity in relation to oneself. The danger of the "pride" in question is a consequence on the one hand of the natural ambition of the man of voluntaristic temperament, and on the other hand of the idea that one must "personally" attain a transcendent goal and a perfect realization, whence a perfectionistic obsession, or an ambitious subjectivism that ends practically by putting the "I" — in the form of a particular "realization" — in place of God. The whole remedy is reducible to the so to speak Vedantic meaning of the *Shahādah,* and thus to the *neti, neti* of the *Vedānta:* "not this, not this"; meaning: "Ātmā alone." This is also expressed, in the Koran, by the story of the child Abraham: seeing a star, he believes it is God; but when he sees it set, he is aware of his error; likewise with the moon and the sun (Sura "The Cattle," 76-78). Unquestionably, this story — like analogous symbolisms — comprises both a specifically initiatory as well as a generally human meaning.

*

* *

The point to be made here is that one ought to distinguish carefully between an "abode" *(manzil)* which one believes is supreme and in which one glories, and an "abode" wherein one remains contented in all piety and in all humility. When certain texts blame those who halt at a given "abode," we can guess that this halting stems from pride since we are told that it causes one to lose everything, according to Ibn 'Arabi; for it goes without saying that contentment with little — a little that in reality is immense — does not result in such a loss, otherwise there would be neither a hierarchy of saints nor degrees in Paradise.

It is possible that we have simplified somewhat the problem of "renouncing something in order to obtain more" — renouncing a particular treasure or dignity — and that this question is in reality much more subtle and complex than we seem to acknowledge, inasmuch as it pertains to the initiatory order; but what justifies our simplification, if it be one, is the theme of "loss" or "fall," which always indicates a luciferian attitude, so that the most refined analyses can add nothing substantial to our interpretation.

There is another version of this myth, with a different meaning since it comprises no luciferianism or fall, found in a German folk tale: the hero goes off to seek adventure on his white horse — which in reality is the spiritual guide or the protective genius, like Al-Khidr in Islam — and he sees on the ground a peacock feather of marvelous beauty; he dismounts in order to pick it up, but the horse tells him: "Leave it on the ground." After some time, the incident repeats itself; the hero renounces a still more beautiful feather; but the third time, he cannot resist and picks up the feather, despite the repeated warnings of the horse. The horse then enumerates, in ascending order, the glories that the hero has renounced, to his advantage in fact; but the greatest glory has escaped him because he has not been able to renounce the preceding glory, which was lesser. The implication here is thus an initiatory possibility altogether different from the one that implies the risk of a fall, even though the symbolism is almost the same.

Having experienced — as far as possible and up to the boundaries of the absurd — the rejection of second causes, which implies the practice of all the forms of asceticism, the disciple has the right to return to these causes without hesitation or suspicion. Henceforth he sees in them — existentially, not philosophically — the Divine causation, and as a result will have access to the mystery of Immanence; this new awareness renders asceticism — but not healthy sobriety — superfluous, and opens the door to a spiritualization of the most noble and therefore most fundamental pleasures, by supernaturalizing and disindividualizing them, precisely.[4] Neither Islam in general nor Sufism in particular can be understood without taking into account this perspective of Immanence which com-

4. Which Ibn ʿArabi has dealt with in his *Fuṣūṣ al-Ḥikam*, in the chapter on the "Muhammadan Wisdom."

pletes, whether paradoxically or harmoniously, the exclusive and austere perspective of Transcendence.[5]

*

* *

It follows from all the preceding that the two major infirmities of the human soul are the forgetting of God — of the immanent divine Cause — and the appropriation, by the individual, of qualities, merits and glories; hence profanity on the one hand and pride on the other; "association" *(shirk)* both objective and subjective. A phenomenon that seems to contradict this verdict is the fact that many Sufis have not feared to speak of the sublimity of their station, which a priori can give the impression of a strange boasting; in reality, it is the inverse that is true: they speak, well or ill, of themselves as if they were speaking of others; and they do so in order to express a victory made miraculously possible, hence in order to glorify God or to exalt the Path, and not in order to attribute a merit to a personality which, to the extent that this is possible, is no longer their own.

But let us return to the question of secondary causes and their spiritual reduction to the one Cause: each religion possesses an energetic aura — a *barakah* — which brings forth phenomena that are consonant with the perspective of that religion; in Sufi surroundings, miraculous phenomena occur — or have occurred — which corroborate supernaturally the perspective we have described, namely, trust in the single Divine Cause, and which occasionally encourage recourse to attitudes that are on the whole senseless but heroically pious. Many facts of this kind seem implausible from the Christian point of view, but that is because the style of Christianity is different and

5. Meister Eckhart has expressed the in principle sacramental character of the gifts of nature by which we live; a character that is unveiled or actualized in accordance with the sanctity or wisdom of the subject.

consequently produces different prodigies. Thus it is appropriate to be prudent when judging phenomena situated in a religious world foreign to our own, and whose apparent implausibility merely illustrates in a particularly concrete fashion the profound difference between traditional universes.[6]

*
* *

The way of mystical "attraction" *(jadhb)*, to which we alluded at the the beginning of this chapter, is more direct than that of the methodical "journey" *(sulūk)*, but it deprives him who follows it of the experiences necessary to guide others. The way of those who are "attracted" *(majdhūb*, pl. *majādhib)* requires in fact only two conditions, aside from being qualified and having the vocation: on the one hand the religious framework, lacking which one risks being deprived of divine aid *(tawfīq)*, and on the other hand the practice of the fundamental virtues, which leads us to the "stations" and to "secondary causes," but independently of all methodical succession. Of course, this way also implies, like the other, accomplishment of what — in principle or in fact — brings one closer to God, and abstention from what — in principle or in fact — takes one away from Him; "in principle," that is by its nature, and "in fact," that is by our disposition or our capacity. For there are good things that are not good for everybody, just as conversely, there are things reputed to be dangerous or harmful — but not intrinsically bad — that are not harmful to everybody; all of which evokes especially the symbolism of wine.

As in the "regular" path of *sulūk*, everything in this exceptional path of *jadhb* is based on the sacramental and al-

6. The phenomena in question are doubtless the origin of poetic legends on the one hand and hagiographic absurdities on the other, and yet they do not excuse the latter despite extenuating circumstances.

most eucharistic ternary *Madhkūr-Dhikr-Dhākir* ("Invoked-Invocation-Invoker"), and then, correlatively, on the ternary *Makhāfah-Maḥabbah-Maʻrifah* ("Fear-Love-Knowledge"); these diverse elements are subdivided and combined indefinitely. But everything in this second path is more independent and spontaneous than in the first; the sense of the nature of things takes precedence over the concern for rules or conventions. The emphasis is upon "taste" *(dhawq)* and upon "state" *(ḥāl)*, although, of course, they are not taken for criteria, since the criteria stem in the final analysis from the fundamental Idea (the *Shahādah)* understood in depth, and from the "Remembrance of God" accomplished with sincerity and perseverance; spiritual intuition and the sense of the sacred being more important here than ascetic practices,[7] unless one includes in this latter category the retreat *(khalwah)*, accomplished in solitude and combined with fasts and vigils. The music and dance of the dervishes — supposed to favor, if not ecstasy in the proper sense of the word, at least its anticipation — pertain to this same perspective of "tastes" and "states," although not exclusively, it being a question of affinities, not of prerogatives.

At the extreme limit, the *majdhūb* appears as a "fool" *(majnūn)* of whom one accepts a behavior situated more or less outside the Law; but at the opposite extreme one finds on the contrary the man who conforms to the primordial nature *(fiṭrah),* (the "knower through God") *(ʻārif bi-Llāh)*, with similar intrinsic or practical consequences as regards the literal Law.[8] This is to say that "attraction" is not neces-

---

7. Hasan ash-Shadhili, father of the Shadhilite line, did not require his disciples — in spite of the problem of secondary causes — to renounce their livelihood, even a princely one, or to scandalize ostentatiously a society that was after all honorable since it was made of believers.

8. It is appropriate not to forget that in any case legalism comprises the danger of pharisaism: the replacement of virtues by prescriptions and the forgetting of what the nature of things requires or allows.

sarily a phenomenon of emotional mysticism, it can equally be linked to pure gnosis, given that in Sufism there is *Ma'rifah* as well as *Maḥabbah;*[9] one will recall here the two ternaries mentioned above. In other words, the path of liberating attraction can be the fact, not only of a Grace coming as it were from without and from above, and which occasionally can cloud the mind, it can also act *ab intra* and through the pure Intellect — uncreated center of the immortal soul — and bring about an awakening made of clarity or evidence.

9. It seems almost superfluous to add, firstly, that it is not enough to have no master in order to be one of the "attracted," and secondly that the fact of being "attracted" does not prevent one from having one or more masters; all the more so in that all combinations are possible. Let us add that the superior type of the "attracted" — extremely rare in fact — is none other than the "solitary" *(fard)*, who more or less corresponds to the *Pratyēka-Buddha* of the *Mahāyāna*.

Transcendence and Immanence in the Spiritual Economy of Islam

Dogmatic and exoteric Islam insists fiercely on Transcendence, which is separative; esoterism, on the contrary, is based on Immanence, which is unitive. Basically, exoterism admits only its own point of view, whereas esoterism necessarily admits two complementary perspectives, its own and that of exoterism, which is that of the Law. But esoterism has erected, again necessarily, a barrier between them that is at once protective and misleading: namely ascetic zeal, which on the one hand clothes esoterism with a mantle of religious intelligibility — since this zeal presents itself as the "sincere" consequence of the Law — but on the other hand risks taking the means for the end, that is, risks favoring a confusion between ascesis and gnosis. The Arabic word *barzakh* means "isthmus": it is a dividing line between two domains, and this line appears, from the standpoint of each side, to belong to the other side;[1] and that is why excess of legalistic scruple can take on the appearance of esoterism from the standpoint

1. The archetype of the *barzakh* is the half-divine, half-cosmic frontier separating, and in another sense uniting, Manifestation and the Principle; it is the "Divine Spirit" *(Rūh)* which, seen "from above" is manifestation, and seen "from below" is Principle. Consequently, it is *Māyā* in both its aspects; the same thing appears, in a certain manner, in the Christian expression "true man and true God."

of legalism — the excess being a way of sublimating legalism through sincerity, hence by the absence of hypocrisy — while from the vantage point of gnosis excessive scruple appears on the contrary as an element of exoterism, since in fact no formalistic zeal can lead to knowledge. This ambiguity, which has its basis in the complexity of a society dominated by a necessarily anthropomorphic, voluntaristic and sentimental religion, is the permanent source of misunderstandings and confusions; it is even what may be termed the classical misunderstanding of average Sufism.

We have just noted that the "exoterization of esoterism" is the reduction of esoterism to religious zeal, especially to legal scrupulousness, and to asceticism. This simplification or this confusion necessarily goes hand in hand with an "esoterization of exoterism," namely the mystical sublimating of ritual acts — their assimilation to "degrees of contemplation"; from this standpoint, it is as if believers who perform the prescribed acts while being unaware of these mystical interpretations were insincere, or it is as if their acts were invalid, or again, as if mystical graces were the criteria of ritual validity, *et cetera*. However, the religion cannot require believers to walk on initiatory stilts, for by definition it is addressed to all, and conversely, initiates, who by definition are situated at the center and in the inward, have no need for projecting their spiritual tension into an outward zeal, all the more so in that such a projection, to the extent that it is inevitable, is necessarily manifested by the spiritual quality of the prescribed acts. All the errors under consideration here result from the strange idea that "the common Law *(Sharī'ah)* is esoterism *(Ṭarīqah)*," an idea in which mystical sublimism meets legalistic scruple and confessional zeal.

Obviously, Sufi asceticism in itself is independent of these misinterpretations and misuses. Its normal function is to be at once a discipline, an argument and a veil; a discipline rightly intended to make the soul more supple in view of knowledge; an argument intended to make Sufism plausible in the eyes of the doctors of the Law; and finally, a veil intended to hide gnosis and its "extraterritoriality," hence all that is dangerously and blessedly above the narrownesses of the letter that "killeth." The latter two intentions are extrinsic and result from the immanent wisdom which regulates the economy of sacred things but which does not forestall the classical disparagement that consists in attaching to the domain of Transcendence factors which in reality pertain to that of Immanence. In other words, the moral incoherence — whether real or apparent — that is encountered in Islam is due in the final analysis to the presence of two domains which are at once complementary and relatively antinomic, that of the Transcendent and that of the Immanent; of obediential and separative piety on the one hand, and of participatory and unitive spirituality on the other.

These three elements, Transcendence, Immanence and intermediary ascesis, are prefigured in the personality of the Prophet, and even explain it; in him, evidently, they are present in an intrinsically homogeneous and substantial manner, and this homogeneity has allowed Islam to realize an unshakable equilibrium, from its beginnings down to our times; and this is necessarily so, since what is involved is a religion. However, this equilibrium could not preclude partial, and in a certain sense providential, disequilibriums, as we have just shown.

*

* *

As for asceticism, it is necessary to distinguish between an ascesis that is physical, and indirect in relation to its end, and another that is moral, and direct in relation to its end: the former is purgative and aims at mastering the passional element, but not at destroying it, insofar as it is pure energy. The latter on the contrary aims at conforming the soul to the demands of contemplation and thus

189

seeks to develop receptive and participatory perfection; it affects not only the character but also the intelligence, in the sense that lack of virtue — or of a particular virtue — limits or paralyzes the very organ of knowledge. It is in fact a matter of common experience that the capacity for knowledge or for comprehension depends upon character: that it can come to a halt brusquely and "mysteriously" in an intelligent man who lacks a particular moral quality, and who for that reason falls into aberrations that are logically inexplicable because they are incompatible with his intellectual scope. The essential — and not merely vocational — virtues are at once moral qualities and contemplative attitudes, hence they are beauties of soul and of mind, and for that reason keys for gnosis; it is precisely from this fact that is derived the traditional notion of the *maqāmāt*, of the "stations," which are at once simultaneous and successive.

It has been said that "Sufism *(taṣawwuf)* is sincerity *(ṣidq)";* now sincerity is the passage from the cerebral to the cardiac, from the intellectual to the existential, from the partial to the total. The content of this transfer is the idea of Unity, and it is realized with the concurrence of the virtues, which for their part are so many modes or proofs of sincerity. In average Sufism, the virtues even appear, along with the practices of orison and asceticism, as the pre-eminent means, often to the detriment of the purely intellective and contemplative keys, whose sacramental and transformative efficacy is then underestimated.

*

* *

This last remark obliges us to pause for a moment, and once again,[2] on the problem of excess. One Sufi master requires his disciple, a city notable, to wear a patched robe

---

2. We have done so above all in our book *Sufism: Veil and Quintessence;* the excesses in question are precisely the veil.

and a ridiculous cap and to beg at the door of the great mosque, on Friday, when the entire city attends. We object: firstly, because a man who requires such treatment, or for whom such treatment is useful, is not qualified for esoteric knowledge; secondly, because such a spectacle — that of a highly respected notable begging in extravagant garb — is totally lacking in charity towards the community and only causes scandal, as well as making Sufism and its representatives hateful and worthy of scorn, all the more so in that such excesses are perfectly contrary to the principles of Islam, all question of "sincerity" aside. Another example: a Sufi is entreated by his friends to leave a city with his family because there is a danger of epidemic, and if the epidemic is declared he will no longer have the right to leave the city, according to the law; now, this Sufi refuses to leave on the pretext that "everything is written"; the epidemic arrives, and the ten children of the Sufi die from it. And yet, the Prophet said to someone: "Tie your camel and trust in God," in other words: Heaven helps those who help themselves.

One of the greatest Sufi masters, Hasan Ash-Shadhili, was in no wise a partisan of such extravagances; considering Sufism to be an inward treasure, he permitted his disciples to live like everyone else, to wear elegant dress and to fill high and lucrative positions. And similarly Rumi, like David, preferred music and dance inspired by God and offered to Him, to ostentatious exhibitions of poverty and virtue; all the more so in that the Prophet, though poor, was so beautifully and without ostentation.

Non-Moslems have great difficulty in grasping the spiritual or typological originality of the Arab Prophet, whereas they have no difficulty in grasping that of Christ or the Buddha. This is because the latter two each represent a synthetic radiance easy to perceive in its dazzling simplicity and univocalness, whereas the Prophet manifests a range of very diverse virtues, close to human experience; and it is precisely this unfolding of humanly

191

graspable, and both noble and imitable, qualities which constitutes the Muhammadan originality. Thus the cult of the virtues and their ramifications is a salient feature of the Arabo-Moslem mentality, and this explains — but does not always excuse — the inordinately moralizing symbolism of Islamic hagiography; whereas the Christian is inspired by the ternary humility-charity-sacrifice and does not analyze the more relative or more situational virtues except a posteriori.

*

* *

In Immanence as well as in Transcendence, it is necessary to distinguish two aspects, one objective and one subjective: objective Transcendence is that which is indicated by the word itself; but it may be termed "subjective" when its situation at the core of our personality is considered, in which case it indicates the Transcendence of the Self which, although subjective by definition, is nonetheless transcendent in relation to the "I." As for Immanence, it is termed "subjective" when it indicates the Self which is situated within us, as well as the continuity which exists in principle between the "I" and the Self, or more precisely, between the latter and the former; but Immanence may be termed "objective" when, in the beings and things surrounding us, we discern Immanence as the existentiating and qualifying Substance.

Now esoterism, by contrast with the exoteric perspective, is based on this double Immanence, without thereby failing to recognize the validity of the complementary perspective. The *Shahādah* — "There is no divinity (reality, quality) but the sole Divinity (Reality, Quality)" — which in the first place signifies the exclusive and thereby extinguishing primacy of the Sovereign Good, assumes in esoterism an inclusive and participatory signification; applied to a given positive phenomenon, it will mean: this particular existence or this particular quality — this miracle of being or of consciousness or of beauty — cannot be other than the miracle of the Existence or the Consciousness or the Quality of God, since precisely there is no other Existence, Consciousness or Quality, by the very terms of the *Shahādah*. And it is this truth that lies at the basis of such theopathic expressions — of the highest level — as "I am the Truth" *(anā'l-Ḥaqq)* of the illustrious Al-Hallaj, or "Glory be to me" *(subḥanī)* of the no less illustrious Abu Yazid al-Bistami.

It goes without saying that in ordinary language, the first *Shahādah* — of which we have just spoken — is connected with Transcendence, without in any way excluding a certain causal, existentiating and efficient Immanence which is essential for Islamic unitarianism. But it is in the second *Shahādah* — "Muhammad (the perfect Manifestation) is His Envoy (His unitive prolongation)" — that we meet with the direct expression, or the formulation-symbol, of Immanence and thus of the mystery of Union or Identity.

The same difference in divine dimensions, so to speak, is expressed by these two formulas of the Koran: "God is greater" *(Allāhu akbar)*; "And verily the remembrance of God is greater" *(wala-dhikru 'Llāhi akbar)*.[3] These formulas establish symbolically the identification of *Allāh*, God, with *Dhikru 'Llāh,* the remembrance of God; this remembrance being quintessential orison or unitive concentration. In fact, *Dhikru 'Llāh* is one of the names of the Prophet, who in the Koran is presented as "a fair example of him who invoketh God much," and of whom this saying is related: "Who hath seen me, hath seen God (Truth or Reality: *man rā'anī faqad rā'a 'l-Ḥaqq)";* and this brings us back to the mystery of the theopathic expressions of a Hallaj, an Abu

---

3. "Greater" *(akbar)* than the canonical prayer, according to the text. It should be noted that the word *akbar* expresses, not merely a comparative, but also a superlative; God is "supremely Great," and so is the remembrance of Him.

Yazid and others; above all, it testifies to the presence of the mystery of Immanence in the soul of the Prophet of Transcendence.

There is a world of "sobriety" *(ṣaḥw)* and a world of "intoxication" *(sukr)*[4] and although Sufism claims both climates, and although Islam as such recognizes itself in the former, it may be said that sobriety pertains to Transcendence, and intoxication to Immanence.[5] Therein lies the reason for the prohibition of wine, music and dance in exoterism, and for the symbolism of wine, the practice of music and dance — not to mention poetry — in esoterism. Here lies the whole difference between the domain of the "outward" *(ẓāhir)* and that of the "inward" *(bāṭin)*, or between the "Law" *(Sharī'ah)* and the "Path" *(Ṭarīqah)* or the "Truth" *(Ḥaqīqah)*.

All this certainly does not mean that "sobriety" or "lucidity" pertains exclusively to the Law, and "intoxication" to the Path; for metaphysical discernment, and consequently esoteric science, pertains essentially to "lucidity," whereas exoteric piety with its aspects of sentimentality, excessiveness and fanaticism is unquestionably ranged on the side of "intoxication," on a purely psychological level, of course. This is yet another illustration of the principle of compensatory inversion, of which the most well-known symbol is the *Yin-Yang* of the Chinese tradition.

---

4. The word *ṣaḥw* means literally "lucidity," as opposed to the obnubilation of "intoxication." As for the word *sukr*, it comprises on the one hand the idea of gentleness, and indicates on the other hand, in another form of the same root, a relationship with death *(sakrat al-mawt)*, which evokes a very important spiritual symbolism, that of "disappearance" *(fanā')* or "extinction," or of ecstatic "death."

5. It should be noted that Shiism, by its personal dramatism and its claim to esoterism, tends to introduce the element intoxication into exoterism itself, whereas Sunnism, on the contrary, tends to ignore it — even to excess when it confronts esoterism — in accordance with the general intention of Islam.

The reason for linking "sobriety" to Transcendence, and "intoxication" to Immanence — aside from the compensatory inversion just pointed out — is that Transcendence is objective and static in the sense that the element object dominates everything, whereas Immanence is subjective and dynamic since it engages the subject. Now the divine "Object," the content of Transcendence, is immutable, and as a consequence the adequacy, the objectivity, precisely, of our intellective perception is also objective; whereas the divine "Subject," which comes into play in Immanence, along with the human subject, which is its plane of refraction, are dynamic owing to their unitive reciprocity; mystical union being our participation in the "divine Life." If, on the one hand, the Transcendent fixes, immobilizes and crystallizes us, in conformity with "fear," the Immanent, on the other hand, attracts, vivifies and, in the final analysis, reintegrates us in conformity with "love"; this is the "dilating" and "intoxicating" return of the accident to the Substance, or of the drop to the Sea.

Concerning Delimitations
in Moslem Spirituality

The fact that Islam intends to represent a terminal synthesis, implies that it must contain and emphasize in its fashion all spiritual possibilities. Now there are fundamentally three paths: that of works and asceticism, then that of love and trust, and finally that of gnosis and unitive contemplation. The first, by itself, is linked to exoterism; the second extends from exoterism to esoterism; the third cannot but be esoteric in its substance, but of necessity includes elements that in one way or another pertain to the two preceding paths, namely the elements of operative activity and ascesis, and those of affectivity or love.

The first perspective is that of "fear" *(makhāfah =
karma-mārga);* in the context of an anthropomorphist, voluntaristic, individualistic and sentimental piety, it will give rise to the emphasis upon fear of chastisement and consequently to an excess of formalistic and legalistic scruple; it is here that is situated the surprising mysticism of sadness encountered in some Sufis.[1] In a climate of religious solidarity and exoteric-esoteric symbiosis, the temp-

---

1. This kind of sensibility can be formally attached to a given fragmentary teaching of the Tradition, but not to its integral teaching; setting aside the question of necessarily relative rights of mystical subjectivism, which is vocational and not normative.

tation is great to have the path of fear, obedience and works enter without any modification into esoterism; as if knowledge could be the fruit of action — which the Vedantists deny expressly — and as if an extravagant piety could substitute for metaphysical adequation.

The second of the three fundamental perspectives, that of "love" *(mahabbah = bhakti-mārga)*, gives rise, at the level of a *de facto* individualistic piety, to a practically unrestrained sentimentalism, hence contrary to pure and discerning intelligence, something which no euphemism can mitigate; intelligence then represents the sin of pride, only belief and zeal count. It goes without saying that this perspective readily combines with the preceding one, in a manner conformable to its own standpoint.

By contrast, the third path, that of "knowledge" *(ma'rifah = jnāna-mārga)*, excludes by its very nature the excesses of the other two; its excess will be an overemphasis upon theory to the detriment of practice; upon speculation to the detriment of contemplation. Nonetheless, this way could exclude neither operative activity nor purgative ascesis, nor *a fortiori* the element "love": namely, the sense of the sacred as well as intellective and contemplative serenity, not to mention the ecstatic modes of union.

It is easy to understand why an exclusive perspective of love cannot help but reject gnosis out of an instinct for self-preservation, when one takes into account the fact that the path of love as such is dualistic and based upon Revelation, whereas gnosis is monistic and based upon Intellection; the latter implying the immanence of the whole Truth in the pure Intellect.[2] Thus *mahabbah* allies itself to *makhāfah* — penitential asceticism — insofar as it

---

2. Some Catholic zealots have even said that gnosis is worse than all other sins taken together, which goes even beyond Thomist sensualism, and which in any case implies a singular limitation of the power of the Holy Ghost, to say the least.

closes itself to *ma'rifah,* and this is something that can be observed in Islam as well as elsewhere, even though oppositions of this kind are not at all systematic in Moslem spirituality.[3]

Gnosis contains everything, but it does not follow that everything can enter gnosis, despite those who confuse it with confessional fanaticism and who seem to wish to say, in the name of the *sophia perennis,* that "all that is sublime is ours." It is not enough to exaggerate a religious practice to be a Sufi, any more than one is profane because one does not exaggerate it.

*

* *

When Monotheism is envisaged as a great cycle comprising three successive religions — which does not preclude their being simultaneous in another respect[4] — a certain analogy between them and the triad "fear-love-knowledge" can be noted, and this is corroborated by the Islamic feeling of being, in the face of the preceding religions, the Truth pure and simple, or of being the Truth more than anything else. The most direct expression possible of this awareness is the testimony of faith, the *Shahādah,* which is like the very symbol of the element Truth.

---

3. Vishnuite *japa-yoga* as well as devotional Buddhism are examples of a *bhakti (= maḥabbah)* that in a certain respect — paradoxically at first glance — is closer to *jnāna (= ma'rifah)* than to *karma-mārga (= makhāfah),* owing to the fact that the emphasis upon Mercy and trust is based in the final analysis on the idea, not of a transcendent Judge, but of the immanent Self. Let us note that the Sanskrit terms quoted are not in every respect the equivalents of the corresponding Arabic terms, but what is in question here are the fundamental principles and not the modalities.

4. Given that every religion, by definition, is a closed, self-sufficient system.

Now, just as the perspective of knowledge contains the two perspectives which prepare and introduce it, as a final synthesis and by essentializing them, so Islam intends to be a synthesis of what has preceded it; in consequence, it intends to include quintessentially and in an appropriate manner, both the perspective of love and that of fear. Moreover, beyond Judaism and Christianity, Islam aims at rejoining primordial Monotheism, that of Abraham and the patriarchs; but whereas Abrahamism was undifferentiated, Islam is differentiated, precisely because it recapitulates, more or less separately, the perspectives actualized by Moses and Jesus.

And this to a certain extent explains the tendency, on the part of average Sufism, to bring the entire religion into esoterism. Because Islam, while analogically corresponding to the element "knowledge" in the triad of the Semitic messages, is nonetheless a religion and not a gnosis; a religion: that is to say, a system intended to save the largest possible number of souls, and to realize, within this same intention, a social equilibrium capable of withstanding the trial of centuries; now this intention has no direct connection with knowledge. In wishing a priori to esoterize exoterism, Islam will necessarily tend to exoterize esoterism; not gnosis in itself, which is inviolable, but Sufism in general; already the simple fact of its enormous diffusion is completely disproportionate from the point of view of gnosis. In such a context, esoterism becomes synonymous with moral sublimation, while moreover culminating in a mystico-political sectarianism.

Be that as it may, the fact that the perspective of fear was the first to be manifested in Sufism, or in Islam generally, reflects the initial position of the "purgative path" in the initiatory order: "The beginning of wisdom is the fear of God," which is to say that the unitive path cannot be approached without having acquired the sense of the Divine Majesty and without having satisfied its requirements; it is above all a matter of removing "the rust from the mirror of the heart." Just as in the cycle of Monotheism, legalistic and formalistic Mosaism had to precede mystical and interiorizing Christianity, so the perspectives of fear and love had to succeed each other within Islam, notwithstanding the fact that there had to be simultaneity as well, there being nothing absolute about the order of succession. Islam, as we have noted, intends to represent "knowledge" in the monotheistic cycle; and similarly, within the Islamic tradition, the perspective of gnosis will be the last to blossom.

But there is also a more contingent reason for the impossibility for gnosis to assert itself widely at the outset of the religion: if on the one hand religion must save souls, on the other it must educate the collectivity; it must forge a mentality and therefore an ambience allowing for the flowering and radiation of superior spiritual possibilities. The mysticism of love, on Islamic soil, had to await the coming of a Rabi'ah Adawiyah and a Hallaj to be able to expand fully; and similarly, gnosis could not explictly assert itself prior to the coming of an Ibn Masarra, a Niffari, an Ibn 'Arabi; not to mention the philosophers who — quite paradoxically in some respects — pertain more or less to the same family. It is true that all the spiritual possibilities were able to manifest themselves from the beginning of Islam, but they could only do so elliptically, almost inarticulately, and so to speak sporadically.

*

* *

What is curious in Islam is not that it comprises the three perspectives, but that they are manifested in a manner which is *de facto* incoherent; that is, they appear to be incompatible and on many points seem to ignore the overall teaching of the Koran and the Sunna, while eagerly basing themselves upon particular isolated elements of this teaching. As regards incoherence — whether doctrinal or simply dialectical — one has to take into account the fact that the ancient Arabs possessed no intellectual culture and that their thought was much more impulsive and empiricist than logical.[5] The Prophet had a presentiment of this when he said: "Seek knowledge, be it in China" (= to the ends of the earth); in fact, "China" was ancient Greece, the legacy of Plato, of Aristotle and of the Neoplatonists. Be that as it may, the disappointing features of a certain type of pious literature — undisciplined impulsiveness, gratuitous exaggeration, platitude, infantilism combined with mercantilism — plainly had their roots in the mentality of the human group to which the religious message was addressed.[6] Yet the simple fact that the religion had to educate so barbarous a collectivity and in time bestow upon it a certain congeniality — we speak of the collectivity as such, not of every individual in it — explains the fact that at the beginning of Islam, dialectic could not have been satisfactory from the standpoint of impeccable logic; this is an extenuating circumstance for many a heaviness and extravagance.

It has to be stressed that incoherence in no way stems from diversity pure and simple; it stems from a thinking which on the one hand tends to isolate and to be discontinous, and on the other tends to intensify and overemphasize. It could be said that in average Sufism different religions are to be found side by side; according to some of them — let it be said without euphemism — God appears to be a capricious and vindictive tyrant, *quod absit;* according to others, the very substance of God is the de-

5. Although the ancient Arabs were rationalists in their fashion, but on a very elementary and outward level.
6. A curious phenomenon that must be taken into account is the reccurrence, even in the greatest writings, of imperfections of this kind; a recurrence which in a sense is inevitable since the cult of the ancients obliges one to close one's eyes to their shortcomings, or even to take these shortcomings as an example. As in the case of Christian art or in the case of scientific and other kinds of progress, the absence of a critical sense becomes a virtue.

sire to forgive even mountains of sins; moreover, the sincere believer cannot be damned — even though he may pass through a purgative fire — whereas fire could not even touch those affiliated with a given *Ṭarīqah*, and so on. The distant and positive cause of the disparity in standpoints is, as we have said, Islam's character as a terminal synthesis; the near and negative cause is an undisciplined sense of the Absolute, combined with an impulsive temperament; in short, a kind of "henotheism" which plunges into one mystery while forgetting all others.

But there is another thing: to say that each of the fundamental perspectives had — or has — to be manifested within the Islamic tradition, means practically that each had — or has — to find a saint personifying it; the first Sufis had to incarnate "provisionally necessary" attitudes in a quasi-sacrificial manner and in order to "pave the way"; certain excesses had to be manifested by way of examples, and had to be exhausted by being manifested. The most problematical aspect of pious incoherence is that "a given perspective equals a given God"; it is true that all the Divine qualities are mentioned in the Koran, but they are in equilibrium or are mutually compensated, whereas the exclusive and excessive emphasis upon one of them by a particular perspective amounts to presenting a particular God, and one Who is exclusively severe in most cases; whereas gentleness, which is obviously more plausible in the context of sanctity, does not give rise to the most notable absurdities.

*
* *

If the perspective of *makhāfah* incites some to weep almost methodically at the idea of the Last Judgement — which is unrelated to the "gift of tears" of Christian mystics — the perspective of *maḥabbah* on the contrary minimizes the notions of heaven and hell: that is, it allows one to disdain both in virtue of the love of God alone, so that one would rather go to hell loving God than to be in Paradise without loving Him, or without loving Him enough, since there are the houris and other delights. Such extravagances — and such carelessness — are explained in part by a turn of mind that replaces logic and the sense of proportions with associations of ideas or images, and that is more attached to symbols than to exact facts; a turn of mind moreover that is fundamentally moralistic; common sense can perish if the moralizing intention and efficacy are saved. It is as if one strained one's ingenuity in order to think all that is thinkable, provided it be to the glory of the one God or in the interest of a moralizing piety, or that it serve some religious sublimation.

Be that as it may, there is a point one must not lose sight of: if stereotyped opinions — attesting to a pious automatism in thinking — are encountered even in eminent spokesmen of the perspective of *ma'rifah,* this may be in large part due to a religious solidarity which sacrifices the critical sense to the sentiment of spiritual fraternity, given that in a religious climate the boundary between truth and charity is often imprecise. We have some difficulty in believing that a Ghazali for example was the dupe of all the naivities he repeats, unless in his mind the symbolism and the basic intention compensated for shortcomings of form; which moreover does not exclude a concern for charitable concession. This hypothesis, however, has a limited bearing, for it applies to stories or images of religious or Sufi "folklore" and not to all theologico-mystical speculation.[7]

7. According to Jili, evildoers are happier in hell than they were on earth, for on earth they forgot God, whereas in hell they remember Him, since they encountered Him at their particular judgement; now nothing is sweeter, argues Jili, than the remembrance of God. In the same style of thought, some have asserted that Satan will be forgiven since, in refusing to prostrate himself before Adam, he attested to the Divine Oneness, God alone being worthy of adoration; it seems to be

As for the question of Paradise — since we broached it above — we shall add that it gives rise to two points of view that are logically opposed but sometimes combined in fact: according to the first point of view, Paradise is a place of pleasure which the true lover of God ought to disdain; according to the second, the idea of Paradise is susceptible of extension or transposition, which is to say that the "Garden" (or "Gardens," *Jannāt*) comprises degrees and that it opens onto the most demanding Union. We would say without hesitation that it is the second point of view that is objectively correct and traditionally legitimate, since it safeguards the symbolism, and therefore the dignity, of Scripture.

*
*　*

Some Sufis, and not the least, have believed it possible to affirm that Islam is the "religion of love," which is surprising to say the least, but which indicates two things: firstly, that Islam inasmuch as it is a synthesis *(jam')* intends to emphasize every fundamental spiritual possibility and, secondly, that it has the tendency — in Sufism — either to reduce or to bring the entire religion to esoterism; a tendency particularly marked in the Shiites, who go so far as to make gnosis a confessional article of faith. What seems to be lost sight of is that the Law could not of itself be esoteric, but that it nonetheless participates in esoter-

---

forgotten that the refusal to do homage was prompted, not by the idea that God alone merits a prostration, but by Satan's conviction of being better than Adam. This does not prevent the opinion from referring to the Apocatastasis and thereby being among the symbols that confirm a truth; an analogous excuse could be made for the Sufic opinion according to which Pharaoh was pardoned, in the sense that this thesis can refer to the orthodoxy of the Egyptian tradition, of which Pharaoh was after all the incarnation.

205

ism to the extent that one's attitude is esoteric, and not otherwise.[8]

It is perhaps not superfluous to insist, once again, on the following point: at the beginning of Islam and during the immediately following periods, there was the need to counter pagan tendencies: to thwart their indifference, self-sufficiency and horizontality. That is why in certain Sufis there is a propensity, surprising in itself, towards sadness and pessimism alien to the overall teaching of the Koran and the Sunna. There was a need to awaken in very profane men the awareness of the Divine Majesty; for the idols did not commit anyone to anything, they were requested only to fulfill earthly desires. The sense of the sacred is everything: after having provoked in souls the fear of the Divine Majesty *(jalāl)*, the way was clear to allow speaking of the Divine Beauty *(jamāl)*, and finally of the mystery, at once terrible and peace-giving, of liberating Immanence.

The element "knowledge" which, according to the theory of the three religious phases of the monotheistic cycle, determines in a certain fashion the Islamic religion, is manifested not only by the saving importance of the idea of Unity or of the Absolute, prototype of metaphysical discernment; it is also manifested by way of consequence in contemplative serenity which confers upon the believer "resignation" *(islām, taslīm)* to the Will of the One; a resig-

---

8. The canonical prayer of Islam, like the Lord's Prayer, is a discourse addressed to God; now Sufism managed to distinguish three degrees in this discourse: "service" *('ibādah)*, "proximity" *(qurb)* and "union" *(ittiḥād)*. That prayer brings about a "proximity" follows from the reason for its existence; but we do not see how it could be merely a "service," and still less how it could accede to the dignity of "union" when by definition it is a dialogue; unitive alchemy disposes of other supports. However, it is plausible that the prayer of the "sage" *('ārif)* has a quality different from that of the "vulgar" *('awwām)*, which does not mean that the latter cannot be fully agreeable to God.

nation which precisely gives Islam its name. Now serenity of soul, like the sense of the Absolute, pertains quintessentially to Intellection; it is a conformation to the nature of things, hence to the nature of That which is, and which alone is.

The Mystery of
the Prophetic Substance

There are several relationships between a substance and its accidents: first of all, it must be borne in mind that the accidents necessarily manifest the substance, and then, that they can manifest it in varying degrees or in different ways. For gold projects its royalty into an object, not only by its matter but also to the extent that the object is royal by its form and its function, which is precisely why it is made of gold; however, not every object made of gold has to be a throne, a crown, a scepter or a chalice, it may also be a utensil that by its nature neither requires nor justifies the use of this noble metal; nonetheless gold will communicate its radiance even through modest objects.

"By their fruits ye shall know them": this saying expresses in the most concise manner possible the relationship of cause and effect that exists between substantiality and accidentality. It is by the properties of the drop, the wave, or the fountain that we recognize the nature of water; it is by the properties or effects of the flame, whether warming or consuming or illuminating, that we recognize the nature of fire. The same holds true for every spiritual manifestation: the substance it vehicles necessarily communicates itself through the accidentality, no matter what the latter's mode — direct or indirect, evident or paradoxical, open or veiled. And this diversity of modes is ontolog-

209

ically necessary — and thus is not a cause for surprise —
owing to the play of *Māyā*, that is to say, to the inexhaustible diversity of Divine and cosmic Possibility.

*

*   *

The concrete content — and thus the origin — of Islamic spirituality is the spiritual Substance of the Prophet,
the Substance whose modalities Qushayri, Ibn al-'Arif and
others have tried to catalog by means of the notion of
"stations" *(maqāmāt)*. Sufism is the realization of Union,
not only by starting from the idea of a Unity that is both
transcendent and immanent, but also, and correlatively,
by being reintegrated into the hidden and yet ever-present Muhammadan Substance, directly or indirectly or in
both ways at once: thus the mystical "traveler" *(sālik)* may
"follow the example of the Prophet" in a way that is either
formal or formless, hence indirect or direct; for the Sunna
is not just the multitude of precepts, it is also the "Muhammadan Substance"[1] of which these precepts are the reflections at various levels, and which coincides with the mystery of the "immanent Prophet." In principle or in themselves the intrinsic qualities are independent of outward
comportment, whereas the latter's entire reason for being
lies in the former; rather as, according to the Shaykh
al-'Alawi, the sufficient reason of the rites is the remembrance of God, which contains all rites in an undifferentiated synthesis.

Man has two kinds of relationships with the Divine Order, one direct and the other indirect: the first encompasses prayer and, more esoterically, intellectual discernment and unitive concentration; the second goes to God
through the door of the human Logos, and it comprises
the virtues of which the Logos is the personification and

1. "And verily thou art of a supereminent nature" *(la'alā khuluqin
'azīm)*: that is, of a most lofty character (Sura "The Pen," 4).

model. At issue here are not only the elementary virtues which may be natural to man or which he can draw from himself, but also and above all the supernatural virtues, which on the one hand are graces and on the other require that man transcend himself and even cease to "be" in order to "become." No path exists without reference to a human manifestation of the Logos, just as, with all the more reason, no path exists without a direct relationship with God.

Outwardly, the Prophet is Legislator, and he can easily be grasped as such; inwardly, in his Substance, he represents esoterism at every level, whence a duality that is at the source of certain antinomies and which in the last analysis has given rise to the schism between Sunnites and Shiites. The Legislator points out the way and sets the example on the formalistic plane of legality and morality, whereas the Muhammadan Substance — the soul of the Prophet insofar as it is accessible in principle — is a concrete and quasi-sacramental presence that prefigures the state of Salvation or of Deliverance and that invites, not to legality or to the social virtues, but to self-transcendence and transformation, hence to extinction and to a second birth.

*

* *

The governing idea of Islam is the concept of Unity; it determines not only the doctrine and the organization of society but also the entire life of the individual and in particular his piety which, moreover, cannot be dissociated from his legal comportment. It is not merely a question of accepting the idea of Unity but also of drawing from this idea all the consequences that it implies for man; this is to say that one has to accept it "with faith" and "sincerity" in order to benefit from the saving virtue it contains. Thus in the last analysis the idea of Unity fundamentally implies the mystery of Union; just as, in a related order of ideas, Unicity complementally implies Totality. To be able to grasp the geometric point is to be able to grasp all of space; the Unicity of the Divine Object demands the totality of the human subject.

And yet, despite the clarity of this relationship of cause and effect, Islamic spirituality presents an enigma in that its theoretical and practical expressions often seem to draw away from Islam as such,[2] notwithstanding the efforts of the Sufi authors to emphasize the legality of their opinions and methods, even those most foreign to the overall perspective of Islam. The entire enigma lies in the fact that there is here a dimension which the Law has not articulated, or which it only suggests covertly; this enigma stems from the very person of the Prophet, who privately — if one may say so — practiced an *ascesis* which he doubtless recommended to some but did not make mandatory, and which moreover in his own case could not signify the "purgative way" as it did with those who have emulated him. This *ascesis,* readily confused with Sufism — whereas it may merely be a preparatory trial at the threshold of the mysteries — is far from constituting the Substance itself of the Messenger; being a spiritual beatitude and thus a state of consciousness, the Prophetic Substance remains independent of all formal conditions, even though the formal practices can be rightly considered as paths towards participation in it.

*

* *

The spiritual nature of the Prophet is determined, illumined and vivified by two poles, which we might designate, quite synthetically, by the terms "Truth" and "Heart": the Truth of God, of the Sovereign Good, and the Heart-Intellect that mysteriously houses it; Transcendence and Immanence.

2. Not that we must therefore accept the inadmissible hypothesis of borrowings from Christianity and Hinduism.

The Mystery of the Prophetic Substance

The Muhammadan Substance comprises all the qualities or excellences which the Sufis term "stations" *(maqāmāt)* and which in principle are innumerable, given that it is always possible to subdivide them and thereby extract new modes from them. But simplicity also has its rights: starting from a given plurality, one can always proceed from synthesis to synthesis towards pure substantiality, which here is none other than the love of God in the widest as well as the deepest meaning of the word; we are then at the source, but lacking differentiated points of reference that could impart the internal riches of this love. It is appropriate therefore to halt at a golden mean between synthesis and analysis, and this mean, far from being arbitrary, is offered by traditional symbolism as well as by certain cosmic structures: Paradise contains four rivers flowing from the Throne of *Allāh*, and there are four Archangels at the summit of the angelic hierarchy; the Kaaba has four sides, and space has four cardinal points.[3] But before considering the Muhammadan Substance in its aspect of quaternity, we must explain the meaning of the numbers that precede it. In relation to unity, this Substance is the love of God; in relation to duality, it is the tension between the two poles Truth and Heart, Transcendence and Immanence; and in relation to trinity, this same Substance reveals the mystery of the Prophetic quality: it comprises first of all perfect conformity and receptivity with regard to the Lord, then the prophetic Message as "content" of the Prophet and as the quasi-hypostatic link between him and God, and finally the perfect knowledge of Him who gives the Message.

The odd numbers are "retrospective" in the sense that they express an infolding towards Unity, or the Divine Origin, whereas the even numbers are "prospective" in the sense that they express on the contrary a movement in the

---

3. When a believer is outside the Kaaba, be it near or far, he prays towards it, hence towards one of its four walls; when he is inside it, he must pray towards each of the cardinal points.

213

direction of Manifestation, the world or the Universe. In the First *Shahādah* ("There is no divinity but God alone"), which in Arabic comprises four words, the Truth of the Principle penetrates so to speak "prospectively" into the world; in the Second *Shahādah* ("Muhammad is the Messenger of God"), which in Arabic comprises three words, the Prophet is defined "retrospectively" in relation to his Divine Source. The number four in particular (the words of the First *Shahādah: lā ilāha illā 'Llāh*) expresses the radiation of the Principle with respect to the world and is therefore the number-symbol of Radiation. When, correlatively, we consider the Source — or the Center — of the Radiation, we arrive at the symbolism of the number five; and when we take into account the two poles determining the quaternity, namely the Transcendent and the Immanent, we come to the symbolism of the number six.

As for the quaternity, which is the mean of our synthesis or analysis — for every number lies between these two poles — its inner significance becomes clear in the light of the symbolism of the cardinal points: the North is negative perfection, which is exclusive, surpassing or transcending; the South is positive perfection, which is inclusive, vivifying and deepening; the East is active perfection, which is dynamic, affirming, and realizing and, if need be, combative; and the West is passive perfection, which is static and peace-giving. We say "perfection" rather than "principle" since we have in view the Prophetic nature, which is human.[4]

*

* *

But let us leave aside for now these more or less abstract preliminaries and consider concretely the principal aspects of the spiritual Substance of the Prophet, which sum

4. But "like coral amongst pebbles," according to an ancient formula.

up all the "stations," and by the same token all the Sunna, at least as regards its subjective and spiritual motivations. In the soul-intelligence of the Prophet there is, first of all, the quality of serenity; this perfection rises above the turmoil of the contingencies of the world and is linked to the Divine mystery of Transcendence; to be serene is to situate oneself above all pettiness, just as in the Divine Order — in Vedantic terms — *Ātmā* is above *Māyā*. Serenity is, accordingly, not only an elevation, but also an expansion *(inshirāḥ,* "dilation of the breast");[5] in consequence it evokes the limitlessness of heights and the luminosity that fills them and gives them their natural and glorious content. This station — or category of stations — is often represented, in various traditional symbolisms, by the eagle soaring above the accidents of a landscape, in majestic solitude, alone towards the sun. Snow is another image of this station; pure and celestial, it covers the accidents of a landscape with a white, crystalline blanket, reducing all diversity to the undifferentiation of *materia prima*. This same mystery of elevation, limitlessness and transcendence finds a religious expression in the call to prayer from the top of the minarets, reducing as it does all earthly agitation and turmoil to a celestial undifferentiation; an undifferentiation that is the opposite of leveling, for the former is qualitative while the latter is quantitative. These considerations pertain to the mystery of Purity,[6] symbolized by the North and thus also by the polestar;[7] and to this order

5. "And whomsoever God willeth to guide, He dilateth his breast unto Islam ("resignation" to the Will of God)." (Sura "The Cattle," 125). — "He (Moses) said: Lord, dilate my breast. . ." (Sura *"Ṭā Hā,"* 25). — "Have We (God) not (O Prophet) dilated thy breast?" (Sura "The Dilation," 1).

6. By "mystery" we mean a spiritual reality inasmuch as it is rooted in the Divine Order.

7. One can see the relationship with the Virgin Mary, who is *Stella Maris:* immutable and primordial in her inviolable purity, and at the same time inspiring hope and certitude.

of ideas belong the sacrificial attitudes of abstention, renunciation, poverty and sobriety; or the virtues of detachment, patience, resignation and impassibility; or again, the conditions of solitude, silence and emptiness — qualities or stations whose flavor is not one of sadness, but of the calm and already celestial joy that is serenity.

Although the "vertical" complement of the North is the South, we prefer to consider first the message of the West which, inasmuch as it is static and pertains to "passive perfection," prolongs in a certain way the static message of the North; at the same time its quality of mildness, which it shares with the South, distinguishes it from the rigor of both the North and the East.

The message of the West, then, is that of recollection, contemplation, peace. Like serenity, recollection implies holy resignation, but in a manner that is gentle, not rigorous, so that immobility here is conditioned, not by a void, or by the absence of the world with its noise and turmoil, but on the contrary by a plenitude, namely the inward and peace-giving Presence of the Sovereign Good. Recollection is intimately linked to the sense of the sacred; within the realm of material things, it evokes not the luminous and cold heights of the boundless sky, but rather the sacred and enclosing intimacy of the forest or the sanctuary; it thus evokes that reverential awe — fascinating and immobilizing — which holy places, works of sacred art and also various manifestations of virgin nature can provoke in the soul. The idea of recollection calls to mind all the symbols of contemplative immobility, all the liturgical signs of adoration: lamps or consecrated candles, bouquets or garlands of flowers; in short, all that stands before God and offers itself to His Presence which is Silence, Inwardness, Beauty and Peace. It is this atmosphere that is suggested and created in mosques by the prayer niche *(miḥrāb)* — often adorned with a lamp recalling the tabernacle of the Blessed Sacrament in Catholic churches — the same prayer niche which is the abode of the Virgin Mary, according to the Koran; now Mary personifies mystical retreat and prayer, hence the mystery of recollection. All this refers to that holy repose *(iṭmi'nān,* "appeasement of hearts") of which the Koran conveys the echoes.[8]

Recollection, like serenity, is indicated by the word "Peace" in the eulogistic formula concerning the Prophet: "Upon him be Blessing and Peace" *('alayhi 'ṣ-Ṣalātu wa 's-Salām);* from the element "Blessing" stem the two qualities of which we shall now speak, namely fervor and certitude. Fervor, in spatial symbolism, is the "horizontal" complement of recollection, certitude being the "vertical" complement of serenity; on the one hand, the East is complementally opposed to the West, and on the other hand, the South is opposed to the North. These considerations, while not indispensable, can nevertheless be useful for those receptive to the language of symbolism and analogies.

The quality of fervor seems to be opposed to that of recollection, as action seems opposed to contemplation; nonetheless, without sacramental and actualizing activity, contemplation lacks support, not necessarily at a given moment, but as soon as duration makes itself felt. The quality of fervor is in fact that disposition of soul which induces us to perform what can be termed "spiritual duty"; if this duty is imposed by an outward law, that is because it is imposed inwardly and a priori by our own "supernatural nature"; a Hindu would say that it is our *dharma* to liberate our soul, just as it is the *dharma* of water to flow or of fire to burn. In Islam this immanent law is manifested as the "Remembrance of God" *(dhikru 'Llāh);* now the Koran specifies that it is necessary to remember God "much"

---

8. "Those who believe and whose hearts are set at peace by the remembrance of God; is it not by the remembrance of God that hearts are set at peace?" (Sura "The Thunder," 28). — "O thou soul at peace, return unto thy Lord, satisfied and accepted." (Sura "The Dawn," 27 and 28).

(dhikran kathīran) — "without ceasing," in the words of the New Testament — and it is this frequency or this assiduousness, together with the sincerity of the act of orison, that constitutes the quality of fervor.[9] For not only must the sacred act dominate the moment in which it arises, it must dominate duration as well; the perfection of the act requires perseverance as its logical consequence and complement; it is not enough to be a saint "now," one must be one "always," and that is why the Sufi is the "Son of the Moment" *(ibn al-waqt)*. The comparison between spiritual activity and holy war *(jihād)* will be readily understood: for to establish the sacred in a soul by nature exteriorized — dispersed and at the same time lazy — necessarily implies a combat, and one could even say a fight against the dragon, to use an expression belonging to initiatory symbolism. All spirituality requires in consequence the virile virtues of vigilance, initiative and tenacity; thus fervor is a fundamental quality of the Man-Logos, and it can be said that the intensity of the victory of Islam proves the immensity of the strength of soul of the Prophet.

As for the quality of certitude, which takes precedence over that of fervor since it provides the latter with its reason for being, it is the liberating "yes" to realities that transcend us and to the consequences they impose upon us; whether this "yes" be a gift of heaven or a merit of our own — and the one does not preclude the other, of course — makes no difference psychologically. Certitude

9. "O Maryam, remain in prayer before thy Lord; prostrate thyself and bow with those who bow." (Sura "The Family of 'Imran," 43). It is in these terms that the Koran presents fervor as belonging to the very substance of Mary, the Divine Command being here, not an order given a posteriori, but an existential determination. It is noteworthy that the Virgin is *Stella Matutina*, an allusion to the East, which in our symbolism denotes fervor. Aside from this particular meaning, the East expresses the coming of light, and it is thus that the Christian tradition interprets the Marian title "Morning Star"; now fervor derives from light just as in principle light and heat go together.

of God implies certitude of our own immortality, for to be able to know the Absolute is to be immortal; only the immortal soul is proportionate to this knowledge. Moreover, he who appeals to the Divine Mercy must himself be generous, in accordance with the *ḥadīth:* "Whosoever hath no mercy, unto him shall be given no mercy." *(Man lam yarḥam lam yurḥam).* And this defines the connection between faith in God and charity towards the neighbor, or between hope and generosity, particularly as the acceptance of the Sovereign Good implies or requires the gift of self, hence a kind of generosity towards Heaven.

It is true that on the plane of metaphysical intellection the transcendent Invisible makes itself evident to our mind in such a way that we cannot but accept it; but this impossibility of resisting the Truth lies then in our nature, and consequently the gift of self to the Divine Real lies in our very substance; the *a contrario* proof of this is that there are men who, while capable in principle of admitting the highest Truth, refuse to admit it owing to the tendencies of their passional nature. The sincere "yes" to that which transcends us always presupposes beauty of soul, just as the capacity of a mirror to reflect light presupposes its purity; such was the *fiat* of the Virgin Mary — and she is essentially beautiful and pure — at the moment of the Annunciation; the "yes" to the supernatural and to the incommensurable, to that which slays us and at the same time delivers us.

Thus, whether it be a matter of elementary belief, of ardent faith, or of metaphysical knowledge, certitude always goes hand in hand with beauty and goodness of soul. Closely related to faith is trust and therefore hope: to trust in the Divine Mercy without a moment's despair, and yet without temerity — while abstaining from what is contrary to it and accomplishing what is in conformity with it — is a way of saying "yes" to the Merciful, and no less so to the deiform nature of our immortal soul; it is to say "yes" at once to God and to immortality. And it is in this sense that the Koran tells the believers: "Verily ye have in the Messenger of God a fair example for him who hath hope in God and in the Last Day, and who remembereth God much" (Sura "The Clans," 21); a saying which combines the mystery of certitude with that of fervor. "I am black, but beautiful," says Wisdom in the Song of Songs: she is black because she transcends and thereby negates our all too human plane, but she is beautiful because, in revealing herself to us, she reveals the Sovereign Good and thereby its saving Mercy. If the Koran testifies to the "supereminent nature" *(khuluq 'azīm)* of Muhammad, it is because, as a Prophet, he realizes the greatest possible receptivity with regard to the highest Reality.

*

* *

Even in pure intellection the "obscure merit of faith" has its place: with all speculative knowledge, there is still a gap between the knower and the known, otherwise the former would be identified with the latter, which indeed is necessarily the case in a certain dimension, that of intellection precisely; but intellection does not encompass the entire being of the subject, or at least it does not encompass it at every moment. Besides, passive union is one thing, while active union is another; therein lies all the difference between a "state" *(hāl)* and a "station" *(maqām)*. At all events, to have certitude is not yet, in every respect, to be that of which one is certain.

Clearly, the value of faith is more than simply moral; not only is faith good because of the merit entailed by its aspect of obscurity, it is good also and above all because of the certitudes it brings about in souls of good will. Otherwise expressed, not only does faith imply that its object is hidden from us because our nature comprises a veil, but also that we see this object despite the veil, and through it; the element of obscurity remains since the veil is always there, but at the same time this veil transmits certitude be-

220

cause it is transparent. Thus, if the *Shahādah* signifies a priori that a given quality is unreal since God alone is the Good, it signifies a posteriori that a given quality, since it is not non-existent, is of God; either the created quality "is not," or else it is of God to the extent that it "is"; for to "exist" is a manner of "being." Seen from this perspective, the Divine Beauty manifested through earthly beauties never ceases to be itself, in spite of the limitations of relativity. It is within this context that one must situate that feature of the Muhammadan Substance which could be called "Solomonian" or "Krishnaite," namely its spiritual capacity to find concretely in woman all the aspects of the Divine Femininity, from immanent Mercy to the infinitude of universal Possibility. The sensorial experience that produces in the ordinary man an inflation of the ego, actualizes in the "deified" man an extinction in the Divine Self.

But the "obscure merit of faith" includes still another and altogether different meaning resulting from the relationship between the subject and the object: on the one hand, the subject — being contingent — has limits that prevent it from knowing in an absolute, hence exhaustive, manner; on the other hand, there appears to be, on the part of the object, a "desire" as it were to conceal itself after a certain point, a will not to be known totally; not to be divested of all mystery of aseity, or violated and emptied so to speak by the knowing subject.[10] The relative subject as such cannot know everything, which amounts to saying that it does not need to, even from the standpoint of the adequacy of knowledge. This also amounts to saying that the object is by definition inexhaustible, and that the more one dissects and systematizes it abusively, the more it will avenge itself by depriving us of its "life," namely that something which, precisely, is the "gift" of the object to

10. There is a certain connection here with the principle of tithing, or of sacrifice in general; to guarantee fertility, the Divine gift must not be exhausted.

221

the subject. Total knowledge exists, certainly, for otherwise the very notion of knowledge would lose all its meaning, but it is situated beyond the complementarity between subject and object, in an inexpressible "beyond" whose foundation is the ontological identity of the two terms; for neither term could be other than "That which is," and there is but one Being. Total knowledge means that the absolute Knower knows Himself, and that there is within us a door which opens onto this knowledge; "within ourselves," yet "beyond ourselves."

In metaphysics there is the principle of the "sufficient point of reference," namely the awareness of the limit separating sufficient and useful thought from thought that is wrong and useless; it is the former that furnishes us with points of reference enabling us to transcend the indefinite plane of thought as such. For the man insensible to the provisional character of concepts it is natural to ask thought to provide what it cannot, and to reach the conviction that thought is vain and that man can know nothing; but it is not normal for man to take thought as an end in itself.

These reflections may all help to clarify the idea of certitude; but a clearer idea of certitude may also be obtained by calling to mind its contrary, which is doubt: "For the man given up to doubt," says the *Bhagavad Gītā* in substance, "there is no salvation either in this world or in the next." To doubt what is ontologically certain is to not want to be; it is thus a kind of suicide, that of the spirit; and to doubt in the Divine Mercy is a disgrace as great as to doubt in God. Spiritual certitude implies the liberating "yes" to that which transcends us, and which in the last analysis is our own essence; whence, the relationship between self-knowledge and the knowledge of God, and also between the knowledge of God and the workings of Mercy.

*

* *

Serenity, recollection, fervor, certitude; this quaternity summarizes the Muhammadan Substance — even if other systems of synthesis-analysis are equally possible; and it extends, as described earlier, between two poles, the Truth of the Transcendent and the Heart as seat of the Immanent. It is thus that the four cardinal points are spatially situated between the Zenith and the Nadir; strictly speaking, it is not the Substance of the human Logos which retraces the features of the cosmic order, rather is it the latter which in reality testifies to the "supereminent" and universal nature of the Man-Logos.

In order to situate correctly the diverse relationships between the contemplative qualities and the virtues properly so called — the moral and social ones — it is necessary to start with the following universal Qualities: Purity, which governs serenity and resignation; Strength, which governs fervor and vigilance; Beauty, which governs recollection and gratitude; Goodness or Love, which governs certitude and generosity. Resignation to trials — to the "Will of God" — and serenity both derive from Purity since they transcend all pettiness and weaknesses, but resignation is exercised with regard to personal experiences whereas serenity transcends the world as such, and this constitutes an essential difference despite a semblance of identity. Similarly for vigilance and fervor: both stem from Strength, but the first in moral and social mode, and the second in spiritual, operative, sacramental and alchemical mode: vigilance is the strength of soul focused upon duty, the capacity to be implacable in connection with duty, and this is a crucial virtue, for goodness is a virtue only so long as it is not weakness.[11] Fervor, on the contrary, concerns spiritual activity alone, it is Strength directed solely towards God.

11. Some have reproached the Prophet for his harsh treatment of traitors, and they have not always resisted the temptation to make *prima facie* accusations against him or to falsify history, losing sight of the fact that generosity is not applicable in every case — otherwise justice could never be exercised — and also that generosity can be applied even within the framework of justice, of which the life of the Prophet, precisely, offers us examples.

As for gratitude and recollection, both of which stem from Beauty, their difference lies in the fact that gratitude responds to men and objects, whereas recollection is turned exclusively towards God; nonetheless, this latter quality or attitude is unthinkable without the virtue of gratitude, thanks to which man appreciates, like a child, the value of little things; the man who is noble, who has a sense of the sacred, is situated at the antipodes of the blasé and trivial man who respects nothing. Whoever does not appreciate the gifts of God in the world is incapable of appreciating them in the heart; there is no contemplativeness without gratefulness, thus without humility. "Suffer the little children to come unto Me."

As for the relationship between generosity and certitude, the Bible furnishes us the key: the first Law is to love God with all our faculties, and the second — which is "like unto it" — is to love our neighbor as ourself. This is to say that the acceptance of the Truth, hence the Certitude of God — be it moral or intellective — coincides with the love of God to the extent that it is sincere or real; to know God is to love Him, and not to love Him is not to know Him; and the love of God includes or requires *ipso facto* the love of the neighbor, hence generosity.[12]

We have said above that the four qualities of the Substance of the human Logos lie between two poles, the Truth and the Heart; one could as well say: between Intelligence and Holiness. To the first of these poles belongs the virtue of veracity, while sincerity belongs to the second: veracity is the propensity to accept the primacy of the true or the real, thereby acknowledging that no right is su-

12. However, as has often been repeated, love of the neighbor cannot be absolute or unconditional as is the love of God, since the former is subordinate to the latter which, precisely, determines it; one loves "in God," and one loves that which by its nature is lovable to God; in another respect, nonetheless, charity is not altogether excluded from what our love has the right or the duty to exclude.

perior to the right of the Truth, whereas sincerity is the
inclination to accept and realize totally that which by its
very uniqueness requires totality; sincerity is likewise to do
what is just, and not simply what flatters, and to do it to
please God, not men.

These four spiritual qualities or attitudes are at the
same time beatitudes, and this calls to mind the four rivers
of Paradise, consisting of water, milk, wine and honey.[13] It
is easy to conceive the relationship between serenity and
water, and between fervor and vivifying wine; also, between recollection and milk — here suggesting maternity
and the Marian mystery of *lactatio*, which Saint Bernard
experienced. This still leaves the relationship between certitude and honey: nothing is sweeter than certitude of the
Sovereign Good and of the Salvation which it implies; not
forgetting that honey is a medicinal nourishment, just as
certitude is what heals us and makes us live.[14]

*
* *

The qualities, attitudes or virtues of which we have
spoken are rooted in the Logos and consequently pertain
also to the "Muhammadan Substance," which can be de-

13. The Koran speaks of rivers in the plural for each of the four
substances, whereas other versions mention four rivers springing, in
the form of a cross, from beneath the Throne of *Allāh*. In Jewish and
Christian texts describing the same four rivers, oil takes the place of
water, which is not surprising considering, on the one hand, that water
is precious to the Arabs of the desert but not — empirically speaking —
to Palestinians or to Europeans, and on the other hand, that oil, a sacramental substance, symbolizes purification and illumination.

14. The contemplative beatitudes symbolized in the four rivers are
represented also by the the "pool" and the "fountain" of Paradise,
Kawthar and *Tasnīm*, which no doubt delineate a principial complementarity; according to the commentaries, the pool evokes the idea of
"proximity," and the fountain, that of "inexhaustibility"; the Absolute
and the Infinite, in beatific vision.

225

fined as a crystallization of the love of God, in a mode that unfolds, like a fan, the fundamental qualities of the soul. According to 'A'ishah, the "favorite wife," the soul of the Prophet is similar to the Koran; in order to understand this comparison, one has to know that this Book possesses, parallel to the literal wording and in an underlying fashion, a supraformal "magic," namely a "soul" extending from the moral qualities to the spiritual mysteries; whence comes the sacramental function of the Text — its *mantra* nature, if one will — a function independent of its form and contents.

While this magic, for a person receptive to it, can be used as a way of approaching the Muhammadan Substance, there is nevertheless another way of this kind, more readily accessible because far less demanding, and this is the concrete example of holy men in Islamic countries; certainly not hagiography with its stereotyped moralism and its extravagances, but rather the living men who can communicate the perfume of the *barakah muhammadiyyah* of which they are the vehicles, witnesses and proofs. For without the qualities of the Prophet, these men would not exist — neither in his time nor, with all the more reason, a millenium and a half later.

Another testimony of this order — and it will come as a surprise to those who fail to see the profound connections between the most diverse traditional phenomena — is of necessity provided by the arts and crafts of the Moslems, above all in architecture and dress, which relate respectively to ambience and to man. As with Christian or any other traditional art, the important thing to know is not from what source the Moslem peoples took the *materia prima* of their art; what is decisive as regards worth and originality is what they have made of this *materia,* the spirit and the soul they have manifested by means of it, or starting from it. Now Moslem art in its most authentic and thus most characteristic realizations — such as calligraphy, architecture, mosque ornamentation and dress — is the very expression of the soul and the spirit of the Prophet, of his serenity and his recollection before God ever-present.

In summary, and leaving aside all considerations of the mystical character of Muhammad, we can say with historical accuracy that the Prophet was generous, patient, noble and profoundly human in the best sense of the word. No doubt, there are those who will point out that this is all very well but hardly significant and the least that could be expected of the founder of a religion. Our reply is that on the contrary, it is something immense if this founder was able to inculcate these qualities into his disciples, both near and distant, if he was able to make of his virtues the roots of a spiritual and social life and to confer upon them a vitality that would carry down through the centuries. Herein lies everything.

*

* *

According to a *ḥadīth* as enigmatic as it is famous, "women, perfumes and prayer" were "made lovable" *(ḥubbiba ilayya)* to the Prophet. Since that is so, we have to admit that these three loves, at first sight disparate, necessarily enter into the Muhammadan Substance and consequently into the spiritual ideal of the Sufis. Every religion necessarily integrates the feminine element — the "eternal feminine" *(das Ewig Weibliche)* if one will — into its system, either directly or indirectly; Christianity in practice deifies the Mother of Christ, despite exoteric reservations, namely the distinction between *latria* and *hyperdulia*. Islam for its part, and beginning with the Prophet, has consecrated femininity, on the basis of a metaphysics of deiformity; the secrecy surrounding woman, symbolized in the veil, basically signifies an intention of consecration. In Moslem eyes, woman, beyond her purely biological and social role, incarnates two poles, unitive "extinction" and "generosity," and these constitute from the spiritual point of view two means of overcoming the profane mentality, made as

227

it is of outwardness, dispersion, egoism, hardness and boredom. The nobleness of soul that is or can be gained by this interpretation or utilization of the feminine element, far from being an abstract ideal, is perfectly recognizable in representative Moslems, those still rooted in authentic Islam.[15]

As for the love of "perfumes" mentioned by the *ḥadīth*, it symbolizes the sense of the sacred and in a general way the sense for ambiences, emanations and auras; consequently it has to do with the "discernment of spirits," not to mention the sense of beauty. According to Islam, "God loves beauty" and He hates uncleanness and noise, as is shown by the atmosphere of freshness, harmony and equilibrium — in short of *barakah* — to be found in Moslem dwellings which have remained traditional, and above all in the mosques; an atmosphere which also is clearly a part of the Muhammadan Substance.

The *ḥadīth* then mentions prayer, which is none other than "remembrance of God," and this constitutes the fundamental reason for all possible love, since it is love of the source and of the archetypes; it coincides with the love of God, which is the very essence of the Prophetic nature. If prayer is mentioned in third place, it is by way of conclusion: in speaking of women, Muhammad is essentially speaking of his inward nature; in speaking of perfumes, he has in mind the world around us, the ambience; and in speaking of prayer, he is giving expression to his love of God.

Regarding the first of the three enunciations in the *ḥadīth*, an additional explanation is called for, and it is fundamental. The apparent moral inconsistency in Islam has its source not only in the antagonism between the public Law on the one hand, with its concern for equilibrium and

15. It is always this we have in view, and not so-called "revivals" which monstrously combine a Moslem formalism with modernist ideologies and tendencies.

harmony, and private *ascesis* on the other, intent on detachment and self-transcendence, it has its source also in the personality of the Prophet himself, in what appears at first sight as the divergence between his *ascesis* and his sexual life. Tradition mentions in fact the virile power of the Prophet as well as his voluntary poverty, his virtually constant hunger and his regular vigils. This apparent contradiction, which in reality is a positive bipolarity, could not be peculiar to Muhammad alone — although it characterizes him among the Semitic founders of religions — since it manifests a universal phenomenon and thereby an archetype: Hindu mythology in fact presents Shiva, god of destruction as well as of generation, as the model both of ascetics and of lovers. This is because Shiva expresses both Transcendence and Immanence, and in like manner, the Prophet of Islam pertains typologically to the same mysteries, if one can so express it; his Message testifies to the Transcendent, whereas his personality — his *barakah* — manifests as it were a "Krishnaitic" participation in the Immanent.

Islam like Hinduism holds in view two aspects of femininity: glorified woman and woman as martyr;[16] it situates two examples outside Islam, in the past, and two other examples at the beginning of its own history. The martyrs are Asiyah, the believer-wife of Pharaoh the unbeliever, and Fatimah, harshly treated by her father and her husband, and unjustly — from a certain point of view — by the first caliph;[17] whereas the glorious women are Maryam — whom "God hath purified and chosen above

16. In Hindu mythology, the story of Sita is characteristic of this second aspect; other myths illustrate the glorious aspect.

17. It is partly from this drama of frustration and misunderstanding, which also involved the sons of Fatimah and above all her husband, that Shiism has arisen. The antagonism between these personages stems from a providential and inevitable antagonism between perspectives; the exclusivism and ostracizing tendency of the exoteric spirit accomplish the rest.

all women" — and Khadijah, first wife of the Prophet and his guardian angel so to speak, as well as "protectress" of the Revelation at the outset of the Prophet's career.

But let us return to the third enunciation of the *hadīth,* the love of prayer: a frequently used canonical formula proclaims that "prayer is better than sleep."[18] Now the Koran enjoins the Prophet to keep vigil part of the night in order to give himself up to prayer, and this reference to the night signifies far more than mere practical advice: more profoundly it means that knowledge is born in the night of the soul, that is, in the perfect receptivity that is "poverty," "humility," "extinction" or *vacare Deo;* a gift can be given only to a hand that is "below" and opened to what is above, according to Eckhart. From another perspective, wisdom is a night compared with the profane mentality, just as it is "folly" in the eyes of the world; the same holds true, within the framework of religion, for esoterism, which transcends religious, formal and psychological limitations; thus there is a certain relationship, at once principial and historical, between the Prophet's nights of prayer and esoterism in Islam. This also brings us back to the two caves of the Prophet, that of Mount Hira where he used to meditate prior to his mission, and the cave of Thawr where during the Hegira he taught his companion Abu Bakr the science of the Divine Name; within the same order of ideas, and pre-eminently, one should mention the *Laylatu 'l-Qadr* and the *Laylatu 'l-Mi'rāj,* the night of the "Descent" of the Koran and the night of the "Ascension" of Muhammad during the "Night Journey."[19]

18. The *tathwīb,* which is uttered during the call to the dawn prayer *(fajr).* Sleep is profane heedlessness, and prayer, spiritual wakefulness.

19. A saying analogous to the *tathwīb* is the following Koranic verse, which also refers to a "best" and to an "awakening": "And in truth, the Hereafter is better for thee than the here-below." (Sura "The Forenoon," 4).

This vigil that God imposed upon His Messenger has two contents, the recitation of the Revelation and the remembrance of God: "Keep vigil a part of the night, a half thereof or a little less or more thereof, and recite the Koran with care . . . . Invoke the Name of thy Lord and devote thyself with a total devotion." (Sura "The Enshrouded One," 1-8). The difference between the two practices — the recitation of the Koran and the Invocation of the Divine Name — is that between the qualities and the essence, the formal and the nonformal, the outward and the inward, thought and heart; and it is this passage concerning the two nocturnal practices which basically inaugurates the Sufic tradition. It is to be noted that the recitation must be done "with care" *(tartīlā)*, whereas the invocation demands that the worshiper "devote himself totally" *(tabtīlā)* to God, the first expression referring to the zeal that satisfies the requirements of the formal plane, and the second, to the totality of dedication needed for the realization of the supraformal element, this being the Essence, or the immanent Unity.

*

* *

The Prophet of Islam possesses two hundred and one names and titles; the most fundamental, those summarizing all the others, are the two names *Muḥammad* and *Aḥmad,* and next, the designations or titles *'Abd, Nabī, Rasūl* and *Ḥabīb.*

The name *Muḥammad* designates more particularly the mystery of Revelation, of the "Descent" *(tanzīl)*, hence of the "Night of Destiny" *(Laylatu 'l-Qadr)* during which this Descent took place. The name *Aḥmad* designates correlatively the mystery of the Ascension *(mi'rāj)*, hence of the "Night Journey" *(Laylatu 'l-Mi'rāj)* which transported the Prophet before the Throne of *Allāh.*

The title *'Abd,* "Servant," refers to the quality of Rigor *(Jalāl)* and expresses the ontological and moral submission

231

of the creature to the Creator, hence "fear"; whereas the title *Ḥabīb*, "Friend," refers to the quality of Gentleness or "Beauty" *(Jamāl)* and expresses by contrast the participation of the deiform being in its Divine Prototype, hence "intimacy."

The title *Rasūl*, "Messenger," refers to the quality of Activity and expresses the affirmation of the True and the Good; whereas the title *Nabī (ummī)*, ("unlettered") "Prophet," refers to the quality of Passivity and expresses receptivity with regard to the heavenly Gift.[20] The first function relates to "duty," and the second to "qualification."

The initiatory means of assimilating the Muhammadan Substance[21] is the recitation of the "Blessing on the Prophet" *(Ṣalāt ʿalā ʾn-Nabī)* whose constituent terms indicate the different modes or qualities of this Substance;[22] these terms are the following: *ʿAbd, Rasūl, Ṣalāt* and *Salām;* "Servant," "Messenger," "Blessing" and "Peace." Now the disciple, "he who is poor before his Lord" *(al-faqīr ilā Rabbihi)*, must realize the perfection of the *ʿAbd*, following in the footsteps of the Prophet, by a thorough consciousness of the relation between contingent being and "Necessary Being" *(Wujūd wajīb* or maṭlūq) which is *ipso facto* "Lord" *(Rabb);*

20. These two titles correspond respectively, in the universal order, to the supreme "Pen" *(Al-Qalam al-Aʿlā)*, which writes out the cosmic possibilities, and to the "Guarded Tablet" *(Al-Lawḥ al-Maḥfūẓ)*, upon which they are inscribed.

21. *Barakatu Muḥammad*, the "spiritual aura" — beneficent and protective — of Muhammad. The terms *Nūr Muḥammadī* and *Ḥaqīqah Muḥammadiyyah* refer, with different shades of meaning, to the Logos itself.

22. One could say as much for the *Ave*, whose expressions *gratia plena* and *Dominus tecum* refer respectively to the perfections of container and content, hence to *Salām* and *Ṣalāt*, and also in a certain fashion to *ʿAbd* and *Rasūl*. The first term denotes the primordial state — the "immaculate conception" — and the second, the Divine gift and the mission.

correlatively, the perfect and normative man is "messenger," that is to say "transmitter" of the Divine Message, by his radiation, for a perfectly pure mirror necessarily reflects the light. This precisely is expressed by the terms *Ṣalāt* and *Salām;* the latter being the purity of the mirror, and the former, the ray of light. Now purity is also a gift of God; it includes all the receptive, stabilizing, preserving and peace-giving graces; without it, as the Shaykh al-'Alawi pointed out, the soul could not bear either to receive or to vehicle the "vertical," illuminative and transformative graces offered by the Divine "Blessing" *(Ṣalāt).*

Other points of reference for the knowledge of the Prophetic nature are to be found in the words of the Second Testimony of Faith: *Muḥammadun Rasūlu 'Llāh;* "Muhammad is the Messenger of God." The first word — the name of the Prophet — indicates Immanence, and by way of consequence Union; the second word connotes the perfection of Conformity or of Complementarity, one could say Piety; and the third — the Name *Allāh* — indicates Transcendence, and more especially the Muhammadan knowledge of this mystery.

*
* *

The Muhammadan Substance is the love of God combined, by the nature of things, with contemplativeness and nobleness of character; as also with a sense of outward or practical values, such as the beauty of forms, and cleanliness,[23] or the rules of propriety infused with generosity and dignity. The sense of outward things — although in no wise "vain" — stems in the final analysis from the emphasis on "discernment," or from the element "Truth"; for one who discerns initially between the Absolute and

23. These last betoken an element of primordiality; they are to be found, moreover — with the same meaning and long before Islam — in Hinduism, for example, and notably also in Shinto.

the contingent, between necessary Being and possible being — and this is the very content of the *Shahādah* — will readily apply analogous discernments in the sphere of contingency. As for the sense of beauty, it is related to the mystery of Immanence.

It is from this Substance and its deepest dimensions, as we have said, that Sufism draws its life, with a consistency that sometimes contradicts — or seems to contradict — the general formalism of Islam. Also the ulemas, who are strangers to Sufism, are all too prone to insist that it is contrary to tradition, in which they are mistaken, though with extenuating circumstances; the Sufi authors for their part affirm the contrary, and sometimes with too much zeal since esoterism, while formally rooted in the traditional system, constitutes by definition an independent domain, its essence being situated outside all temporal or "horizontal" continuity.[24]

We can liken the particular mode of inspiration and orthodoxy that is esoterism to the rain falling vertically from the sky, whereas the river — the common tradition — flows horizontally in a continuous current; in other words, the tradition springs from a source, it goes back to a given founder of a religion, whereas esoterism refers in addition, and even a priori, to an invisible filiation, one which in the Bible is represented by Melchizedek, Solomon[25] and Elijah, and which Sufism associates with al-Khidr, the mysterious immortal.

24. Zen Buddhism offers a particularly striking example of this spiritual and structural "extraterritoriality."

25. Who was also "king of Salem," as his name indicates; but in biblical history he is presented in terms of the exo-esoteric antinomy.

The Two Paradises

The Vedantic notion of "Deliverance" *(moksha, mukti)* evokes, rightly or wrongly, the paradoxical image of a refusal of Paradise and a choice of Supreme Union, the latter seeming to imply — according to some formulations — a dissolution of the individual and the identification of the intellect-nucleus with the Self. If such an outcome is presented as the object of a strictly human option, it is right to object that no individual could have a motive for choosing anything except his own survival and happiness; the rest is pretentiousness and bookish speculation, and so has nothing to do with the Vedantic notion in question.

To begin with, the following two points must be borne in mind: firstly, that the idea of "Deliverance" or "Union" corresponds to a metaphysical truth, however much its true meaning may have come to be altered by pedantic or extravagant interpretations; secondly, that there are in man two subjects — or two subjectivities — with no common measure and with opposite tendencies, even though there is also coincidence between them in a certain sense. On the one hand there is the *anima* or empirical ego, which is woven of contingencies, both objective and subjective, such as memories and desires; on the other hand, there is the *spiritus* or pure Intelligence, the subjectivity of which is rooted in the Absolute and which therefore sees in the empirical ego only a shell, something outward and alien[1] to the true "myself," rather, to the at once transcendent and immanent "Self."

Now if it is incontestable that the human ego normally desires happiness and survival in happiness, to the point of having no motive for desiring more than this, it is equally true that pure Intelligence exists and that its nature is to tend towards its own source. The whole question is one of knowing, spiritually speaking, which of these two subjectivities predominates in a human being. One has a perfect right to deny that the choice of a supra-individual state has any meaning for the individual as such; but one cannot deny that there is something in man which goes beyond individuality and which may take precedence over the latter's aspirations and thus tends towards the fulfillment of its own transcendent nature.

We speak of taking precedence over the individuality's aspirations, not of abolishing them, and here we touch on another aspect of the problem, and by no means the least important. When traditionally one speaks of a "dissolution" or an "extinction" of individuality, it is the negative limitations of the ego that are meant, not its existence as such. If there is no common measure between the ego of one who is "delivered in this life" *(jīvan-mukta)* and his spiritual reality — so much so that one can say of him that he "is Brahma" without thereby denying that he is a particular man — the same incommensurability and, together with it, the same compatibility or the same parallelism, is to be found in the next world; were it not so, we would have to conclude that the *Avatāras* have totally disappeared from the cosmos, and this has never been admitted in traditional doctrine. Christ "is God," but this in no way prevents him from saying: "Today shalt thou be with me in Paradise," or from predicting his own return at the end of the cycle.

---

1. Despite the fact that everything is *Ātmā*, although this is true in an altogether different and as it were opposite respect.

The world is the plane of phenomena or contingencies; the ordinary ego, the *anima*, is thus an integral part of the world and is situated "externally" for one who is able to see it from the point of view of the *spiritus* which, by definition, belongs to the *Spiritus Sanctus;* and this could never be a matter of ambition or of affectation, for it is a question of real understanding and of an inborn perspective. In other words, subjectivity may be conceived, or realized, according to three degrees, which correspond precisely to the ternary *"corpus," "anima," "spiritus."* The first degree is that of animality, albeit human; the second is that of the microcosm of dreams, in which the subject no longer identifies himself with the mere body, but with that ever-growing mirage that is imaginative and sentimental; the third degree is that of pure Intelligence which is the trace, in man, of the one "transcendentally immanent" Subject. The soul is the inner witness of the body, as the spirit is the inner witness of the soul.

The nature of Intelligence is not to identify itself passively and as it were blindly with the phenomena which it registers but, on the contrary, to reduce these to their essences and thus to come in the end to know That which knows. By the same token, the sage — precisely because his subjectivity is determined by Intelligence — will tend to "be That which is" and to "enjoy That which enjoys," which brings us back to the Vedantic ternary: Being, Consciousness, Beatitude *(Sat, Chit, Ānanda)*. There is in reality but a single Beatitude, just as there is but a single Subject and a single Object. The three poles are united in the Absolute, and separated insofar as the Absolute engages itself in Relativity, in accordance with the mystery of *Māyā;* the final outcome of this descent is, precisely, the diversification of subjects, objects and experiences. Object, Subject, Happiness: all our existence is woven of these three elements, but in illusory mode; the sage does not do otherwise than the ignorant man, that is, he lives on these three elements, but he does so in the direction of the Real, which alone is Object, Subject, Happiness.

In the Face of the Absolute

*

* *

When the Sufis say that "Paradise is inhabited by fools,"[2] one must take it as referring to subjects attached to phenomena rather than to the one and only Subject, which is its own Object and its own Beatitude. All paradoxical expressions tending to make a distinction between the "saved" and the "elect" are to be understood, above all, as metaphors which affirm a particular principle or a specific tendency. The paradox is occasioned by the fact that the image is naively human, and therefore psychological, while the principle itself has no common measure with psychology. Two subjectivities, two languages: herein lies the whole enigma of esoterism. A doctrine is esoteric to the extent that it appeals to "inward subjectivity" and thereby puts aside "outward subjectivity"; by contrast, it is exoteric insofar as it accepts the empirical ego as a closed system and an absolute reality and confines itself to subjecting this system to prescriptions that are equally absolute. For the Sufis, the attestation that there is no god but God is esoteric because it ultimately excludes outward egoity; "ultimately," that is, when it is understood "sincerely" *(mukhliṣan),* and therefore totally. The traditional expression "knowing through God" *('ārif bi-'Llāh)* — and not "knowing God" — is characteristic in this connection, the preposition "through" serving to indicate the practically divine subjectivity within pure intellection.

The outward ego is by definition nourished on phenomena, and is in consequence thoroughly dualistic; to it corresponds the revealed and objective religion whose Prophet is a particular historic personage. The inward ego

2. This idea is plainly inspired by the saying of the Prophet: "Most of the dwellers in Paradise are simple-minded *(bulh),*" that is, free from cunning and from malice. The sense is thus positive, whereas it becomes pejorative in the interpretation we have pointed out.

looks towards its own transcendent and immanent Source; to it corresponds the innate and subjective religion[3] whose *Avatāra* is the heart; but this wisdom is in fact inaccessible without the concurrence of objective and revealed religion, just as the inward ego is inaccessible without the concurrence of the sanctified outward ego.

The crystallization of metaphysical truth into a religious — and therefore dogmatic — phenomenon results from the principle of individuation: by falling into the human atmosphere, Divine Truth is coagulated and individualized; it becomes a point of view and is personified, so that it is impossible to reconcile one particular religious form with another on the very level of this personification, just as it is impossible to change one's own human ego for another human ego, even though we know perfectly well that our neighbor's ego is no more illogical nor any less legitimate than our own. On the other hand, this passage from one form to another, and so from one metaphysical-mystical subjectivity to another, is always possible if one reascends to the source of religious coagulations, which precisely belongs to universal Subjectivity or, if one prefers, to Intelligence as such; man has access to it in pure intellection; in principle or also in fact; and it is to this subjectivity that "Deliverance," in the Vedantic sense of the term, applies.

*

* *

When Sufis disdain Paradise and want only God, it goes without saying that they mean Paradise inasmuch as it is

3. "Know" — God reveals to Niffari — "that I will accept from thee nothing of the Sunna, but only that which My Knowledge brings to thee, for thou art one of those to whom I speak." Not everyone possesses this station, to say the least, and to attribute it to oneself is to risk an irremediable fall; if we speak of it here it is to satisfy the needs of doctrine.

created, and therefore "other than God," and not inasmuch as it is divine by virtue of its substance and its content, independently of its existential degree; otherwise, the Sufis could not speak perfectly logically of the "Paradise of the Essence," which precisely is situated beyond creation. Analogously, if the Sufis sometimes appear to reject good works or even the virtues, they do so insofar as these values appear to be "theirs" and not insofar as they belong to God. Or again, when some Sufi asserts that he is equally indifferent to good and to evil, this means that he is envisaging them in relation to the contingency which they have in common; and this contingency in its turn appears as "evil" in comparison with that one "good" which pertains to Absoluteness alone. If we compare good to light and evil to an opaque stone, whitening the stone does not transform it into light; the stone may be striped white and black in terms of "good" and "evil," but it will not be, by reason of its opaqueness and its heaviness, any less a kind of "evil" in relation to the luminous ray.

The two human subjects, the outward or empirical and the inward or intellective, correspond analogically to the two aspects of the Divine Subject, the ontological or personal and the supra-ontological or impersonal; in man, as *in divinis,* duality is perceptible, or is actualized, only in relation to the element *Māyā.*[4] Or again, to return to the ternary *corpus, anima, spiritus,* these three subjectivities reflect respectively the three hypostases — if indeed this term is applicable here — Existence, Being and Beyond-Being. Just as God is "absolutely Absolute" only as Beyond-Being, so man is totally himself only in the Intellect; while the empirical ego is nourished on phenomena, the intellective ego burns them up and tends towards the Essence. However, this difference in principle does not imply an alternative in fact, precisely because there is no

4. In Sufism, the key notion *Māyā* is expressed by means of the terms *ḥijāb,* "veil" and *tajallī,* "unveiling" or "revelation."

common measure between them; the norm is equilibrium between the two levels, and not a "dehumanization" inconceivable in concrete terms.

The paradoxical expression "absolutely absolute" calls for certain explanations. Orthodox theologians, according to Palamas, make a distinction in God between the Essence and the Energies; error, say the Catholics, for the Divine nature is simple; no error, reply the Orthodox, for the laws of logic do not concern God, who is beyond them. A dialogue between the deaf, we say, for logic in no way prevents one from admitting that the Divine Nature comprises Energies, even while being simple. To understand this, it is enough to possess the notion of Divine Relativity, which is precisely what the theologians' totalitarian cult of sublimity precludes by refusing to allow any combination of the antinomic relationships which, in pure metaphysics, are part of the nature of things. There can be no symmetry between the relative and the Absolute; in consequence, if there is clearly no such thing as the "absolutely relative," there is nonetheless something that is "relatively absolute," and this is Being as Creator, Revealer and Savior, Who is absolute for the world, but not for the Essence which is Beyond-Being or "Non-Being." If God were the Absolute in every respect and without any hypostatic restriction, there could be no contact between Him and the world, and the world would not even exist. In order to be able to create, speak and act, it is necessary for God to make Himself "world" in a certain manner, and He does so by the ontological self-limitation which gives rise to the "personal God," the world itself being the most extreme and also the most relative of self-limitations. Pantheism would be right, in a way, if it confined itself to this aspect of things without denying transcendence.

Monotheistic exoterism readily loses sight of the aspects of inclusiveness, but it has the advantage — and this is its reason for being — of placing man as such face-to-face with this "human Absolute" that is God the Creator; it

241

must however pay the price for this simplification with theological "dead ends" which the Christians explain in terms of "mystery" and the Moslems in terms of God's "good pleasure," and which testify to the need to account in one and the same breath for both the unity of God and the antinomic complexity of Divine intervention in the world. Now this complexity can never be explained in terms of unity; it is explained, on the contrary, by relativity *in divinis,* that is, by hypostatic gradation with a view to the unfolding of creation; this relativity in no way affects unity, any more than the dimensions of space affect either the oneness of the central point or the homogeneity of total space which derives from that point and deploys it.

The situation of the theologies, faced with the paradoxical complexity of metaphysical Reality, can be summarized as follows: first, there is the axiom that God is the Absolute, since nothing can be superior to Him; then follows the logical observation that there is something relative in God; finally the conclusion is drawn that, since God is the Absolute, this apparent element of relativity can only be absolute. The fact that this is contrary to logic proves that logic does not attain to God, who is "mystery" (Christianity) and who "does as He wills" (Islam). Now we have seen that the solution of the problem rests upon two points: objectively, the Absolute is subject to gradation, at least unless one prefers not to speak of it; subjectively, it is not logic that is at fault, but the opaqueness of our axioms and the rigidity of our reasoning. Certainly, "God does as He wills," but this illusion of arbitrariness springs from our inability to discern, on the phenomenal level, all His motives; certainly He is "mystery," but this is because His Subjectivity — ultimately the one and only Subjectivity — is inexhaustible and yields up its secrets only to the extent that it embraces us in its light.

*

* *

It stands to reason that the ego is not wholly itself to the extent that it is determined by objects, which are "other than myself"; the true ego, the pure Subject, bears its object within itself, like the Divine Essence, which "tends towards its own infinite Center" — if this inadequate image is admissible — whereas Being tends towards creation, but obviously "without going out from itself" and without being affected by the world and its contents. Like Beyond-Being, the subject-intellect bears its object within itself; but the empirical or psychic ego, like Being, has its object both outside and within itself; and just as Existence has its object outside itself, namely in the things that exist, so the sensory ego has its object outside and tends towards the outward. Now God can be simultaneously Beyond-Being, Being, and even Existence if we speak from the point of view of *Māyā,* for in the final analysis Beyond-Being cannot be exteriorized, It contains everything within Itself in a state that is undifferentiated but infinitely real. Although man is made in the image of God, it is nonetheless possible for him to be unfaithful to this image, since he is not God and since he is free; having in fact committed this act of infidelity, and bearing it in his inborn nature he must — to become theomorphic once again — tend towards the Divine Inwardness. The subject as *anima* must make itself independent of the corporeal subject, and the intellectual subject must make itself independent of the subject anima, in conformity with this teaching: "Whosoever shall seek to save his life shall lose it; and whosoever shall lose his life shall preserve it" (Luke 17:33); and again, "Except a corn of wheat fall into the ground and die, it abideth alone; but if it die it bringeth forth much fruit. He that loveth his life, shall lose it; and he that hateth his life in this world shall keep it unto life eternal" (John, 12:24-25).

The "life" or the "soul" to be sacrificed is, we repeat, the ego as passional nucleus and not as a particular subjectivity; nor is the criterion of a spiritual degree the absence of consciousness of the "I," which could not be a habitual condition — otherwise Christ could never have moved in the world — but rather it is to be rid of passional entanglement rooted in desire, ostentation and optical illusion. The first spiritual phase is isolation, for the world is the ego; its summit is to "see God everywhere," for the world is God. In other words, there is one spiritual perfection in which the contemplative sees God only inwardly, in the silence of the heart; and there is another that is superior to this and derives from it — for it can only be conceived as an extension of the first perfection — in which the contemplative perceives God equally in the outward,[5] in phenomena; in their existence, then in their general qualities and then in their particular qualities, and indirectly even in their privative manifestations. In this realization, not only does the ego appear as extrinsic — which happens also in the case of the first perfection — but the world appears as inward by revealing its Divine substance, things becoming as it were translucent. It is to this realization, at once radiating and all-embracing, that the Sufis allude when they say, with Shibli: "I have never seen any thing but God."[6]

5. This state corresponds to the station of the *Boddhisattva*, whereas the preceding state is that of the *Pratyeka-Buddha*. To transcend the *Pratyeka-Buddha's* need for solitude and to become a *Boddhisattva*, is to remain in the state of union in a harem as well as on a battlefield; and that is independent of the active and creative function of the *Samyaksam Buddha* who represents, not a spiritual degree — he possesses by definition the supreme degree without being the only one to possess it — but a cosmic phenomenon of superlative greatness because it is of the order of Divine manifestations.

6. Tradition attributes analogous words to the four "rightly guided" Caliphs: one of them saw God before a created thing, another saw Him after the created thing, the third simultaneously with it, and the fourth saw only God. Again, Hujwiri in his *Kashf al-Mahjūb* says: "One saint sees the act with his bodily eye and, seeing it, he perceives the Divine Agent with his spiritual eye; another saint finds himself separated from all things by his love for the Agent, so that he sees only the Agent." This is not unrelated to the words of St. Paul: "To the pure all things are pure."

But to "see God everywhere" may also have a more particular meaning, which in a sense coincides with the understanding of the "language of the birds" and at the same time brings us back to the principle that "extremes meet": the intelligence which is penetrated by what is most inward may thereby be graced, as with a charisma, with the faculty of understanding the secret intentions of outward things and so of forms in an altogether general sense.

*

* *

Above, we quoted the words of Christ on "life": those who wish to save it lose it, and those who are willing to lose it save it for eternity. No doubt this teaching makes a first, entirely general, distinction between worldly and spiritual men; but it refers equally, since it is sacred and therefore polyvalent, to the two subjectivities which we have considered, namely the phenomenal and the intellectual, or the empirical "I" and the transcendent "Selfhood." In the latter case, the notion of "perdition" has to be transposed, that is, it refers simply to the ambiguous situation of the "psychic": whereas the "pneumatic" is saved by his ascendant nature, his subjectivity being intellective, the "psychic" risks perdition by reason of the contingent and passive character of his egoity.

But it is in the nature of things that spiritual subjectivity should give rise to an intermediate solution which is more sacrificial than intellectual and for which the subject, without being the microcosmic prolongation of the "Self" in Shankara's sense, is nonetheless not limited to being the empirical "self": this is the heroic subjectivity of the way of Love, which tears itself away from phenomena without however being able to integrate itself into the transcendent and immanent Witness. It is then a ray of Mercy that enters into the subjectivity withdrawn from the world; deprived of the worldly "I," the immortal soul ultimately lives on the Grace which upholds and adopts it.

The distinction between the two subjectivities being essential, no spiritually complete tradition can be without it. Even if we did not know of a Meister Eckhart, we would nonetheless have to admit that this distinction is not absent from Christianity. Meister Eckhart, with characteristic audacity, prayed God to free him from God, but made it clear that this referred to God as the origin of creatures and that our essential being is above God envisaged in this fashion; "the Essence of God and the essence of the soul are one and the same," he said, thus providing the key to the enigma.[7] This way of putting things expresses a compensatory reciprocity between the Absolute and the Relative, or between *Ātmā* and *Māyā:* for joined to the mystery of incommensurability (in Islam: *Lā ilāha illā 'Llāh*) is the compensatory mystery of reciprocity (in Islam: *Muḥammadun Rasūlu 'Llāh*). In other words, there is in *Ātmā* a point which is *Māyā*, and that is Being or the Personal God, while there is in *Māyā* a point which is *Ātmā*, and that is Beyond-Being or the Divine Essence present in the Intellect; it is the immanent absoluteness in human relativity. This brings us back once again to the Taoist symbolism of the *Yin-Yang:* the white part has a black center, and the black part has a white center. The fact that man can conceive of the limitation of Being in relation to the pure Absolute proves that he can in principle realize this pure Absolute and thus transcend the Legislation which emanates from Being, namely formal religion; "in principle," we say, and rarely in fact; otherwise the religions would not exist.

"If I were not, God would not be either,"[8] says Meister Eckhart, and his meaning becomes clear in the light of the

7. The analogy with the Vedantic *Tat Tvam Asi* ("Thou art That") is clear.

8. We would not dream of denying the problematical nature of such an expression; if it is ill-sounding, this is because it is too elliptical, since the relativity of the "God" in this formulation is not explained.

doctrine that has just been expounded; and he is careful to add, for those who do not understand this "stark naked truth which has issued forth from the very heart of God," that they should not "beat their heads against a wall," for this truth is understood only by one who is "like unto it." In other words, the doctrine of the Supreme Subjectivity demands a providential predisposition to receive it; we say a "predisposition" rather than a "capacity," for the main cause of metaphysical incomprehension is not so much a fundamental intellectual incapacity as a passional attachment to concepts that are in conformity with man's natural individualism. On the one hand, the transcending of this individualism predisposes to this kind of comprehension; on the other hand, integral metaphysics contributes to this transcending; every spiritual realization has two poles or two points of departure, one situated in our thinking and the other in our being.

The Sura "The All-Merciful" attributes "to him who fears the Station of his Lord" two paradisal gardens, and then goes on to mention two further gardens. According to the commentators, the first two gardens are destined respectively for men and the jinn,[9] or again, according to others, for each believer, but without the difference in the gardens being explained; as far as the two further gardens are concerned, many tend to think — with Baydawi — that they are for believers of lesser merit or lesser quality. According to others, headed by Qashani, the second two are, on the contrary, higher than the first two, but this

9. The jinn are subtle or animic beings situated between bodily creatures and angelic creatures. Each of these three degrees comprises peripheral states and a central state; on earth there are animal species and there is man, as in Heaven there are ordinary angels and the Archangels, who are identified with the "Spirit of God" *(ar-Rūh)*. There are similarly two sorts of jinn; those of the central state can be believers and win Paradise; it is of these that the Sura "The Jinn" speaks.

question, which depends on the symbolic descriptions of the Paradises, is of no importance here. To us, in any case, it seems admissible to make a distinction in each of the two pairs mentioned, between a "horizontal" garden and a "vertical" one, this second Paradise being none other than God Himself as He communicates Himself or manifests Himself in relation to the degree envisaged; this is the exact equivalent of the distinction between the "celestial body" of the Buddhas and their "divine body."[10]

In the case of the "chosen" or those "brought near" *(muqarrabūn)*, the "vertical" garden is the state of Union; we have already seen that this state could not prevent the personal presence of the "bodies of glory" in a created Paradise, for without this possibility many passages of the Scriptures and many sacred phenomena would be inexplicable. As for the two lower gardens, the higher of the two will not be a Paradise of "Union" but of "beatific vision," this vision being, like Union, "vertical" in relation to a "horizontal" and therefore phenomenal and properly human beatitude.[11] This is the meaning, among other symbolisms of the "crowns of uncreated light" which, according to a Christian tradition, the elect will wear; and this meaning applies first and foremost, at an unsurpassable level of reality, to the "Coronation of the Virgin."

In the celebrated Orison of Ibn Mashish, which is concerned with the Logos or the *Ḥaqīqah al-muḥammadiyyah,* there is mention of "the radiance of Beauty" and "the overflowing of Glory"; apart from other meanings, this may refer to the two "celestial" degrees we have just mentioned. In erotic symbolism, it is the difference between vision of the beloved and union with him; in the second

10. *Sambhoga-kāya,* "the body of heavenly Enjoyment," and *Dharma-kāya,* the "body of the Law," the Divine Essence.
11. We could just as well speak of a "circular" garden and an "axial" garden, in conformity with a geometric symbolism which presents no problem.

case, the form is extinguished as the accidents are reabsorbed into the Substance and as the Divine Qualities become undifferentiated in the Essence. This extinction, or reabsorption or, again, indifferentiation, is connected to what we have called on other occasions* the perspective of centripetal rays as opposed to that of concentric circles.[12] In terms of the first mystery, which is that of continuity or inclusiveness — and here something infinitely more than a "way of seeing things" is involved[13] — "all is *Ātmā*," and direct union is consequently possible;[14] in terms of the second mystery, that of discontinuity or exclusiveness, *"Brahma* is not the world," and separation between the created and the uncreated orders is consequently absolute, and therefore irreducible. It is only on the basis of this irreducibility that it is possible to adequately conceive the inclusive homogeneity of the Real along with its spiritual consequence, the mystery of Identity or of the "Paradise of the Essence."

*See, for example, the author's *In the Tracks of Buddhism*, pp. 26-27. (Translator's note)

12. We have here the complementary relationship between the "axial" dimension and the "circular" dimension.

13. In the principial order, a perspective relates to an objective reality; it is not the "point of view" which so to speak creates the "aspect," unless one risks speaking of a "divine point of view."

14. Precisely because indirect union pre-exists; it is realized in advance by the Divine homogeneity of the Universe, as pantheism would attest if it had the complementary and crucial notion of transcendence. The geometrical symbol of this homogeneity, which is not "material" but transcendent, is the spiral, which combines the perspective of concentric circles with that of the rays.

The Transcendent Unity of Religions, *Faber and Faber, 1953*
Revised Edition, *Harper & Row, 1974*
The Theosophical Publishing House, 1984

Spiritual Perspectives and Human Facts, *Faber and Faber, 1954*
Perennial Books, 1969
New Translation, *Perennial Books, 1987*

Language of the Self, *Ganesh, 1959*

Gnosis: Divine Wisdom, *John Murray, 1959*

Stations of Wisdom, *John Murray, 1961*
Perennial Books, 1980

Understanding Islam, *Allen and Unwin, 1963, 1965, 1976, 1979, 1981*
Penguin Books, 1972

Light on the Ancient Worlds, *Perennial Books, 1966*
World Wisdom Books, 1984

In the Tracks of Buddhism, *Allen and Unwin, 1968*

Dimensions of Islam, *Allen and Unwin, 1969*

Logic and Transcendence, *Harper and Row, 1975*
Perennial Books, 1984

Islam and the Perennial Philosophy, *World of Islam*
Festival Publishing Company, 1976

Esoterism as Principle and as Way, *Perennial Books, 1981*

Castes and Races, *Perennial Books, 1982*

Sufism: Veil and Quintessence, *World Wisdom Books, 1981*

From the Divine to the Human, *World Wisdom Books, 1982*

Christianity/Islam: Essays on Esoteric Ecumenicism,
World Wisdom Books, 1985

The Writings of Frithjof Schuon: A Basic Reader (S. H. Nasr, Ed.)
Amity House, 1986

Having a Center, *World Wisdom Books,* in preparation